Medal of Honor

Medal of Honor

A Vietnam Warrior's Story

M. Sgt. Roy Benavidez, USA SF (Ret.)

with

John R. Craig

Foreword by H. Ross Perot

BRASSEY'S
Washington   London

ISBN 0-02-881098-8

Printed in the United States of America

This book is respectfully dedicated to:

Those who honorably serve their country through military service for the cause of freedom.

Those who serve by caring for and honoring their military.

Those who have lost loved ones in the fight for freedom.

Those men who died beside me on 2 May 1968: SP4 Michael Craig, WO Larry McKibben, SSG Lloyd Mousseau, MSGT LeRoy Wright, and the Civilian Independent Defense Group volunteers.

The POWs, MIAs and their families, for whom the cost of the Vietnam War continues.

To Lieutenant Colonel Robert B. Thieme, Jr., USAF (Ret.), Pastor/teacher at the Berachah Church in Houston, Texas, for his writings and teachings on the principle of freedom through military victory.

Foreword

February 24, 1981, was a special day in the life of Master Sergeant Roy Benavidez. On that day, the nation watched proudly as this brave soldier was awarded the Medal of Honor by President Ronald Reagan, a recognition given only to very special service members who have displayed courage well beyond that expected of our citizens.

I find Roy's life one with which I can empathize and one that should make all Americans proud of the opportunities America offers to those strong enough to seize the chance. Roy's is a classic study of success in America—born poor in South Texas, an orphan harassed for his mixed Mexican-Indian ancestry. As a boy, Roy was helped by his relatives and his community. As a young man, he found the U.S. Army the perfect place to exhibit his burning desire to contribute to the country he loved despite his difficult beginning. Sent to Vietnam as an adviser, he became known as "Tango Mike/Mike," a radio call sign his fellow soldiers made up for "That Mean Mexican." He was mean in the best sense: tough and burning to fight America's and his unit's designated enemies. Roy soon earned a reputation for courage that bordered on recklessness, and he was wounded so badly that army doctors said he would be paralyzed for life. They didn't reckon with Tango Mike/Mike.

After months of grueling and determined rehabilitation, Roy Benavidez not only could walk, but qualified for the elite Army Special Forces—the Green Berets. He was soon back in action in Southeast Asia, on the Vietnam–Cambodia border. It was here that he rose to the challenge that made him a respected member of a very special group of heroes. On the morning of May 2, 1968, twelve soldiers from his unit became trapped during a special reconnaissance mission in Cambodia that had been authorized under special presidential orders. This time, the troops were surrounded by a North Vietnamese regiment. Three helicopters tried to get them out but met such heavy fire that they were unable to land. It appeared we would lose those brave soldiers—Roy's friends. Guess who volunteered to climb into a helicopter to go help them? Tango Mike/Mike was on the way.

The rest is American history. Sergeant Benavidez and a small band of heroes came to the rescue. Despite numerous wounds—he was shot five times, riddled with shrapnel, and bayoneted and clubbed during hand-to-hand combat—Ray returned again and again to lead the wounded survivors to the rescue chopper and retrieve the bodies of his dead comrades. In a final act of patriotism, he pushed his bullet-ridden body back to the ambushed soldiers' highly classified documents and electronic gear and destroyed them to keep them out of enemy hands. Only then did he allow himself to be pulled into the helicopter.

The U.S. military does not just pin Medals of Honor on its heroes. Their actions have to be written up, documented, and passed through an appropriately difficult and skeptical review process. Because of the sensitive nature of the Green Berets' reconnaissance mission in Cambodia, Roy's medal did not come quickly, and as a result he became the last warrior of the Vietnam era to receive this great honor. That gave many of us the opportunity to enjoy an especially memorable day when President Reagan hung the medal around the neck of this great Mexican–Indian–*American* hero.

As a fellow Texan, I have known about and admired Roy's courage and his fulfillment of the American dream. I was delighted to be asked to write this foreword for his inspirational, truly American story. It is one he tells to groups around the country—to veterans, to the military, and especially to future Medal of Honor recipients in the ranks of the less fortunate children of America. We remain very proud of him and his devotion to our country and his fellow soldiers. I am pleased to salute him as a special American.

H. Ross Perot

"The unfailing formula for production of morale is patriotism, self-respect, discipline, and self-confidence within a military unit, joined with fair treatment and merited appreciation from without. . . . It will quickly wither and die if soldiers come to believe themselves the victims of indifference or injustice on the part of their government, or of ignorance, personal ambition, or ineptitude on the part of their military leaders."

General Douglas MacArthur, *Annual Report of the Chief of Staff*, U.S. Army, June 30, 1933

Contents

Acknowledgments

I wish to thank the many individuals who have contributed to this book. Due to the nature of the material, many who contributed were asked to recall people, places, and events that produced painful memories. Without the willingness of the contributors to delve into their memories, much of the history of the conflicts described in this book would be lost.

Roger Waggie, Bill Armstrong, and Jerry Ewing are among those who contributed their memories to the re-creation of the battle scene during which my action was deemed worthy of the Congressional Medal of Honor.

Roger Waggie was the unsung hero of the Cambodian ambush of May 2, 1968. He saved my life by piloting the helicopter that landed in Cambodia and brought me and others to safety. Roger is among the many silent heroes in my life, and his story of service to his country is one that should be told.

Brigadier General Robin Tornow (USAF Ret.) was the forward air controller on May 2, 1968. Colonel Howard Hanson and Colonel Robert Knopoka (both USAF Ret.) flew the mission that saved me and others from certain death. Lieutenant Colonel Fred Jones, USAR SF, was the officer in charge of the entire operation on that day. All contributed to the reconstruction of the events that took place, and all have my heartfelt thanks.

I wish to thank our publisher, Brassey's. Frank Margiotta, president, and Don McKeon, senior editor, gave me and my biographer invaluable support and encouragement. Thanks also to Steve Fayne, pro bono lawyer for the Medal of Honor Society, and his assistant, Paula Palmer.

I am grateful to those who contributed research and technical skills to the preparation of the book. Captain Donald R. Craig, USN (Ret.) and Raul Herrera contributed to the military research. Carol Lumpkin, senior editor at Craig Literary Group, provided skillful advice on the arrangement of the material. She and John R. Craig, my co-author and agent, also provided for use in this book research material they had compiled for the screenplay based on my life: *Duty, Honor, Country.*

I especially thank two others without whom the book could never have been written. Jennette Craig, John's wife, spent untold hours preparing the manuscript. Hilaria Benavidez, my wife, cooperated in innumerable ways, helping to locate long-packed-away material, giving interviews, and providing me with the support that has been my mainstay since the day of our marriage.

I owe a special debt of thanks to my children, Denise, Yvette, and Noel, for supporting me and sacrificing our time together for a common cause.

Prologue

My given name at birth was Raul Perez Benavidez. I changed Raul to Roy when I joined the army. The Alpha code name given to me by the United States Army Special Forces is Tango Mike/Mike. I am as proud of my second name as I am of my first name. The second name was bestowed on me by my brothers-in-arms. They were all the bravest men in the world and I loved them. Most of these men died or were wounded for you and me. I want you to meet some of them in this book.

The following written words chronicle far more than my life. This is a story of the cost of freedom. It is the story of the American values that keep this nation a free democracy and of the people whose sacrifices must be remembered and relearned by each generation of Americans.

When my friend, co-agent, and biographer, John R. Craig, approached me about writing this book we discussed the purpose and motives behind the project.

Since we are both military veterans from the same era, we share many common bonds. We also share a desire that my life and this historical period of our country be chronicled in such a manner that successive generations may use the record as a positive influence upon their lives.

John convinced me that the message I have been sharing with those who will listen should be shared in this writing.

This book is for you guys. This is for the ones who didn't come back and the ones who came back in pieces. It's also for the ones who wished that they hadn't come back at all and for those who have lost children, husbands, fathers, wives, and loved ones in service to this country. I dedicate this book to the youth of this and future generations. My heart's desire is that they never experience war. But they must be vigilant and prepared to pay any price for the preservation of their freedom.

When President Reagan placed the Congressional Medal of Honor around my neck, it all came racing back to me. The blood flooding the floor of the helicopter and gushing out the doors as we banked and ran from that Cambodian jungle. The sights and sounds of my six hours in hell. The agony of the wounded and dying kept repetitively flashing through my mind while I watched the honor guard and heard the president, my commander-in-chief, read the details of the award. I was not ashamed of the tears that blinded my eyes.

I am one blessed man. Frankly, I don't believe in luck. Everything happens for some purpose.

To begin with, I'm alive. I shouldn't be; I should have been dead many times over. No, I can't walk too well, I'm missing one lung, and I lock up like an old rusty gate if I sit too long, but I am alive. Most of my buddies aren't; almost all of them are gone. Over fifty-eight thousand other guys that I didn't know died with them, but I'm alive, and I'm here, and I owe them the telling of this story.

Every one of them had his own story. Maybe he just stepped off a plane one day and got it from a misplaced mortar round. Maybe he was walking back from the latrine when a sniper got him. Maybe he's a bigger "hero" than I'm supposed to be, but few are alive to tell the tale. Every one of those guys sacrificed his life, or his limbs, or his humanity, or his youth, or his mind, and I'm alive to tell about it.

Up until now, nobody has really cared too much about hearing our side of it, our stories. Maybe it's different now. But I can't tell everybody's story. I can only tell mine. This is not a story about war. It is a story about freedom and its cost.

Medal of Honor

An American

Most people probably hear my name, Roy P. Benavidez, and think that I'm a Mexican, or a Mexican-American, or a Hispanic, or a Chicano, or a dozen more names that I'd rather not mention. I call myself an American. But, like every other American, I am an American with a heritage. My heritage is Mexican and Yaqui Indian.

My father, Salvador Benavidez, Jr., met my mother, Teresa Perez, at a dance held in an old wooden hall near the community of Lindenau in the rolling hills of South Texas. He was a tall, graceful man who loved to dance and was much sought after as a partner. He also had a beautiful singing voice and was in demand to entertain. He sang the "old" songs like *"La Noche Sereno"* ("The Serene Night") and *"Las Quatro Milpas"* ("The Four Cornfields"). My parents decided to marry, a simple enough proposition when taken at surface value. Grandfather Salvador, with whom I would live in the same house for most of my youth, never said much about what happened when my father broke the news of their engagement to the family. The best I can tell from the little pieces of information and the few words that have slipped out through the years is that the Benavidez family's reaction made the battle of the Alamo seem like a peace conference.

The reason for their consternation was that my mother, though seeming just another Mexican to many Anglos, was a Yaqui Indian. The Yaqui were about the toughest, meanest, and most ornery group of Indians that ever lived. Back when Cortés was conquering most of Mexico he wisely chose to avoid the northern deserts where the "wild men of the desert" lived. The Yaqui had killed and eaten whole armies of Aztec and Toltec who had been trying to conquer them for hundreds of years.

The Yaqui had their own system of clan government, and they engaged the Mexican government in warfare for three hundred and fifty years. The Spanish, French, Mexican, and American armies were defeated time and time again when they set foot into the mountains and deserts inhabited by the Yaqui. Even the fierce Apache would not enter Yaqui territory. Finally, right after the turn of the century, a combined army of United States and Mexican troops got the Yaqui to make a fragile peace with them. Not a surrender, just a peace of sorts. Still today that peace holds—with some unusual terms. The Yaqui don't recognize the border between the United States and Mexico, and both governments accept that. Yaqui lands and reservations cross that border at many places, and all Yaqui are considered dual nationals and are not required to observe the boundary, just as my impetuous parents refused to acknowledge some boundaries that had been set for them.

Today the Yaqui in this country are recognized for being industrious. They import and package fish, charcoal, and a variety of agricultural products. But even today, these businesspeople get a little crazy once in a while and go off to the mountains of Sonora to live the old life for a few weeks until they're ready to come back to the twentieth century.

My mother was born in Monclova, Coahuila, in northern Mexico, when it was still very wild. The peace was still new. The Yaqui didn't trust the outside world, and the rest of the world knew as much about them as it did about little green men from Mars. Her people came into South Texas looking for land to farm alongside the land owned by the settlers of German descent who had come there when Texas was still a republic. My mother's people were done with raiding and stealing and killing. However much they had reformed, though, they didn't fit in, even in the part of the community considered Mexican. A proud group of people, they stayed to themselves.

Because of my mother's background, the Benavidez family's reaction to my father's announcement that he intended to marry my mother was severe. He was Grandfather Salvador's youngest son and his namesake. He, like any Benavidez son, was to carry on the Benavidez tradition, which was quite different from that of my mother's family. And he was going to do it with a "savage."

Grandfather Salvador was like many others who were designated "Mexican," but in fact, his grandfather, Nicolas Benavides, had received a land grant of one-fourth league near Victoria, Texas, in 1833. The name was spelled "Benavides" with an *s* by my family then, but they later began spelling it "Benavidez" with a *z*, a change that would work to my advantage many years later when I wanted to prevent a three-star general from identifying me with a young soldier he had come close to court-martialing in Germany.

Nicolas Benavides's brothers, Placido and Ysidro, fought in the Texas army in the war for independence from Mexico, and Nicolas was loyal to the Texas cause. Records show that all of the brothers contributed horses, cattle, tobacco, rum, salt, and gunpowder to the effort.

Following the Texas War for Independence from Mexico, a great deal of anti-Mexican sentiment sprang up in Texas, and the new settlers who were rushing into the republic didn't distinguish between Mexicans and Hispanic Texans. Neither did those in power. In 1836, General Thomas Rusk, commander of the Texas army, issued an order for the detention and removal of all Mexicans suspected of sympathy with Mexico.

My great grandfather's brother, Placido, had been a captain in the Texas army and had participated in the siege of Bexar under the command of General Stephen F. Austin, which inspired the Mexican general Antonio López de Santa Anna to travel to San Antonio in Bexar County and teach the Texans a lesson. The battle of the Alamo ensued.

In spite of the loyalty of the Benavides brothers, they were in danger after the war was won. Placido went with his family to San Landry Parish in Louisiana, and Nicolas moved to Edinburg, Texas, near the Mexican border.

The Benavideses were *vaqueros,* cowboys who had practiced their craft for two hundred years before the *gringos* came to sit at their feet and learn to be cowboys themselves. My father's family members were also sharecroppers. The term *sharecropper* has

taken on a negative connotation because of the abuses that hold-
ers of large parcels of land visited upon those workers, mostly in
the Deep South.

In my grandfather's and my father's day, farming "by share"
was honorable, if backbreaking and not especially lucrative,
work. Grandfather Salvador was a sharecropper, not rich, but
prominent in his community and well respected by Anglo and
Mexican alike. He was a hardworking, rigid man who lived by
old-country values and customs. And his son Salvador Junior
was going to marry a Yaqui. He could hardly have been more
shocked if his son had announced his intentions to marry one of
the daughters of the German settlers whose descendants still pre-
dominated in the area.

Marry my parents did, and their union pleased my mother's
family even less than it did my father's. My parents started their
married life independent and separated from both their families.
Like his own father, my father farmed "by share" near Lindenau,
not far from Cuero, Texas, on the Wallace ranch. Carrying on
the tradition of his *vaquero* ancestors, he also worked cattle.

I was born on August 5, 1935, in my mother's bed with the
help of a midwife. When the sun set on the day of my birth, the
only light in the farmhouse was that of candles and lanterns. In
that same year, the Rural Electrification Administration was created to make loans to finance the cost of electric distribution
systems. Two years later, in 1937, a young congressman who had
grown up in country similar to that around Cuero—and not too
far from it by Texas standards, about 150 miles—was elected to
represent the state in the United States Congress. Lyndon B.
Johnson worked to get Texas its share of REA money, and electric poles were finally set, bringing electricity. With it, families
such as ours were finally able to enjoy such amenities as electric
irons and refrigerators. Perhaps most important was that they
could have more practical radios than those that required batter-
ies, and the people were brought into closer contact with the rest
of the world.

The world I was brought into, however, was more frontier
than rural. Even though one of the first hydroelectric plants in
Texas had been built on the nearby Guadalupe River in the late
nineteenth century, its benefits did not extend to our farm. My
parents lived in relative isolation from the outside world. They
did things the old way.

They cultivated a little vegetable garden near our unpainted frame house. They raised chickens that ran as free as the wild turkeys that were so plentiful in the region. They kept a milk cow, which my father milked. My mother churned butter from the rich milk and served it and the milk to us. Pasteurization, a process that had virtually eliminated tuberculosis in the cities, was too new an idea for them to know of.

In 1937, my brother, Rogelio, was born, and in that same year my father died of tuberculosis, his disease contracted from the product of the seemingly harmless and generous creature, our milk cow. When he lay on his deathbed, his sister Isabel was with us to help care for Rogelio and me. She rocked us to try to make us feel secure while mysterious events were taking place. One day, while she was holding us both, a rocker on the old wooden chair broke, and we fell backward. Still Aunt Isabel held on, and we all got our heads well bumped. I tell her now that my head still hurts from the injury, which was her fault because she was not holding us securely.

My father was buried in a coffin made by a neighbor, and his body was transported in the back of a truck to the cemetery on the ranch where he had worked. My mother, left alone with two small children, had few choices. She moved into Cuero and took a job as a domestic worker.

In Cuero, I found a world that offered a small boy a bounty of opportunities for adventure. Cuero is on a branch of the Chisholm Trail, and cowboys had gathered their cattle there before the long drive north. The town's name is fitting, for *cuero* is the Spanish word for "leather" or "hide"—more appropriately "rawhide" where Cuero, Texas, is concerned.

By the time I came to Cuero, the cattle were transported to market by train, but cattle ranching was still one of the principal industries. Even in the late thirties and early forties, Cuero had many saloons for the convenience of the cowboys and ranchers, for the cattle buyers, and for the cotton buyers, the latter seeking bales to fill the vast warehouses of Mr. W. L. Moody in Galveston, Texas. Residents sometimes complained that every other business in town was a saloon.

Most of the saloons had swinging doors, their installation made a necessity by the barkeepers' frequent need to toss drunken troublemakers into the street. Solid doors were simply in too short a supply and too expensive to risk splintering them every time a barkeeper found it necessary to eject a patron. Swinging doors also facilitated evacuation of the saloons in times of great peril, for contrary to western legend created by Hollywood, customers didn't hang around inside to watch a shootout. They hightailed it to the street through the swinging doors when bullets started flying.

My friend Bill Namie, who still lives in Cuero, tells the story about his own father's adventure in Banks' Saloon. Banks' was one of the safer establishments in which to drink because the proprietor required that his patrons check their firearms, which most carried, before being served. The guns were placed summarily into a bucket and lowered into a cistern just above the water line, providing safety for both them and the men in the saloon.

Bill Namie's father, George Namie, was the proprietor of a grocery and dry goods store. He was also a friend of the high sheriff of DeWitt County, John Pace. George Namie got wind that a local outlaw was in town and had stated his intentions to kill Pace before going home, and he hurried to Banks' Saloon, where the sheriff frequently "conducted business," to warn him. George leaned across the sheriff's table and was just whispering the threat to his friend when the outlaw materialized in the doorway and opened fire. George took a shot in the leg, but the sheriff was saved by men in the saloon who jumped the outlaw—who had just reserved himself a room in the county jail.

About a year after my father's death, my mother married a man named Pablo Chavez, and in another year I had a baby sister, Lupe. My stepfather was not cruel to Rogelio and me, but neither did he pay us much attention. We were Teresa's children, and she was busy with household duties, a new baby, and her job as a domestic worker at the town doctor's house. This left me free to savor the delights of Cuero.

Rogelio and I went to the home of our neighbor Lula Jackson any time we knew she was home. Lula was a big, warmhearted black woman who cooked the best beans and corn bread I've ever tasted. At her house I developed a taste for soul food. She would fill my plate with beans, often remarking that I was not "as big as a washin' of soap." I wasn't then and I never did grow tall like my father; I have the small stature of my mother's people.

I developed another kind of soul at Lula's, a feeling that all men are brothers, just as my fellow Green Beret LeRoy Wright and I were brothers at schools in the States and in Vietnam, where he saved my life. I loved to be at Lula's house late in the evening when, her day's work done, she told us stories. Sometimes when she and other black neighbors of ours gathered in their yards to enjoy the coolness of the end of the day, they began to sing the hymns of their faith, harmonizing sweetly. Hymns such as "Amazing Grace" echoed throughout the neighborhood, and hearing them gave me, a Catholic, an insight into my neighbors' spiritual beliefs and faith. Those experiences with Lula Jackson endure to this day.

One of my favorite occupations was to go to the cotton gin where my stepfather worked. The gin was near the mostly Hispanic neighborhood where we lived. In the fall of the year when farmers brought their cotton to the gigantic tin building to have the seeds removed from it, the floor of the gin would be covered with seeds, a fuzzy nap of cotton still clinging to them.

With a group of kids, I'd sneak into the gin. We'd climb into the loft and leap, shouting "Ayeeeee," into that cloud of soft, gray seeds piled on the floor of the gin. World War II was raging, and I had seen newsreels of paratroopers at the local movie house, which I could enter for nine cents and where I had to sit in the Mexican section in the balcony. I've often wondered if those jumps into the cotton seeds were some kind of prophecy of my fate, of the day to come at Fort Bragg, North Carolina, when I would finally realize my dream of becoming airborne and would jump thirty-four feet from a jump tower.

I never got—or needed—a sergeant's foot in my back, as I'd gotten the first time I went off that tower, to make me leap into the cotton seeds. They were as soft as cumulus clouds look from an airplane, a whole lot softer than the ground I hit when I jumped in the army. We kids didn't even need a parachute.

A time that it was fun to be in town was when the turkey farmers drove their birds through the streets to market. Turkey farming was a thriving industry in the area. In fact, Cuero was once known as the turkey capital of the world. When I was a boy the turkeys, like the cattle, were range creatures. They were descended from the many wild turkeys that existed in the area and were cultivated somewhat casually by the farmers. These turkeys were tough old fowl that hunted their own grasshoppers and acorns, not the plump, butter-soaked birds people buy today.

On the day of the turkey market, sometime near Thanksgiving, the farmers would drive as many as ten thousand of the birds through the streets of town. People came from all around just to watch the Turkey Trot. The square around the old stone courthouse would be lined with the pickup trucks and Model-T Fords in which the spectators had come to town. At last, the turkeys would come, filling the street as far as a person could see and squawking their resentment at being herded into that hostile environment.

Eventually, Cuero would have a turkey festival and name the high school football team the Gobblers, but then there were just the turkeys, enough of a spectacle without any frills. The turkeys took their revenge on the town for the indignity perpetrated on them. Turkey excrement stinks as bad as any filth I encountered as a soldier in foreign countries. Anybody who ever smells it might consider changing the Thanksgiving menu. For days after the Turkey Trot, Cuero smelled like turkey manure.

My life in Cuero wasn't all fun and games, though. When I was five, I was sent to the Spanish school to learn to speak English before going on to regular school. It was a public school, the legendary one-room schoolhouse, presided over by one Miss Prisby, and its facilities were rather primitive. The toilet was an outhouse.

Now I've heard stories about children who came from homes where only Spanish was spoken being punished for speaking their mother tongue. I remember being punished when I was at that school . . . but not for speaking Spanish. Another boy and I conceived of a way to have some fun one day when a couple of girls were inside the outhouse. We pulled some long weeds from a field adjacent to the school ground, and while the girls were taking care of their needs, we sneaked behind the outhouse and tickled their bare fannies with the weeds.

Miss Prisby made me wish I'd found another form of entertainment. She cut a switch of her own from a tree on the school grounds and lashed my bare legs vigorously. Miss Prisby's switching made me dance around a lot more than my trick with the weeds had made those girls jump.

When I was six, I was sent to St. Mary's Catholic School, where I had no opportunity to repeat the weed trick, but I found ways to annoy the nuns who were my teachers there. I can still feel the red-hot pain that came when they twisted my ears. I guess they managed to teach me something, for when I was seven, wearing white pants and a white shirt and looking saintlier than I was, I celebrated my First Communion.

Mine was not the only war that was being fought in 1941. Around Christmas that year, two of my mother's nephews, Alisteo and Jacinto Ramirez, came for a visit. They were much older than I, and they wore army uniforms. There was talk of the war and Pearl Harbor, none of which meant much to me, but I was fascinated by their uniforms. I hardly thought I'd ever seen men looking so well dressed.

By then, I also worked in the streets to earn the nine cents I wanted for admission to the movie theater and the nickels I wanted so that I could buy an ice-cream cone. I scrounged the roadside for Coke bottles that people had thrown from their cars and took them to Vela's store, where Mr. Vela would pay a penny for each bottle. Each time, I hoped that he would give me an apple or a banana as he sometimes did. The stockyard was one of the best places to earn a few pennies for running errands or cleaning up. It was the busiest part of town, with strangers coming in to sell their cattle.

On my way to the stockyard, I tried again and again to enter a nearby house that was peculiarly popular with the cowboys and the cattle and cotton buyers. If they liked it so much, I figured I would too. Several bright-haired ladies lived in the house, and I wanted a closer look at them. Their clothes were much shinier and their lips much redder than my mother's, and the eagerness with which the men entered the place led me to believe that the entertainment within was at least as interesting as a Roy Rogers shoot-'em-up movie. The ladies consistently ejected me, laughing and hooting at my tenacity. Several years passed before I learned that the residents of the house were not "ladies."

When I was seven, I discovered a way to increase my earnings and to do something that was no more unpleasant to me than hauling water or mucking out stock pens. Piling manure in a corner of the yard and helping the families who came to collect a supply of it to fertilize their gardens earned only pennies. If the people happened to be "city slickers" who had moved to Cuero from someplace like San Antonio to be gentleman farmers, the cowboys would always speculate about whether or not they had enough sense to age that manure about a year, when it would not be so chemically hot that it would burn up their tender tomatoes and cucumbers. In spite of such speculation, I never heard one of the country men befriend a newcomer and warn him of the hazard.

All of the cattle waiting for sale or shipment in those stock pens were range cattle. Today you see a different kind of cattle in the stockyards. They are almost raised by hand. They've been vaccinated, dipped, and dehorned. They are used to the touch and smell of man. Then, however, the cattlemen put their cattle out on thousands of acres of open range to breed and grow, and they went to check them every month or two. Once or twice a year they'd sort out what they wanted to sell and drive them into town.

Those range-bred cattle had seen a man on horseback only one or two times in their lives and might have never seen one on foot. They could jump like deer and fight like bobcats. A lot of experienced cowboys lost lives and limbs to their hooves and horns.

I was leaning up against a post and acting sort of smart-alecky while two ranchers were discussing the finer points of a two-thou-sand-pound range bull standing in one of the pens. The ranchers got tired of my nonsense and of my warting them to give me a job, and one of them dared me to sneak into the pen and grab that huge sack hanging between the bull's hind legs and give it a tug.

"I'll give you a quarter, *neen-yo*," the rancher said.

A quarter was an awful big amount of money to me then, and I accepted the dare. Before long the fence was lined with cow-boys watching me crawl under the bottom rail of the pen and sneaking up on that monster. I yanked the bag. The bull swapped ends of the pen faster than you can count to one, but I was just a mite faster and was crawling under the closest rail while he was still snorting and looking in confusion for his tormentor.

The rancher who had dared me put a shiny new quarter in my hand and patted my head. I stared at the quarter for a long time, figuring it out. Five ice-cream cones. Or two trips to the movies and one ice-cream cone with two cents to spare. The cowboys also paid me numerous compliments for my bravery. They said I was "tough as a boot" and a "crazy little *frijole*," and they had admiration for me in their eyes. One said he thought I'd fight a rattlesnake and give it two bites to start.

The experience changed me. The way they looked at me meant more than the quarter, even as much as I wanted that. Little did those *gringos* realize that running in my veins was the blood of the fierce Yaqui. If there is a crazy, never-give-up, never-quit side of me, I believe that it comes from my Yaqui ancestors. Moreover, I have the blood of the very *vaqueros* who taught their ancestors to ride, rope, and work the wild stock of the rugged Southwest. Maybe if I had been born five hundred miles farther south I would have been a retired bullfighter by now. I might have fewer scars as well.

I had begun establishing the pattern that I would follow for many years to come. I was turning into a tough, mean little kid. I was fighting with kids on the street and turning into a general nuisance for anybody who got in my way. If my mother had been well, she might have been able to change my direction, but she now was ill with tuberculosis, the same disease that had killed my father. And I had started down a path that often leads to the pen, and I don't mean the stock pen but the penitentiary.

2

Songs in the Night

My mother was a beautiful woman. Looking at her photograph makes me understand why my father was willing to go against his family's wishes and marry her. She had big eyes, so dark that they seemed to have no pupils, and a mass of sleek hair.

The doctor she had worked for did what he could for her, but she became increasingly ill. There was a state tuberculosis sanitarium in San Angelo, Texas, where some Anglos went to be treated for the disease, but if its services were available to people of our race, we didn't know it. The year I was seven she died at home.

Her funeral was a simple one. I barely remember the funeral service at Santa Guadalupe's Church in the neighborhood where we lived, or the graveside service in the Cuero City Cemetery, where she was buried in a section reserved for people who couldn't afford a plot. I do recall going to the cemetery in the 1934 Ford my mother's brother Siesto Perez owned, and I recall that there were many other cars around, Fords and Chevrolets that could serve as vehicles in an Al Capone movie.

Perhaps I remember little because I was so frightened. I had heard talk about what would be done with us, the most frightening of it to me that Rogelio and I might be going to different places to live. My stepfather's family was going to take Lupe, but it was clear from the first that they would not take my brother and me. We would be a burden wherever we went.

I felt terribly alone. I was a seven-year-old half-breed orphan.

When the service ended, both Rogelio and I were taken in hand by a man I had seen only a few times. He told us that he was our Uncle Nicholas and that we would be going to live with him. Aunt Isabel tells me that our mother asked Uncle Nicholas to care for us after her death. That Rogelio and I were together was relief enough, and that, after gathering our things, Uncle Nicholas took us to the bus station and bought three tickets to El Campo, Texas, relieved my fears greatly.

By the time we were on the bus—in backseats, of course—I was almost happy. I had never been on a bus before, and I had certainly never been any place as far away as El Campo. I sat in my seat with my nose pressed against the window and watched the hills roll by and the countryside give away to flat fields.

As we traveled—not so far, as it seemed to me, for El Campo is only eighty-five miles southeast of Cuero—Uncle Nicholas told us a few things about our new home. Our grandfather, Salvador, lived there. "He will tell you many stories," he said. Aunt Alexandria was Uncle Nicholas's wife, and they had eight children, our cousins. What a deal! I thought. Just when I was feeling that I could hardly be more blessed, Uncle Nicholas looked down at my scuffed shoes, a piece of cardboard inside providing a patch for the hole in one sole. "Tomorrow we'll take you into town and buy you a pair of new shoes."

When we entered the house, my eight cousins peered at us curiously from the other side of the room. A tall man gave Rogelio a hearty *abrazo,* a Mexican hug, and told us that he was our Grandfather Salvador. "You must always remember that you are a Benavidez," he said. "You must always bring honor to that name." Uncle Nicholas recited the cousins' names: María, Eugenio, Elida, Evita, Joaquin, Frank, Nicholas, and Miguel. They were now our brothers and sisters, he said.

"We are not rich," Uncle Nicholas said, "but everything we have belongs as much to you as to anyone. We all work, and we share what we have. You will work alongside us, just as your new brothers and sisters do."

"They go to school and study hard. So must you," Grandfather Salvador said. "There are opportunities in this country for people who get an education."

Just as I was beginning to feel that life in my new home might not be as idyllic as I had first thought, Rogelio and I were rescued by Aunt Alexandria, a woman with a kindly expression whose shoulders were already showing a hint of the stoop that she would have when she was older.

"They are hungry," she said. *"Tienes hambre, Rogelio?"*

"Yes," my brother answered emphatically, and we were taken to the kitchen and given a generous supper of tacos.

A distinct advantage of living in El Campo was that our house was near town. I had soon returned to the bus station that had so fascinated me on my arrival. I worked as a shoe shine boy, and I could get a nickel for a shine and maybe up to a quarter for a good job on a pair of cowboy boots. Years later my army buddies would ask, "Where'd you learn to put a shine like that on a pair of shoes?" I had plenty of practice, not only at the bus station but also when I worked as a driver in the army for various generals who, with their wives, often required a vast variety of services, including polishing boots.

The people who came through the El Campo bus station were a little tamer than the cowboys and cotton buyers I had known in Cuero, but not much. El Campo was called the "Pearl of the Prairie" by the people who founded it in the late nineteenth century as a siding and shipping point on the railroad. It was originally called Prairie Switch. When cattlemen began to camp there, the name El Campo began being used, and it stuck.

At the bus station, I shined the boots and shoes of cattlemen and rice farmers and of men who came to work in the nearby oil fields. The "roughnecks" were well named and had little more polish than the toughest cowboys in Cuero. With all of the coming and going, the single cabdriver in town, a man who spoke only English, stayed pretty busy. Once in a while, someone who spoke only Spanish would come in on a bus and need a ride. That old driver would holler for me, and I'd jump into the cab to translate for him. I really liked those jobs because they were always worth a dime to a quarter, depending on how far out the man wanted to go.

Most of the money I made, I turned over to Uncle Nicholas. Both he and my grandfather were rigid. There was black, and there was white, and there was nothing in between. Grandfather Salvador and Uncle Nicholas laid out very clear lines. I knew that the money was going to feed and clothe me and to buy my school supplies. Aunt Alexandria was the banker. She kept ten envelopes, each with the name of one child on it. Into the envelopes went some of the child's earnings, and when he or she needed something, my aunt took some money from the appropriate envelope. My cousins and brother pitched in, and it gave me pride to do so as well.

Not that this sterner discipline than I had been used to resulted in a complete change in my nature. I'd sneak a nickel once in a while for an ice-cream cone. In fact, my love of ice-cream cones led me to get into several fights. On my way home from school one day, I heard a familiar taunt from across the street. "Pepper Belly," it came. I kept walking, but I glanced sideways to identify my tormentor.

He was a priss-pants white kid I knew at school, and he was showing off for some girls. He wore a white shirt and khaki pants, starched and ironed by his mama, and shiny brown oxfords, probably polished by her, too. What she hadn't done for him was to teach him to leave well enough alone.

"Hey, Pepper Belly," it came again.

I left few imprints of my bare feet in the dirt street as I went after him. He started running, but he was too slow by a long shot. *"Pendejo!"* I said as I grabbed him and threw him into the dirt.

By the time I decided to let him go, he was nearly the same color that I am. His mama had her work cut out for her to get him white again.

Many of El Campo's white residents were descendants of the Swedes, Czechs, and Germans who had been the original settlers of the region. The more Anglo whites who came later blended in fairly easily, but the lines were still pretty well drawn between the whites and the browns when I was a boy, and I was the object of racial taunts that I could not refrain from responding to with my fists.

Whenever I fought and Uncle Nicholas heard about it, he would quit his work in the barbershop or in his garage, where he worked as an automobile mechanic, and proceed to give me a lecture. We kids hated his talks more than the infrequent whippings he administered with his razor strop. He'd begin first with words about bringing shame to the Benavidez name. Then he would go on to explain that up through my grandfather's generation, the Mexicans and Mexican-Americans had been able to live to themselves and get along fairly well. "That has to change," he would say. "My future and yours will be in a different kind of world. We will not give up our heritage, but we won't let it hold us back either. We will be judged by the way we act and by the respect we earn in the community."

I have stood at attention in the army sweating bullets while some Top Kick got in my face and screamed. I've had those old sergeants tell me to hit a brace, meaning to come to a rigid attention, and I knew what was coming. But even when "hitting a brace" I was no more uncomfortable than when Uncle Nicholas preached one of his sermons to me.

Even then, I knew he was right because he was the kind of man who commanded respect. That didn't mean that I followed his instructions, but if I have turned out to be anything worthwhile at all, I owe it to him and, of course, to Aunt Alexandria, who became my adopted mother just as he became my adopted father. Once when Uncle Nicholas finally dismissed me from one of his lectures I turned, even in my flight, to find him smiling mysteriously. I think he knew that I would have preferred that he whip me and get it over.

While we kids avoided Uncle Nicholas's lectures, we gathered around Grandfather Salvador at every opportunity because we loved his stories, even though they, too, were really parables with a point. His favorite theme was that people had to help each other, and one of his stories was especially damning to the people of his own culture. It expressed his belief that they didn't help each other as they should. He told of a man who sold crabs down near Palacious where the Colorado River empties into Matagorda Bay and the water mixes with the salt water of the Gulf of Mexico.

The man had two baskets of crabs for sale, according to my grandfather, one labeled "American Crabs" and the other labeled "Mexican Crabs." The basket labeled "American Crabs" had a wicker lid, firmly tied down, but the basket labeled "Mexican Crabs" had no lid. A man from El Campo stopped his car and, interested in buying some of the crabs, asked what the difference was between the American and the Mexican crabs.

"See those Mexican crabs just sitting down there in the bottom of the basket?" the vendor replied. "They don't need no lid. They don't try to get out. Now these American crabs are a different proposition. You don't put a lid on them, and pretty soon one of them climbs up on the back of another, and another climbs on his back, then another climbs on his back, and on and on, and pretty soon them American crabs are getting out all over the place."

A story we liked much better was of a time when Grandfather Salvador was a young man, living in the mountains. One of his jobs was to take the family cattle to pasture each morning and to return to bring them home each evening. The trip was a treacherous one, along narrow paths on the mountainside. One evening as he was returning, towing the lead cow by a halter rope, he heard a man crying out for help. The man had fallen from the path and was stranded on a ledge beneath it.

Our grandfather told us that he unfastened the halter rope and lowered it toward the man, who reached for it desperately but found it several inches beyond his grasp. Our grandfather then retrieved the rope and attached his belt to it. He lowered the rope again, and the man grasped it with great relief and clung to it while our grandfather pulled him to safety. "Remember," he would say, "people sometimes need help, and when they do you must help them." With that he'd rise and put on the Stetson hat that he always wore, which was to him a mark of his manhood, and leave the house. He'd walk down the street for his daily recreation, a game of dominoes and one beer . . . maybe two.

Sometimes I thought that the best friend I made in El Campo had never heard the stories about helping people, even though he was a grandson of Grandfather Salvador like me. Leo Foisner, my friend and cousin, was an unlikely looking "Mexican." He had blond hair and blue eyes, passed on to him by his father, who was of German descent and who was married to my aunt.

One especially bright day, both Leo and I had enough money to buy hamburgers, which cost a whole quarter then. The trouble was that none of the cafés in town served Mexicans. In fact, one that I remember had a sign on the front door: "NO MEXICANS OR DOGS. COLORED AROUND BACK." Leo didn't see that as a problem because nobody guessed that he had any Mexican blood in his veins.

"I'll just go in and get both our hamburgers and bring them outside," he said. Between the time that I gave Leo my quarter and he entered the café, he somehow forgot our bargain. When the hamburgers were served, he plopped himself in a booth near the window where I waited and slowly chewed his burger, smiling at me between bites. I looked in through the window and drooled. When Leo finally brought my slightly cool hamburger to me, I would probably have tried to kill him if I hadn't been so hungry.

Bigotry was alive and well in El Campo in those days. I remember playing out in the streets with my brothers and sisters and neighbors when a man came by and opened up a roll of dimes. He just threw a handful of them down into the dirt, then stood back and laughed while we fought for them. I was in there fighting for 'em too. Two of those dimes would take me to the movies and buy me an ice-cream cone. I needed those dimes, but I remember the pride I lost getting them.

At Christmastime, the welfare office of Wharton County would send baskets to the school for the "poor" kids on the last school day before the holidays. We would all line up to leave at the end of the day and some county official would hand each of us a paper sack with an apple and an orange and a few nuts in it. We'd say thank-you and walk out of school with our "gift" from the county. Man, I can still see the condescending, do-gooder looks in those people's eyes when they handed us our bags. I can still hear the simpering tone of voice of one man when he said, "Now you have a Merry Christmas, fella." Maybe they thought that without that apple we were gonna starve over Christmas.

Actually, we were usually more prosperous around Christmas than at any other time of the year because we had recently returned from the picking fields of Colorado and West Texas. When we kids entered school in late autumn, we'd all have new jackets and new shoes. At first, I didn't mind at all when we were withdrawn from school in the spring before the end of the term. In fact, I was delighted. We were going on a great adventure.

Aunt Alexandria packed the household goods that we would need—our bedding, cooking vessels, and dishes—and we loaded them into a stake-bed truck. Once the kids were in the truck, too, we'd hit the road for northern Colorado. For a boy who had thought that an eighty-five-mile bus trip from Cuero to El Campo was exciting, our spring odyssey was almost unbearably thrilling. We went through towns I had heard of—Austin, Amarillo—and after a couple of days, we'd cross into Colorado and pass through Pueblo and reach Colorado Springs, camping out nearby for our last stop before reaching our destination.

Little did I know when we camped there and I gazed in wonder at the mountains and canyons that I had begun one of the circles of my life, for I would return to nearby Fort Carson after basic training for advanced infantry training. The journey and the way we lived on the road and in the camps set up for migrant workers seemed like one long picnic to me.

After days on the road we would finally reach Timnath, Colorado, and the sugar beet fields where we were to work. Timnath is in the northern part of the state near Fort Collins, and the migrant camp where we stayed was about two miles from the town.

The houses we lived in when we were working on the road were not luxurious by anyone's standards. They had wood stoves, no indoor plumbing, no hot water. The entire family worked in the fields from "can see" to "can't see." We'd go to the fields when the sun came up and leave them when it went down. The beets were plowed out of the ground, and our job was to pick them up and cut the leafy tops off. Sometimes the sun would move so slowly across the sky that I'd think that time was standing still. Yet, I loved looking at the mountains off to the west. They were incredibly beautiful to a flatland kid from South Texas.

We little ones had our ways of shirking some of the work. We'd make frequent trips to the water bucket and more frequent trips than were necessary to relieve ourselves behind a tree. I soon started noticing the closeness of the family, though—how they all worked together and how the individuals had no idea what they had earned themselves. It was all family money, and it went to put clothes on our backs, shoes on our feet, and beans in our bellies. Soon, I found myself wanting to be part of that team, and I began to take pride in my contribution.

I also noticed that the family members worked without complaining. If anyone had a right to gripe a bit, it was Aunt Alexandria. She was the mess sergeant, the supply clerk, and the chaplain for a family of thirteen. She also had to put up with our nonsense, some of which concerned the *duendes*. The *duendes* were mischievous elves who were capable of rearranging the furniture or tumbling up the bedding, and we never failed to blame every mishap that occurred on them: "The *duendes* did it."

We worked long hours, but we had fun too. We had one red radio that we always took on the trips, and we listened to station XELO, which broadcast out of Villa Acuña, Mexico, just across the Rio Grande River from Laredo, Texas. Late into the night, we'd listen to the country-western songs that were broadcast by the megawatt station that had its transmitter in Mexico because such signals were prohibited in the United States by the Federal Communications Commission.

Lying on my bedroll those nights and listening to Ernest Tubb and Hank Williams, Sr., singing such songs as "Walking the Floor Over You" and "Your Cheating Heart," I developed a fondness for country-western music that I retain to this day. I was less impressed with the advertisements, these—like the station—unrestricted. One was for a tonic made with an extract from goat glands, guaranteed to restore potency to any man having problems in that area. Another was for a picture of Jesus Christ, a bargain at five dollars for it was *autographed.* "'J. C.' on the bottom," the disc jockey would say.

We never needed such souvenirs, for we had a network of our own that provided our connection to the Lord. That was church. We never missed going to mass, no matter how pressing the work load.

We also had celebrations with the other families living and working with us. Whenever a baby was born or a couple married, the women worked together to create a *comida Mexicana,* a feast of enchiladas, tamales, and much more. Sometimes we'd go into the little town of Timnath, and when we walked past the school where the year-round residents' children were still attending classes, the kids inside would stare out the windows at us as if seeing aliens from another planet. For a long time, I felt that I was more fortunate than the kids who were cooped up in those classrooms.

On the red radio, we also heard the news of the death of President Franklin D. Roosevelt, and we learned the name of his successor, Harry S. Truman. Washington and the events that transpired there seemed very far away from us. We learned of VE (Victory in Europe) Day, of VJ (Victory in Japan) Day, and that World War II was over. If Washington seemed a long way off, the distances between us and Europe and Japan were unfathomable.

After the beet fields were cleared it was time to move back down to West Texas and the cotton fields. The fields had rows like waves, and as we dragged our sacks through them, it seemed that each row was longer than the next. The days seemed never-ending, and the nights were way too short to rest up enough for the next day and the next day and the next day.

Twenty years after that, when I was in the jungles of Vietnam, guys would look at me and wonder how I survived so well. They used to say I acted like I was out on a picnic. "I am," I'd say, "and I brought a jar of ants to turn loose so you'll feel like you're on one too." Somehow living in that steaming jungle never seemed quite as rough as all those years as a migrant worker.

Still, we found ways to have fun. Uncle Nicholas was a master psychologist. He divided the family into teams, one headed by himself and the other by Frank, who was the champion at picking cotton. Frank could pull a thousand pounds a day, and we all strove to best him. Not only did Uncle Nicholas make us competitive, he also provided some incentive for us to work. "If you want to work Sunday," he'd say, "I'll give you half of what you make." That was Sunday after mass, of course.

After all the picking seasons were over, we'd return home and go back to school. Being in the fields was more fun, for when we entered school we were far behind the other children. The teachers put us off to the side, where we rarely caught up with the rest of the class. Sometimes it didn't matter much to us because we wouldn't finish that year either. We'd take off again when the next crop needed pickin'.

All the while Grandfather Salvador was saying such things to us as "Getting an education is the most important thing in your life." Sometimes I just wanted to jump up and say "Grandfather Salvador, I believe you, just let me stay home and go to school." Out of respect I never did. We were an old-fashioned family. If one of my elders asked me to bring a glass of water, I obeyed and stood beside him while he drank it so that I'd be ready to return the glass to the kitchen or to refill it.

Grandfather Salvador was right, of course, when he said that machines would put us out of business. One man on a cotton combine today does what a hundred of us did fifty years ago. But back then all we had to live on was thirteen strong backs, so we picked.

I wish I could say that working in the fields gave me a strong work ethic and that my frustration at school created a strong desire in me to achieve, but I took a long time to learn those lessons. Some of my experiences just made me mean, meaner than I had been as a street child in Cuero.

I continued my career as a fighter, mostly in the streets. I didn't fight much at home. Uncle Nicholas broke me of that with those lectures that I hated so much. Anyhow, I didn't have as much reason to fight with my cousins and my brother as with other kids. My relatives were in the same boat that I was—often barefoot. I sometimes avoided fights at school for the same reason that I avoided them at home. Uncle Nicholas would, as we put it, get after any of us who got a bad conduct report at school.

The streets were a different matter. By the time I was ten years old, I fought anybody who looked at me wrong. From kids to grown men. It didn't matter to me. Mostly I fought with the white kids who had new shoes or who had money to buy whatever they wanted. I almost always fought when somebody called me names. Many years passed and I created a lot of problems for myself before I broke the fighting habit.

3

Quick Fists

When I was twelve we had a pretty big change in our lives. Uncle Nicholas was appointed to be a Wharton County deputy sheriff. He was the first Hispanic to hold such a position, and he had overcome great odds to achieve it. The Anglos owned most of the land, held all of the political offices, and made all of the rules. Certain lines had been drawn long ago, and Uncle Nicholas was the first to cross them.

A great deal of prejudice still existed. For example, the restaurant where I took a job as a dishwasher. The owner didn't mind hiring me to wash dishes, but I had to eat in the kitchen, not up front. If I went to the movie theater I still had to sit up in the balcony in the "Mexican Section." In school the teachers knew not to seat us next to an Anglo child. They could lose their jobs for it.

If there was a killing or a robbery on our side of town, the Anglos would say, "You know how those Mexicans are. Leave 'em be, they'll settle it themselves." They called the killings "misdemeanor homicides." In those days other kids would call me a "greaser" or "spic" or "taco bender" right to my face. The kids had heard their fathers use such epithets, and their fathers had heard their fathers use them, so the kids thought it must be all right.

That's the way it was, and I resented it deeply, but Uncle Nicholas didn't see it as the way it had to be. If we got an education, worked hard, and led a clean life of discipline we would earn the Anglos' respect, he told us. "Your futures lie in a world that is controlled by the Anglos," he lectured. "America is a great melting pot."

"What's a melting pot?" I asked.

"*Hijo,* you'll never have any success until you learn to blend your small difference into the whole. You have to prepare yourself to sell your talents to the highest bidder in the large market that will eventually become available to you. Someday, someone will open a door to you, and you must be there saying 'Let me in.' "

He was right, but most Mexicans couldn't understand him, including me. "I can't even go in the front door of the restaurant where I work."

"No, not now. Some of the laws and practices are stacked against us, but we must respect the law. We must get inside the system and enforce the laws fairly."

Uncle Nicholas was not a militant or a rabble-rouser. Instead, he was a peacemaker. Even before he was made a deputy, he resolved problems between the communities. He talked the talk and made the peace. He didn't do it with his hat in his hand and his eyes on the ground asking for favors, and he didn't do it with threats. If our folks were wrong he'd say so and stick to it. If the Anglo side was wrong he'd talk sense until their ears fell off or they agreed, just as he sometimes preached to us until we gave up and did what he wanted.

I believe that his qualities of honesty and honor were the reasons he was chosen to be the first from our community to be "melted" into the larger pot. He kept the good in our culture: language, love of family, and religion; and he adopted what he saw as good in the America that was coming to be: a chance to rise above his present station.

The overt racism didn't disappear overnight, but the door that Uncle Nicholas had spoken of was gradually being opened. My own behavior changed almost as slowly. I was still a fighter. Uncle Nicholas tried to break me of fighting; it just didn't work. I averaged about one fight per day.

There was one kid whom I fought at least once a day for almost six months. I still see him once in a while and we joke about it. It all began one day when he had an ice-cream cone. He guessed that I didn't have a nickel to get one for myself, and he was right.

He came so close to me that I could smell the chocolate and I could almost feel the coolness from the mound atop the cone. His pink tongue came out of his mouth and made a deep trench across the top of the ice cream. He took a long time swallowing, like someone tasting wine. Then he said, "Sure is good. I bet you wish you had a nickel to get an ice-cream cone, Roy."

I shoved that cone down his throat and we went at it. For six months, every time we saw each other, we went at it. Sometimes he whipped me; most of the time I whipped him. Neither of us would call it off. I went off that summer to cut beets, and when I got back neither of us could remember why we'd been so mad at each other. So we didn't start up again.

Uncle Nicholas thought that he could channel some of my fist-fighting into something more acceptable and got all of his boys into the gym and training for the Golden Gloves. My brother and I were the only ones who stuck it out, and I suspect that the program was intended only for us anyway.

I turned out to be a pretty good fighter, but I had a hard time staying within the rules. I was pretty wild on the offense, but I could sure take a punch. I started my career slowly. But, after a while, I started winning match after match and I began moving toward a shot at the state championship.

Rogelio and I rode to Fort Worth, Texas, with our coach. The state championship match was held at the Will Rogers Coliseum there. I'd never seen so many people in one place in all my life. The noise and crowds in that arena were like something I'd only heard and seen from the balcony of the movie theater. I felt that for once in my life I was the one doing the right thing. For once in my life the family was proud of me, not embarrassed by me. This was my big day, but it didn't last long.

I got my butt licked soundly. My opponent made me look like a fool. I was wild and aggressive. He was one heck of a boxer and just stood there and cut me down to size. The more he whipped on me the wilder I got. The referee almost stopped the fight before it was over.

I was still mad back in the locker room when my brother, Rogelio, came in to console me. "Ya did okay, man," he said.

"You're lying. We both know it."

"Naw, man. You tried."

"Tried!" I said. "I got my butt whipped."

While we were talking, the guy who had beaten me walked into the room. He had learned the lessons that the Golden

Gloves tries to teach: Sportsmanship is just as important as box-
ing. The organization tries to channel the participants' aggressive tendencies into something acceptable and teach respect and
the value of following rules.

I wasn't too good at living up to any of those ideals. I still
hadn't figured that part out.

My opponent extended his hand. "You gave me a good
fight . . ." he began, but he didn't get to finish his speech about
what the Golden Gloves is really about because I grabbed him,
dragged him to the toilet, and stuck his head in it.

This episode was observed by the other fighters, coaches, and
parents who were all around us. I had moved too quickly for
anybody to stop us. But I never fought in Golden Gloves again.
I'm still ashamed of myself for that stupid move. I disgraced the
Benavidez name, committing that unforgivable sin so preached
about by my grandfather and uncle.

My fights became increasingly serious, and Uncle Nicholas
became more and more worried about some of the tough guys I
was hanging around with. What would start out as a "friendly
discussion" would end by being a hassle with someone drawing
a knife. One night, Rogelio got word that a buddy of his was
involved in such a friendly discussion, and he went to help him.

After he didn't return for a while, I decided to go help
Rogelio. We all ended up in a sizable brawl that attracted the
attention of a certain Wharton County deputy sheriff. Uncle
Nicholas scattered the other boys, told them to go on home.
Rogelio and me he took to the jail, where he locked us in a cell.
We sat despondent on a ticking-covered mattress for three hours.
Every now and then, Uncle Nicholas would pass the cell and
taunt us, "Oh, you Benavidez brothers sure look nice in there."

One night after a session of beer drinking with some of my
pals, I went to bed in the attic room where we boys slept two to
the bed. I began to feel nauseated and struggled to make my
way down the stairs to the bathroom. Uncle Nicholas met me
at the foot of the stairs and slowed my progress so that I was
unable to reach my destination in time to prevent an accident.
Recovering, I tried to convince him that I had become ill from
eating a hamburger sold by one of the street vendors that oper-
ated behind the post office where the migrant workers parked
in the hopes that some farmer would engage their labor for the
day. Uncle Nicholas discouraged our eating the food sold

there, but he knew that one of their hamburgers had not been the cause of my ailment.

"Booze and bad friends will get you in trouble, Raul," he said. *"Dime con quien andas, y te dije quien eres."* Literally translated, this means "Tell me with whom you walk and I will tell you who you are." I'll bet Uncle Nicholas said that to me a thousand times.

When we checked out of school to go to the Colorado beet fields the spring of 1950 before I was fifteen, I turned in my English literature book to Miss Vera Schram. "I'll see you in the fall, Raul," she said.

"No, miss, I'm not gonna come next year."

She looked at me with real concern. "Raul, I want you to come back. I'll be expecting to see you."

"No, I'm not gonna come back."

"Raul, please come back. You're smart. You'll do all right if you'll keep your mouth shut and stop fighting."

I never did return to the public schools of El Campo, but I saw Miss Schram again years later when I was a member of Special Forces and I was on leave. My wife and I were visiting our families, and we went to church. After the service, Miss Schram told me that the FBI had questioned her about me when I was being investigated for top-secret clearance. "Roy," she said, for I had changed my name from Raul to Roy while I was in the army, "oh, Roy, when the FBI contacted me, I was just hoping that you weren't in trouble."

In the spring of 1950, I was once again in the sugar beet fields of Colorado, and on May 1 of that year, President Truman announced the first installment of military and financial aid to the French in Indochina. The United States had then begun to pump millions of dollars into the French effort, which, as is well known, failed completely. Perhaps I heard the announcement of Truman's decision on the red radio. I know that I heard reports of the fears of Chinese Communist intervention in Korea and other parts of Indochina. I had no idea how my life would eventually be affected by the reports I heard.

By the time I was fifteen I was living the typical life of a school dropout. I was working at a gas station pumping gas and doing odd jobs on the side. I was living at home and giving most of my paycheck to Uncle Nicholas every week. I really considered myself a burden to the family. I was even embarrassed myself about where I was in life after all of the preaching I had received from Uncle Nicholas and my grandfather about the value of an education. I was turning into a living example of what not to be for the younger kids. If you could have bet on me back then the odds were about even that in ten years I'd either still be pumping gas or be in prison, where a lot of my street buddies ended up.

Not that Uncle Nicholas gave up on me. He kept talking: "Real friends don't get friends in trouble, *hijo.*"

Evidently, the angels were still watching over me, because I met another man who, like Uncle Nicholas, would change my life. His name was Art Haddock. He worked at the Firestone tire store in El Campo as the bookkeeper. He was looking around for someone good and dependable to help at the store. He knew I was Uncle Nicholas's "son" and had heard I was a hard worker, so he asked me if I'd come to work with him.

Art was different from any Anglo I had ever met at that time. He wasn't Catholic like we were, but he was an ordained minister. His Bible was always on the desk next to the ledger books, and he often found occasions to read it to me. If he heard me say a curse word when I was trying to loosen the lug nuts on a tire, he would summon me.

"Listen to this, son."

Dreading what was coming, I'd say, "Don't you want me to fix the tire?"

"Tires can wait, Raul. You can't."

"But that man was in a hurry for his tire."

"Come here, son."

Obediently I would go, and Mr. Haddock would open his well-thumbed Bible. "Genesis, chapter twenty, verse seven: 'Thou shalt not take the name of the Lord thy God in vain; for the Lord will not hold him guiltless that taketh his name in vain.'"

"I'm sorry, Mr. Haddock. I'll go fix that tire now."

He would thumb the pages. "Sit down, son. Matthew, chapter fifteen, verse eleven: 'Not that which goeth into the mouth defileth a man; but that which cometh out of the mouth, this defileth a man.' Now those are the very words of Jesus Christ, Our Lord."

I promised to remember and in relief returned to my chores.

Within a year he had taught me so much about having a sense of responsibility and about what the Bible said that I was running the shop while he ran the business. What he was really doing was just reinforcing what Uncle Nicholas had been trying to beat into my hard head for eight years. Somehow it was finally starting to stick.

When he started talking to me about how I could never really make anything of myself without a decent education I began to think that maybe he and Uncle Nicholas had been talking on the side. Neither one would ever admit it.

Our business was mostly commercial. Trucking lines depended on us when they were in the area, and Curtis Reese, who owned the store, had contracts with most of the oil field service companies to fix all of their flats out in the field.

By the time I was sixteen Mr. Haddock had given me the shop truck to take home every night so I could handle any emergency calls that came in after we closed. He gave me responsibilities and treated me like a man. I sure didn't want to miss a call because I was out drinking beer with my buddies. So I guess I grew up some and took those responsibilities seriously. Sometimes when someone treats a person with respect that person automatically becomes deserving of it.

One day, when we were about to close, we got a call from one of the oil field service companies. They were trying to get to a blown-out well, which was a pretty big emergency, and their truck with the equipment had a flat. Art took the call and gave me the directions and told me to handle it quickly but not to break the speed limit getting there.

Ignoring his admonition, I went screeching my tires through town like my own tail was on fire. I saw Uncle Nicholas coming out of a coffee shop, and I slowed down and waved. That was my big mistake.

He waved me over, and I stopped. He propped his arms in the open window of the truck. "What's the emergency, son?"

"Mr. Haddock sent me to fix a flat. He told me to hurry."

"I don't think Mr. Haddock would tell you to drive like that. I don't figure that this flat is reason enough for you to endanger innocent people." Uncle Nicholas backed away from the truck. "You've got a speeding ticket coming. When you get through fixing that tire, you'd better drop by the police station to see me."

It didn't take long to find the truck and fix the tire. At least not as long as I'd hoped it would take, and within an hour I was standing inside the police station. Deputy Sheriff Benavidez asked, "Do you want to pay your fine, or do you want to call your boss?"

Being always broke because I was still handing over my paychecks to the family, I told him to call Mr. Haddock. About fifteen minutes later Art handed over fifteen dollars, and Uncle Nicholas told him, "You know, he's my boy, and I'm real proud of him. But out on the streets he's the same as everyone else." It gave me a real funny feeling. I'd done wrong, and here were the two most important men in my life talking about their regard for me. They sent me on my way and Art never mentioned it to me. Somehow, the way they talked about me, like I wasn't even there, made me feel so guilty that Deputy Benavidez never had any call to treat me the same as "everyone else" again.

I had taken a small step toward growing up, and I was beginning to try to figure out what that future was that everybody kept telling me about.

4

A Better Way

Even though I had begun to try to envision my future, I was still working for Curtis Reese, owner of the Firestone store, and Art Haddock when I was seventeen. While the job wasn't a bad one for a young man, I recognized that it was a dead-end one. That was a dreadful realization for someone my age. I did value the job, though, and because of it, I reduced my one-fight-per-day average to just one or two bouts on weekends when I was not on call.

Mr. Haddock and Uncle Nicholas prodded me to return to school and finish, and I considered it. I decided that I just couldn't go back because I would have felt like a fool walking back into a classroom with people who were much younger than I was. Besides, I needed to work every day. I looked into taking a high school equivalency test with the goal of going to junior college in mind. But I didn't do that either. My failures weren't caused by laziness—I had worked at one job steadily, sometimes holding two or three part-time jobs at the same time. They were caused when my misplaced pride got in the way.

I had some grand ambitions, though. For a time, I wanted to become a truck driver. I loved the sound of the air horns on the Mack trucks, and I liked the idea of being on the road. Foolishly, I thought that I could do that without an education. Because Uncle Nicholas was a law-enforcement officer, I dreamed for a while of becoming a highway patrolman and maybe later a

Texas Ranger. Then I learned that I was not tall enough to qualify for that group.

The seeds of another life ambition had been planted in my mind, too. At church, at weddings, and at various parties, I had noticed a girl named Hilaria Coy. I had been seeing her at such occasions ever since I had come to live in El Campo, but somehow I was now looking at her in a new way.

Not that there was the possibility for anything that vaguely resembled "dating" as it is done today, for Lala, as she was called, came from a family as strict and old-fashioned as my own. Lala was fair-skinned and had glossy brown hair. I thought that she was by far the prettiest girl in town, and I started trying to get her to notice me.

One of the ways I tried to attract her notice was by showing off at the baseball games we had when numerous families gathered for picnics. That often backfired because I'd miss a ball I should have caught when I was looking to see if she was looking at me. I did, though, attract the attention of two girls from the nearby town of Victoria. They learned my name, and some days after a ball game, they returned to El Campo to try to find me.

My luck was running true to form. In their search, they stopped at the store where Lala worked and asked *her* where to find me. When I heard about it, I thought, I was just beginning to make a little progress with Lala, just beginning to climb the fence, that barrier that our culture put between young men and women, and somebody—those girls from Victoria—had pulled me down.

Finally, my luck turned, at least insofar as work was concerned. I got interested in a program that would give me some education, an additional income, and could be worked around my steady job. I heard about the Texas National Guard, and the more I found out about it the more I liked the idea. It seemed to be the perfect solution for someone in my position, and I signed up.

My first taste of military life was basic training at Fort Knox, Kentucky. It reminded me of being back in the labor camps of my youth, only easier. I never could figure out what a lot of the other guys were complaining about. We ate good, most nights we slept under a roof, only one to a bed, and we got a lot of exercise.

The instructors who were cadre, or regular army, got me really hooked on the army. Some of them were Airborne with battle experience in Europe or Korea. Some were Rangers who had jumped behind enemy lines. The stories they told about their adventures thrilled me.

Before going into the National Guard, I was a typical teenage know-it-all; once I met some of those instructors I became more humble about my knowledge. They had been places and done things I'd only dreamed of.

My fellow trainees taught me a few things, too. They came from a variety of backgrounds, and the astonishing thing was that we all worked together as a team. I was seeing some of the ideal that Uncle Nicholas had always told me was possible. The experience was surprising to me, and it opened my eyes to the opportunities for a half-Mexican, half-Indian dropout from South Texas.

The army was still basically segregated during the early fifties. The command made formal and informal efforts to keep the races apart, but that was largely unsuccessful. We were a bunch of young kids, after all, most of us away from home for the first time in our lives, and naturally we all worked together to try to beat the system.

When boot camp was over, I had made corporal, and I could hardly wait to return to El Campo to show those stripes to Art and Uncle Nicholas. I was really starting to feel good about myself.

While I was in the Guard, I also got a chance to meet one of my heroes, Audie Murphy, the most decorated soldier from World War II. I had seen *To Hell and Back,* the movie of his life, about a dozen times when he came to Fort Hood near Killeen, Texas. I was already impressed, but when I actually met him, I was awestruck.

By this time I was nearly full grown and stood only five foot six and weighed one hundred and thirty pounds. Murphy was a little guy, as I was, but everybody was looking up to him. He had come from poverty, just as I had. His family had been tenant farmers in North Texas, and he had picked cotton as I had. Yet he had made something of himself. He was a movie actor when I met him, and he was still a member of the 36th Infantry Division, Texas National Guard, a well-known and highly decorated unit during World War II. In spite of Murphy's celebrity, he was a polite guy who talked to us as if we were his buddies. Audie Murphy became my idol and role model.

After I received the Medal of Honor, his widow, Pam, sent me a photograph of her husband. She signed it "The Murphy family salutes *you* for Audie."

While I was in the Guard, I learned a number of valuable lessons, none more so than the necessity of checking the gas gauge in any vehicle I might be driving . . . or even going for a ride in. I had been assigned to drive Lieutenant Colonel Ken Frankey, the battalion commander of the El Campo National Guard, to an officers' meeting.

I also learned that I shouldn't borrow a mess kit, or at least if I did I should make sure that I borrowed a clean one. I had borrowed a buddy's and had failed to take that precaution, and I came down with a severe case of diarrhea, a common occurrence in the field when soldiers failed to properly sterilize their mess kits.

I checked out a jeep and picked up Lieutenant Colonel Frankey, but en route to his meeting, I had to make frequent stops and repair to the bushes on the roadside. I made elaborate apologies each time I had to stop, but by the third time, the lieutenant colonel lost patience. He took the wheel of the jeep and told me to get back to camp the best way I could. Unfortunately for him, but more so for me, the jeep ran out of gas before he reached his destination.

The lieutenant colonel hitched a ride to his meeting, and I had the unpleasant task of locating the jeep and putting gasoline in it, all the while knowing that I would be on KP for days.

Certainly, I learned many lessons while I was in the Guard, and I would have spared myself a great deal of suffering if I had learned to control my temper. However, I still had a bad attitude. If I thought some guy was looking down at me I'd try to put him down on the ground so I'd be looking down at him. Because of that tendency, and a smart mouth that got me in as much trouble as my fists did, I lost my corporal stripes twice while I was in the Guard.

I always worked hard to earn back my stripes, and I figured I was army material. For two weeks each summer and one weekend each month, I wore a uniform and served as a squad leader. The rest of the time, I was running the store for Mr. Haddock. During those two years in the Guard, I became convinced that my future would be in the regular army. I thought that I had found a home in the military, one that I was already quite well prepared to inhabit.

Mr. Haddock continued to instruct me, in both life and the Bible. "For a nineteen-year-old kid, Raul, this is not a bad job. But is it going to be a good job for you when you're twenty-nine or thirty-nine?"

I hated those talks, but now I see how unselfish Mr. Haddock was. I was good help at the store, and in spite of my other failings I never stole, even though I had ample opportunities to make a few "back-door" tire sales.

Art would go on. "Your cousins are graduating from high school and some of them are passing you by so fast it looks like you're standing still." I'd see his hand move toward his Bible. "Proverbs, chapter four, verses twenty-six and twenty-seven: 'Ponder the path of thy feet, and let all thy ways be established. Turn not to the right hand nor to the left: remove thy foot from evil.' If you're going to have a good future, you're going to have to get more education."

I could see that circumstances had changed since our family had worked in the fields. Grandfather Salvador had been right when he had said that machines would take our jobs as field-workers. The army was the only place that I could imagine that I could get training. They would pay me, house me, feed me, and teach me several trades. The army looked like the best shot I had.

I had talked to some recruiters while I was in the Guard, and they had said that I could qualify for police work—next best thing to being a Texas Ranger. They also encouraged me to go Airborne. They filled my head with their views of the army. "Airborne is the elite, it is the best, it is for you," they said. "What do you want to do? You want to tell your grandkids about bein' a cook somewhere? You want to tell them about shuffling paper in Georgia? Kid, you're a fighter, you go Airborne, you go be a fighter."

The recruiters omitted some of the less glamorous aspects of the fields they recommended, aches and fears that I would learn about later, but they convinced me that I wanted to be army and to be a special part of it.

Once my mind was made up, I had to take one more essential step. I was old enough to enlist without my family's permission, as many young men did, but doing so would have been unthinkable to me. As wild as I was about some things, I would not have dreamed of taking such an important step without having Uncle Nicholas's permission. I was responsible to Uncle Nicholas, and he was responsible for me until I was twenty-one. This was the old-country custom and a basic rule in our family. If such loyalty existed today, our society might have fewer problems, but an abundance of men like Uncle Nicholas would be needed to command such respect.

Uncle Nicholas and I sat in the living room and talked it out. He listened patiently while I laid out all that I had been told by my officers and sergeants. "Raul, I believe that the Guard has done a lot to increase your confidence in yourself, and I think that it has begun to teach you a sense of responsibility; but I want you to be certain that this is what you want to do. Once you're in, there will be no getting out." He wasn't trying to talk me out of it; he was just trying to make sure that I had thought it out clearly and really understood what I was doing.

I assured him that I was certain about the decision, and he gave me his blessing. "I'm very proud of you, Raul," he said, and I think his voice cracked slightly as he said it. To dilute the emotion that we both felt, he said as I left the room, "I'm not sure the army knows what it's getting itself into."

I wonder if Uncle Nicholas was secretly relieved. Of all those kids I had been the hardest to raise, and I still lacked some finishing touches. Maybe it was that Yaqui blood of my mother's that made me so ornery and difficult. Years later, I teased Uncle Nicholas that he had been happy to pass this problem on to the government of the United States, but he always denied it.

Next I went to talk with Mr. Haddock. "I won't leave you high and dry. I'll stay on long enough for you to hire more help and for me to train them as best I can." That was a hard promise for me to make. My mind was a million miles away. It was on the beaches of Normandy and in the frozen foxholes of Korea, places that I imagined to be far more appealing than they were. In my mind I was already gone. I kept my promise, though, for Mr. Haddock had meant too much to me for me to abandon him.

The day I left, he put his hand on my shoulder and said, without opening his Bible, "The Lord bless thee and keep thee: The Lord make His face shine upon thee, and be gracious unto thee: The Lord lift up his countenance upon thee, and give thee peace." Mr. Haddock did something that day that nobody had ever done to me before. He put his arms around me and gave me a hug. My first *abrazo* as a man came from an Anglo. Ours was an emotional parting.

On the bus to Houston, I was a free nineteen-year-old, free of all of my responsibilities, both to my family and to Mr. Haddock. I was sure that the year 1954 would be a big one for me.

The recruiting station in Houston was a big building, the old U.S. Customs House at 701 San Jacinto Street. Thousands of young men had been processed there during World War II and the Korean War. It was the single recruiting office in the area in those days when the smaller offices had not yet opened. In fact, many volunteers from the South Texas area signed their papers there.

The street doors had glass panes in wood frames, and recruiting posters were plastered all over every pane. On the first floor there were offices and desks for all of the branches of the service. Each recruiter competed to get enlistees to join up with the branch he represented. I walked across that creaky old wooden floor and felt as if I were running a gauntlet. A navy recruiter said, "Hey, did you come to see me?" An air force recruiter said, "This is the right place over here."

I walked across the floor like a cocky little rooster with all of my papers from the Guard and all of my records tucked under my arm. I walked straight to the army desk. The sergeant took my papers and leaned back in the chair, and as if I wasn't even present, he started flipping through them. He was reading a little here and a little there. Every once in a while he would look up at me. Finally, I just blurted out, louder than I meant to, "I want to go Airborne."

He started to smile, looked up for a second, then turned his eyes back down to my papers and said, "Boy, I don't think you're big enough for the Airborne."

Jumping up, I leaned over the desk, stuck my fist in his face, and yelled, "I can cut you down to my size quick enough."

A crowd of recruiters gathered. The sergeant just laughed, and that made me one mad son of a gun. I had a marine sergeant with an arm on one shoulder saying, "Son, I think the marines could use a man like you." I also had an army captain with his hand on my other shoulder telling the marine to get lost. "You're army all the way, son. We need tough guys like you."

Those guys did a job on me. I was like a chicken that had walked right into a pack of coyotes. Within a couple of hours, I had taken a test, passed a physical, been sworn into the army by an officer, and I was back on a bus to El Campo to await reporting.

Going home, I pondered the oath that I had taken:

I, Raul P. Benavidez, do solemnly swear that I will support and defend the Constitution of the United States against all enemies, foreign and domestic; that I will bear true faith and allegiance to the same; and that I will obey the orders of the president of the United States and the orders of the officers appointed over me, according to the regulations of the Uniform Code of Military Justice. So help me God.

The words were solemn, and so was I. When I finally settled down and read all of the papers that I had signed and figured them all out, I knew that my education had begun.

I was in the army, and that was all. I shook my head when I realized what they had gotten me to agree to. I would not be Airborne. They had ignored my National Guard experience. I would not be going to advanced infantry school with my current rank of corporal and then going on to Airborne training as I had expected. I had actually signed on to go back to basic training again as a raw recruit. I was back at the bottom again, and I had signed it.

Today I cannot count the courses and seminars and classes that the army sent me to. I was trained as a warrior. I was trained in communications, medical technology, business administration, personnel management, psychology, criminology and police techniques. But the first education that the army gave me for free was the lesson that those recruiters taught me when they enrolled me on their terms rather than on my own. I'll always remember this because I heard it myself and told it to multitudes of recruits a million times: "The needs of the army come first."

5

The Military Way

The family had a get-together for me before I left, a party to which my many relatives all came. That my aunts and uncles and cousins had gathered in my honor to wish me good luck made me feel good. Yet I sensed that some seemed a bit too happy to send me on my way, and that made me wonder if they were glad to be rid of me. I was too immature at the time to understand the pride that people of my culture take when a member of their family chooses to serve our country.

Later, I heard the story of Sara Castro Vara of San Antonio, Texas, who had six sons. All six of her sons served in World War II. When she was approached with sympathy because of this, she said, "If I had a seventh son, I would have been proud to send him too to fight for his country."

I was torn in another way as well. I thought of myself as a tough loner who wanted to build a future away from my family. Yet I was not as much the loner as I imagined. All of the years of being inculcated with the importance of family had left an indelible mark on me. I felt that by going away and doing what I so passionately wanted to do I was deserting my family in some sense. I looked around the room at the smiling faces of my relatives and justified my desire to be gone by thinking, They're glad to see me leave.

When the train blew its whistle and pulled out of Union Station in Houston on its way to Fort Ord, California, I was as excited as I had been as a boy when Uncle Nicholas had taken Rogelio and me on the bus trip from Cuero to El Campo. I had the same feeling of adventure that I used to feel when we'd load up in Uncle Nicholas's truck and head off to the fields of Colorado. This adventure was better. It was my personal enterprise.

Sometimes as we traveled, I lapsed into self-flagellation for my failures. I'd tell myself that I hadn't followed the advice of Grandfather Salvador, Uncle Nicholas, or Mr. Haddock and finished school. The other kids had followed Uncle Nicholas's blueprint for success, and they remained at home. I was the only one who had to leave to make a better life. I think that I was suffering the first pangs of homesickness.

The car in which we traveled was filled with other raw recruits like me. We were accompanied by a few commissioned and noncommissioned officers, who were there to herd us like cattle through the dining cars and the stops and stations along the way. In conversations with my fellow recruits, I learned that most of them perceived this chapter of their lives as a short one—two or three years. I felt lonely because I felt different from them. I already felt that my career would be military; I saw it as my single chance to be successful. If I was not, I knew that I could never look Uncle Nicholas in the eyes again.

The army does little without some reason behind it, and there was a reason for putting a group of recruits into the same railroad car for a three-day trip to California. By the time we reached San Antonio, about two hundred miles from Houston, we were already getting acquainted. A few groups started playing cards.

By the time we reached Fort Ord, we were "buddies." Some of the camaraderie that is typical—and necessary—in the military was already formed. In our case the basis for the closeness was "us against them." "Us" were the recruits, and "them" were the officers who had charge of us.

I felt at home at Fort Ord, comfortable back in uniform, and secure in my second round of basic training. I did not like the way my drill sergeant pronounced my given name, Raul, when he got his big red face in my face. "Ra-oooool," he would yell, his nose almost touching mine. "Ra-oooool." I was changed in several ways by my basic training—one way was that, when it was over, I became Roy P. Benavidez so that no one could ever call me "Ra-ooool" again.

Those drill sergeants were pretty tough characters. In the previous fifteen years many of them had served in both World War

II and the Korean War. They weren't training a peacetime army. They knew that what they were beating into our heads could save our lives, and they never let up on us.

Theirs was the "brown shoe" army, and in it all recruits rotated through the kitchen doing KP duty. One day I was one of the Kitchen Police and was doing a job so common in the kitchen that even to speak of it sounds like uttering a cliché. I was peeling potatoes, vats of potatoes.

One of the cooks was a big fat man whose size belied the quality of the food he dished up. Possibly, he became obese from laziness, for he commanded the recruits to do a lot of work that was rightfully his. While he was goldbricking, he entertained himself by picking on us. On that day, he had chosen me as his favorite target. "Move it," he yelled. "A one-handed blind man could peel more of those spuds than you're doing."

Everybody tried to avoid him, and I kept my mouth shut for a long time. He said, "Get the lead out of your britches, Benavidez." I just kept peeling potatoes. He walked by me and shoved me with his huge butt. Still I kept my mouth shut. He walked by me again and gave me a shove. Still I said nothing. Finally, he came at me from behind and shoved me so hard with his belly that I almost fell headfirst into the potato bin. I still didn't say anything.

I turned around and hit him, and he stumbled back against a stove. He reached back to keep from falling and both of his hands got wedged behind him on a hot grill. I can still smell the flesh burning.

He went to sick call and I went to the drill sergeant's office. I expected to be court-martialed on the spot. The drill sergeant chewed me up one side and down the other. I thought I had heard every derogatory name that existed until I took that dressing-down from him. He laid on me every dirty detail, such as cleaning the latrines, that he could think of.

What he didn't do was put a record of the incident in my file. He might have hated the cook as much as we recruits did. Definitely, we were his men, and he felt that he was the only one who should be allowed to abuse us. That was the old "brown shoe" army way of doing things.

I couldn't figure out what the sergeant was so mad about. Somebody had been picking on me, and I'd let him have it. I still hadn't caught on to who I was and what real discipline was all about. I had the shell of a good soldier. On the surface I looked and acted like a soldier. But, if you scratched the surface, not far underneath you'd find an insecure, tough little kid who fought at any provocation.

Except for a few scrapes off post, I managed to stay out of trouble until the last day of boot camp. We were out on night field maneuvers and I got lost. I was with a man I had become real good buddies with during basic. His name was Broadnax, and he was from Beeville, Texas, about a hundred miles south of El Campo. We made an odd-looking pair, him big and black and me little and brown. The comments occasioned by our looks had started most of the off-post fights I got into. Broadnax wasn't one to hold back either; he had an attitude about as bad as mine.

Broadnax and I had gotten separated from the troop and were cutting across the fields to catch up when we stumbled into a couple of skunks. The ensuing battle was won by the skunks, and when we reached the rest of the troops, they could smell us coming a hundred yards off. That's just about how far back the sergeant made us stay until we got back to camp close to midnight.

The sergeant ordered us to strip as we stood in front of the barracks. Then he ordered some men to burn our clothes. We stood naked and watched our stinking fatigues go up in flames. Everyone else roared with laughter, but not at the sight of us naked—after all of the times we had showered together, that didn't interest them. They laughed at the extent to which Broadnax and I could go to create problems for ourselves.

The sergeant gave us an about-face and marched us off down the road to the football field that doubled as the parade grounds. When we reached the fifty-yard line he ordered us to halt. He put us at ease and told us he'd be back in the morning. He said, "You can sleep out with the other skunks for the night."

The night became so cold that we wished we had our fatigues back, no matter how sickening they smelled. We tried lying down, and standing up, and jumping around. There was nothing we could do to keep warm. About five A.M., the sergeant returned and marched two shivering naked fools back to the showers.

I've had a grudge against skunks ever since. I actually enjoy smelling the aroma of a "road-killed" polecat.

A few hours later I was back on the fifty-yard line. This time

I was in dress uniform and I was getting corporal stripes and orders to report to advanced infantry training out in Fort Carson, Colorado.

I had enough leave coming that I could have gone home to El Campo for a few days, but I saved most of it. I spent a few days in California, then reported early to my new assignment. I wasn't ready to go home yet. I wanted to prove something before I walked back in that door.

In Colorado, where I had last been as a migrant field-worker, I really dug into the training and started to discover that I had a brain as well as a body. The last time I had been in a classroom I had felt like a dumb "Mezikin" kid who wasn't expected to do more than take up a chair. Training with me was Billy Martin, who would later become the great New York Yankees manager. He was one fighting dude. After seeing him in action as a soldier, it was easy for me to understand his later success. Another trainee was Faron Young, who would go on to fame as a country-western singer.

At Fort Carson, I was a squad leader and I was expected to stay one step ahead of my squad. I ate it up. I discovered what a real kick it was to sit in the front of the class and have the first answer rather than to hide in the back and hope that I didn't get called on.

Some other changes in me were taking place during that period. I began to be proud of where I was and what I was doing, and I started wanting to go to El Campo to visit Uncle Nicholas and the rest of the family and to show them that they could be proud of me, too. My only regret was that I still hadn't been assigned to Airborne. To me, Airborne was still the elite. If I was going to be "army all the way," that's where I wanted to be.

The army didn't see it that way. The Korean War was officially over when a cease-fire was negotiated between the parties in 1953. Infantry was needed there to maintain the fragile peace. After all, "the needs of the army come first."

I wanted to see my family, but I was nervous about it as well. Training such as I had been through inevitably rearranges a person's brain, and I feared that I would be a square peg in a round hole back home. I left Fort Carson on a bus, and I had to change in El Paso, Texas. I had become so skittish by then that I almost failed to board the second bus. The final call came over the speaker before I went to the bus door. It was closed, and I banged on it and hollered to the driver to open up and let me in.

I stopped in Cuero to see Lupe, my half sister. I loved her, but while I was visiting with her I had a flash of insight. Her people weren't my family. My family were in El Campo waiting for me, and I could hardly wait to get there.

They didn't know exactly when I was coming in so they weren't waiting for me at the bus station. The old cabdriver I used to translate for was still there, and he took the "soldier boy" over to the sheriff's office at no charge. Sheriff Benavidez wasn't in when I arrived, but he returned to the office a few minutes later. When Uncle Nicholas came through the door and saw me, he stopped and said nothing. His expression was unsmiling but happy. Seeing him look at me that way made any discomfort I had endured during training completely worthwhile.

After a brief pause, we stepped toward each other, and he took my hand as he would take the hand of a man, a man worthy of another man's respect.

Those two weeks with the family were a happy time. My cousins gathered around me, just as we all used to gather around Grandfather Salvador, and begged me to tell them about my experiences. Even he asked me to talk. He said, "*Hijo,* in my day we didn't have many books such as those you read now. We talked. We told our children about the old days. Tell me about the new days. We must always talk to each other."

People were looking up at me without my having to knock anybody down first. I began to realize how much love was in that family that I had sometimes refused to open my eyes to and see. It had surrounded me all of my life. God had given me a "song in the night" after I had lost my father and mother by giving me Uncle Nicholas, Aunt Alexandria, my cousins, Grandfather Salvador, and Art Haddock.

My leave passed so fast it seemed that I had only gotten home when I had to leave for Seattle. I boarded the S.S. *Mitchell* at Pier 91 for the trip to Korea in the fall of 1955. I was seasick for the first time in my life during the twenty-eight days it took us to cross the Pacific, and I was truly homesick for the first time as well. I finally understood the guys I had known in basic training who suffered for the pieces of their souls that they had left back home. In the past when I had left my family, I had felt that I was escaping them; now I felt that I was leaving a vital part of myself behind. With both seasickness and homesickness, the sufferer lacks stability that he has become used to having. I had double sickness during the voyage. The ship pitched and rolled, and I, who had never been a picky eater, who had even found little to complain about in army chow, went to mess fearfully. I would take my tray to the rack where we stood to eat and try to swallow and keep down a few bites. Often I failed.

I was mistakenly glad when I saw the shoreline of Korea at Inchon Harbor. While we waited for high tide so that we could dock, I gazed at the land where I would spend two Christmases, at the surrounding islands and the rugged mountains in the background, and found it beautiful.

The wind was blowing over the terrain, and I noticed a sickening smell. I asked a sailor what the stench was. "The world's biggest outhouse," he responded. "That's Korea." I knew nothing then of primitive agricultural methods, and I knew nothing of being really cold. I thought that I had been cold when the drill sergeant left me naked on the football field. I knew nothing about monsoons, Slicky Boys, Katusa soldiers, and Amerasian orphans. Neither did I know, in spite of my background, about genuine grinding poverty.

6

Land of the Morning Calm

After suffering from seasickness for nearly a month, I developed a severe case of culture shock in Korea. I was a member of E Company, Second Battalion, Seventeenth Infantry Regiment, also known as the Buffalo Regiment. The regiment members carried a buffalo nickel in their pockets as a good luck talisman. The Seventeenth was a regiment in the Seventh Infantry Division. The real shooting war had just ended.

The 1953 cease-fire kept the situation in Korea stalemated. The only conclusion that I could draw was that the country was now divided in half at the thirty-eighth parallel and that America was destined to be a resident military force there for a long, long time.

We had sacrificed over fifty thousand American lives to hold the line, and more than eight thousand soldiers were missing in action. There was a lot of bitterness among the American military for not going all-out to win the war. General Douglas MacArthur had been removed by President Truman as commander of the United Nations forces because he wanted an all-out war instead of the "police action" that we had fought.

About the only aspect of the sixteen months I was there that pleased me was that I stood taller than most of the Koreans. I liked to walk around without having to look up at everybody.

The living conditions of the Koreans shocked me profoundly. Back home we lived in a palace like royalty compared to the way those folks lived following the war. Seoul was still a bombed-out city. Many buildings were mere shells, and the areas around them were off-limits to GI's. In the countryside, the houses were constructed from the refuse of the army. The roofs were often made of flattened beer cans and pork-and-beans cans.

Old men, women, and children were always in the garbage dumps scrounging for not only any refuse that might be usable but also for scraps of meat or lettuce to take home. They gathered another kind of army refuse for their use. During this period, they still used human excrement to fertilize their fields, and they came to clean out the latrines, loading the waste onto a "honey wagon" pulled by either oxen or people toward its destination. Individuals came with pots hung on A-shaped frames that they filled and carried to their farms. These we called "honey pots."

We didn't eat the food grown with this fertilizer. If we had, we would have become gravely ill. At least we would have had medical care. The Koreans had none, except that which was occasionally provided by military medical teams in the area. The "ladies" who conducted business from their residences in the village were periodically rounded up and taken to the medic to be tested for venereal disease.

The lighting in the Koreans' hovels was limited to the cooking fires, most of them made of buffalo dung. During their forty-five years of occupation, the Japanese had stripped the land of timber, so wood was scarce. When night came, the dark was profound.

As might be expected, these poverty-stricken people didn't limit their gathering of supplies to that which was our waste. They were the most accomplished thieves I have ever known. A "Slicky Boy," a member of a "Slicky Gang," would try to penetrate a battery by offering the services of his sister, inevitably a virgin, to the sentry in order to get into the mess halls to steal food or into the motor pools to steal fuel—even a jeep, if we weren't cautious. They were strong people who could carry a fifty-five-gallon drum of diesel fuel or a jeep motor on an A-shaped frame.

The Slicky Boys usually avoided the tents because all of the soldiers were armed. Whenever a theft was attempted at the

ammo dump, we always suspected that the perpetrators were
not Slicky Boys but infiltrators from North Korea. The Slicky
Boys were more interested in acquiring the necessities of life,
and they were extremely good at their jobs. We joked that they
could steal a radio and leave the music playing.

We GI's lived a little better than the Koreans, but not much.
At least each unit had an electrical generator. We lived all year
long in tents. Even with a diesel-fueled stove in the middle of
that tent the subzero air could never be brought to much over the
freezing mark. In fact, the diesel fuel that we burned in our
depot-type stoves, ventilated through a hole in the tent, would
freeze. Then we had to build a fire under the diesel drum in
order to thaw our fuel.

We either wore so many clothes that we sweated on the
inside, or we stayed near the fire, where one side of our bodies
baked while the side turned away from the fire froze. To make
matters worse, a definite pecking order existed at the fireside.
Rank had its privilege there just as it did in the field.

Being out on maneuvers was the worst—trying to hack foxholes out of that frozen, snow-covered, rocky soil so you could
get out of the wind. I gained instant respect and admiration for
those troops who were in the thick of war in Korea. They had to
be tough soldiers to survive in those conditions.

The winter was tough on a guy from South Texas, where winter often passes without the temperature falling below freezing.
My tent mates were Texans from the same area where I had
grown up, and as soldiers do we groused and complained. We
looked forward to summer until it came and we experienced our
first monsoon.

We had been cold. Now we were wet, and we couldn't decide
which was worse. To get anything dry, bedding or clothing, was
simply impossible. We dug trenches around our tents to contain
the water that poured down, but it was not unusual to awaken
and find that our boots were filled with water or had floated off.
We squished about our duties wearing wet socks, and most of us
developed foot fungus so severe that we thought our toes were
going to rot. The ponchos that we were issued to protect us from
the rain were prone to collect water and to dump it in our pants
or down our necks if we made contact with a tree limb. The
standing joke was: "Happiness during a monsoon is a dry fart."

American GI's are resourceful, though, and we made our lives as comfortable as possible by observing the time-honored tradition of "midnight requisitions." Mostly, we requisitioned food, but I heard that Battery C of the Thirty-seventh Field Artillery, Second Division, operating in the DMZ near us, availed itself of an even more cherished supply—whiskey.

Korea was becoming somewhat civilized, at least for the commissioned officers stationed there. An officers' club had been established near the artillery company's camp, and a three-quarter-ton truck was en route to it carrying a supply of liquor. The truck broke down, and foolishly the driver decided to go for help. I was told that a GI named Gotch-Eye Ireland happened on that truck while the driver was away from it, examined it, and discovered its contents.

Gotch-Eye hurried back to his battery, then went to the motor pool to obtain a three-quarter-ton vehicle and some help in order that he might "liberate" that whiskey. The people in the motor pool, of course, had to be involved, for the motor pool sergeant had to sign off on the truck.

The soldiers "liberated" the bourbon, scotch, gin, and vodka, leaving sissy liquor such as crème de menthe and sherry for the officers. They hid the truck, and when night fell they removed the bottles from it and took them into the hills.

At daylight, MP's conducted a tent-to-tent search but found no trace of the liquor. The captain who commanded the battery called a meeting of all of the noncoms. "I am upset," he said, "but I will be even more upset if I do not have periodically in my tent a bottle of bourbon. If I do not, I will take further action. I will see that another search is conducted and that the perpetrators of this incident are court-martialed."

Needless to say, the captain got his bourbon. Apparently, he thought as the dogfaces, who could only get three-two beer, did—that the liquor would be wasted on some of the shavetail second lieutenants who drank at the officers' club. The enlisted men used to say of the second lieutenants that their motto was "We're gentlemen because we're officers." The GI's response was "Yeah, but it took an Act of Congress to make you one."

Serving in Korea was not all misery for me. I felt more a part of something than I ever had in my life. I was a U.S. soldier. Maybe I was a little shorter, or a little darker, or had a different-sounding name from some, but to the other troops I was just one of them. A poor dogface freezing his butt off, too. It did me good. The army had always separated me a little bit as a Hispanic, and I had always separated myself a little, too. Now they didn't have the choice and neither did I.

Once I was out on patrol in the mountains with two other guys, one black and one white. The three of us had separated from the main group, and night was coming on. To try to follow the mountain paths at night was too dangerous. Even in 1955 North Korean ambush and intelligence-gathering patrols regularly infiltrated south across the thirty-eighth parallel. Often, their mission was to plant land mines and engage in firefights in an effort to provoke U.N. forces. Thus, infantry duty for U.S. army forces was still dangerous duty—we were still taking casualties. If we continued our movement, we might be spotted by enemy patrols or by snipers, or we might step on a land mine. We decided to hole up and wait for morning. By the time we got to sleep we looked like three Eskimo dogs curled up in the snow. Nobody cared if the other was black, brown, or green; we shared our warmth and we survived.

This was what the military was all about. I was equal. I was simply "Benavidez, Roy P.; E-455-02-5039; O Pos; Cath." That was what was embossed on my dog tag, and I had the same opportunities as any other soldier. If I screwed up or if I succeeded it wasn't because I was brown or black, or white. It was because of what was in me, Benavidez, Roy P.

The Koreans treated us all the same, too. A lot of them liked us, or tried to. Most Koreans really appreciated the American blood that was spilled on their soil to help maintain their freedom. Some didn't. To some few, a distinct minority, we were just another group of invaders, like the Japanese in the last war and the Chinese before them. They could hardly be blamed for feeling that way after living for so many years with foreigners in their land.

Getting to know the Koreans helped me to begin to develop an understanding about the cost of freedom. Not all of the Koreans were Slicky Boys. The Korean soldiers I worked with were excellent. The ROK army soldiers and marines were much less well equipped, fed, and paid than we were, but they were committed to doing what they could to preserve their five-thousand-year-old culture. They had an intense hatred for communism that I would see again when some of them fought in Vietnam.

Our men developed strong compassion for the plight of these proud, independent people. The desire to be free from oppression seemed to extend to the last man, woman, and child. The greatest tragedy of war could be seen in the children, and they touched everyone. We were soldiers, but we were human beings, too.

Our toughest, meanest sergeant often visited the kids in the orphanages to take them gifts and to clown around with them. If a word was ever said to him about this contrast in his behavior, he would give a look so mean and threatening as to make anyone shut up fast.

Some guys adopted kids and sent them home, and some married Korean women who had borne their children. Some claimed their Korean children and had them shipped back to the States when their tour ended. The children left behind by American soldiers were a horrible reminder of the price paid for occupying foreign lands. Many soldiers never considered the consequences of fathering these children, who were left to a life of despair. They were abandoned by their fathers and scorned by the people of their mothers' culture. I had never been an orphan in the sense that those kids were.

I sort of adopted a young orphan by the name of Kim. I gave him little assignments and paid him with scrip and food. Once when we had an inspection coming up, I was sent with a squad to police the area and get rid of all of the trash. By the time we were done we had a couple of truck loads of junk, and we hauled it back to the big garbage pit a few klicks down the road. We dumped it, then sent Kim out with a five-gallon can of gasoline to set it on fire.

Maybe my instructions to Kim got lost in translation. What I told him to do was to sprinkle a little here and a little there, not to throw it all on one spot. The next we saw he was on the opposite side of the pit from us, and he was lighting a match.

He must have dumped the whole can in one place because when he dropped that match, it looked like he'd been consumed by the fires of hell. We went running toward the plume of fire and smoke and all I could hear was Kim yelling, "Benavito, Benavito." (He couldn't pronounce my name very well.) We ran to him and put out the flames by rolling him on the ground. When we could examine him we saw that he had lost his hair and eyebrows, most of his clothes, and he was completely black from the soot. That boy was a pure mess, but fortunately, he wasn't seriously hurt.

Later in the day the first sergeant called me to his office. He accused me of trying to burn that boy up along with the garbage. He yelled and screamed about my creating an international incident and causing him a mountain of paperwork. I was in trouble again, this time for trying to help someone.

Much of the talk among military personnel in Korea in those days was about what should have been, or should be, done there. Some sided with Truman, who saw what we were doing as a United Nations police action. He didn't want World War III with the Chinese. The guys who were in the field and directly responsible for the lives of their men wanted an all-out offensive to end things quickly and save American lives that were still being lost in 1955 in spite of the war officially being over. I heard all sides, and to me they all made sense.

As for me, I was a soldier. I did as I was told. I was freezing my butt off, and I often wished that they'd just abandon the whole idea and send me to someplace where it was warm. I was a young kid in a strange country, and I figured just doing my job as well as I could do it was all that was expected of me. I sure didn't feel qualified to make any decision past how deep to dig the latrine.

We were surrounded by suffering and controversy, and we were either cold or wet, but we did "soldier things" to lighten the mood. We short-sheeted cots; we hung buckets of water over doors; we chained jeeps to tents so that when they drove off the tents went with them—just innocent pranks. Somehow the army never saw them as only boyish fun, the way I intended them. Soon I began to be blamed for everything that did go wrong, whether I caused it or not.

One day the first sergeant called me in and said, "Benavidez, we feel that you need a little guidance. We've noticed that you attend church regularly, and the captain feels that two weeks in a religious retreat just might straighten you out. Here's your orders, you're on the flight to Tokyo tomorrow."

Hot dog, I thought. I'm going to Tokyo for two weeks. They better ice down a lot of beer. I'm on my way.

That's what I thought. What I got was closer to two weeks in jail. The retreat was held in a monastery at the base of Mount Fuji and was put on by a Catholic chaplain whose authority came from God and the MP's who assisted him. They got us up around five so we could pray before breakfast. Then we were sent to prayer after breakfast. That session lasted almost until lunch. After lunch we prayed again until it was time to go back to our rooms and meditate privately until it was time for supper—then evening prayers. After a while, all I was praying for was a wet, frozen foxhole in Korea.

Somehow all of the praying seemed to help me. Feeling very like a monk, I returned to Korea and just bided my time and counted the days left until I was to rotate home.

7

Revelations

Back in the States, I reported the second week of February to Fort Chaffee, Arkansas, where my orders were being cut. On Friday of that week, I was told that they would be ready the following Monday and that I would be billeted at the fort until then. I expected my orders to be thirty days leave plus five days travel time and a stateside assignment for the next sixteen months. The weekend was to be a fateful one for me.

Before I left the office I heard the first sergeant there chewing out one of the other guys. He called all of us together and told us that we wouldn't get our orders until we got a haircut and looked military. Those of us who were returning from Korea did look scroungy compared to the men who had spent the last months stateside, and we still reeked of the smells that we had absorbed during our tours in that land. We smelled of Korea and Cashmere Bouquet talcum powder, which we had been able to get. We had poured it into our clothing and sleeping bags so that we could bear the smell of our own bodies. After a while, the Cashmere Bouquet came to smell as bad to us as a "honey pot."

Okay, I thought, we're stateside, I'll try to look like it. I started looking for the post barbershop. Man, I couldn't even get near it. Some guy by the name of Elvis Presley had just been drafted, and he was at the barbershop getting all his hair chopped off. There were more people and cameras than I had ever seen in my life. None of us knew much about this Presley kid. When we asked, someone told us that he was some kind of blues or rock-and-roll singer. From the look of the crowd around the barbershop, I thought the president of the United States was inside.

My buddy and I decided we'd head into the nearby town of Fort Smith and get a haircut there. We located a barbershop but decided to stop for a beer before getting our hair cut. That cold U.S. beer and all those people in the bar talking English sure made us feel at home. They told us about Elvis, and we fed some quarters to the jukebox and played some of his songs, "Hound Dog" and "Love Me Tender." One thing led to another and pretty soon the barbershop was closed. Well, at least I had tried to get a haircut.

A couple of hours later we were still sitting in the bar when a guy in civilian clothes walked over to us. He looked us up and down, and when I turned to ask him what his problem was, he said, "You boys better get a haircut."

I corkscrewed off that bar stool and got right in his face. "I just spent sixteen months in a tent in Korea. Who do you think you are, trying to tell me what to do?" I was just about to throw a punch at him when my buddy grabbed me and dragged me out of there while I was still yelling at the man.

Monday morning I was spit-shined and waiting for my orders to go home. The sergeant called my name and I stood at attention in front of him.

The first thing he said was, "Didn't I tell you to get a haircut?" I tried to explain about Elvis and all and he just cut me off. "No, if you had time to go to town Saturday you had time to get a haircut. Here's your orders—five-day pass, then you're going to Germany."

"Germany," I yelled, "I just got back from Korea. I'm supposed to have thirty-five days, then a stateside post."

"You got your orders, soldier. Get moving."

I was halfway back to El Campo before I realized that the sergeant who cut those orders was the same guy I almost popped in the bar Saturday night. I hadn't recognized him out of uniform. Man, when was I ever going to realize that it was sergeants who ran the army? When was I going to learn to keep my mouth shut? I didn't mind going to Germany, but my failure to get that lousy haircut had cost me a month at home. I was burned up.

Counting two days travel time, that gave me only three days with the family. It was like I had just got home when it was time to leave. But I accomplished a couple of things. For one thing, I saw Lala Coy as often as possible even though we had nothing that amounted to a real date. Before I left, we agreed to write to each other.

The night before I left I went out to try to track down a bunch of my old friends, the kids I had run with on the streets when I was younger and wilder. The ones Uncle Nicholas had warned me about so often.

They weren't hard to find. They were still working on the streets doing odd jobs for drinking money. When I had hung out with them, they were still kids; now they were like the drunks and bums that we used to make fun of when we were kids. I learned that a couple of my old friends were in the state pen now. I learned that a few more had joined the army like me. But they hadn't joined by choice.

Back then, if a kid got in trouble at seventeen or eighteen, the judge many times would give him a choice of jail time or joining up. A lot of those old judges figured that military service would make a man of a troublemaker and teach him some discipline. Sometimes it worked. Most times it just helped fill the military stockades when those boys couldn't break their old habits.

I sat with my former pals, now twenty-two- and twenty-three-year-old bums, and listened to them saying the same things about life that we were saying when we were twelve and thirteen and didn't know any better. All I could think about was, was I ever that stupid? At last I understood that Uncle Nicholas had been afraid that I would turn out like them.

I could still hear them making ridiculous statements when I was on the plane to Europe, and those echoes gave me a lot to think about on that long trip.

My visit at home had been good for me, even if it had been too brief. Again the family had been eager to hear my news. Uncle Nicholas had treated me like an equal, asking me about my experiences instead of lecturing me. He had treated me like a man, and once in a while I would see him just looking at me and smiling. I didn't notice that much of a change in me, but I guess he did.

While I was on the plane, I realized that I had neglected to do something important while I was at home. I sat back and wrote

Uncle Nicholas the longest letter I had ever written. It was almost ten pages long by the time we landed, but if all of the thank-you's and the I'm-sorry's had been deleted, it could have been written on the back of a postage stamp.

The plane landed in Frankfurt, and I traveled by truck to Augsburg. There, I had none of the culture shock that we all experienced in Korea. Augsburg was like any quaint U.S. country town except that the residents didn't speak English. Well, I thought, I speak English, Spanish, and passable Korean. German should be no problem. Augsburg looked like a place that I could really get to like. The post at Augsburg was the home base of the Eleventh Airborne Division. They also had a jump school there. I thought that I had finally made it; I would be going Airborne. That's not what my orders said, but I knew that I could make it happen. I was assigned to the non-Airborne support troops.

As soon as I got there, I ran into a couple of buddies I had gone through basic training with. They were already Airborne and arranged for me to talk to the top sergeant, who said "No problem" and was getting set to cut my papers for jump school.

That's how the week started. It didn't end so well.

I walked into a bar with my Airborne buddies, Ernie Trujillo and Frank Montoya, and we sat down and ordered a round of the local brew. At the table next to us were some other soldiers. They were "legs." Now, a "leg" is anybody who is not Airborne. The Airborne troops look down on them and don't feel that they ought to have to buy the first round of drinks when there's a leg around to buy it for them.

I was a leg too, but I was sitting with Airborne, and I was about to start jump school, and, well you know how those things happen. When the waitress came back with our beer, I told her the legs over there would pay for it. She had been through this before and started getting nervous. The two groups exchanged insulting remarks for a minute or two; then all of a sudden the biggest son of a gun I had ever seen in my life gets up and walks over to teach me and my big mouth a lesson. That guy was eight inches taller than I was and a good hundred pounds of muscle heavier.

I launched myself out of my chair and kicked up with my heavy boot for my favorite target. While he was sinking to the floor we were heading out the door at double time. His buddies were about his size too and, legs or not, we were out-matched, and we knew it.

I thought it was all a big joke until I was up in front of the first sergeant the next morning. The man I had kicked had ended up in the hospital, and Colonel Patrick Cassidy had reached the end of his rope. I had walked into the tail end of an ongoing battle between the legs and the Airborne. My fight had been the last straw.

The legs were talking some pretty healthy revenge against me, and all the officers wanted to do was get me the heck out of there and try to regain control of the discipline again. The bottom line was that this "war" was going to end. If I were transferred out and gone in the next ten minutes they could end it now. If I didn't get my gear and get out, it wouldn't end until after the legs had put me in the hospital. Sergeant Villareal himself said that the colonel wasn't so sure that he just shouldn't turn me over to them. "You're a grade A troublemaker and you deserve it. You're lucky he didn't decide to court-martial you."

Under the circumstances, I didn't have to be told to leave twice. As fast as my legs could move I was on my way to Berlin. I had done it again, and my dream of going Airborne was on the shelf once more. I kept asking myself, When will I ever learn? Mostly I blamed myself when I was unhappy, but sometimes I blamed Elvis Presley. If he hadn't been in the barbershop at Fort Chaffee, I wouldn't be in Germany. As if to pour salt on my wounds, the Armed Forces Radio Network seemed to play "Hound Dog" every other record.

I traveled by train for almost two days before reaching Berlin. Those of us traveling had been warned to keep our shades closed and not to look out because we were near the Eastern Zone, which had come under the Russians after Germany surrendered unconditionally to the Allied forces on May 7, 1945. The country had been divided by declaration in June of that year into four sections, with the United States, Britain, France, and the U.S.S.R. each having supreme authority over one section. The purpose of the division of the country was stated in the Potsdam Protocol, issued in August 1946, after the meeting of "The Big Three"— President Truman, Marshal Stalin, and Prime Minister Atlee. The stated purpose of Allied occupation was "the extirpation of German militarism and Nazism and to ensure that Germany never again will threaten her neighbors and the peace of the world."

I was met in Berlin by a soldier who said as soon as he realized that I was the person he was looking for, "I thought I was waiting for a great big Texan. They're all six feet tall, aren't they? What nationality are you anyway?"

Berlin, the capital of Germany, was divided among the Allies in a similar way to the division of the entire country, but tensions soon began to mount between Russia and the other Allies about political and economic policies in the country. By 1949, Germany was split into two rival states and governments. In 1957, when I was sent there, that situation still existed.

I would begin to learn to control my temper in Berlin. It was a strange city to be in during the heart of the cold war. The Berlin Wall had not yet been erected to divide the city, but it was divided nonetheless. There was constant tension between the Russians who controlled East Berlin and the Westerners who controlled West Berlin. The U.S. troops were on constant alert, and we were required to maintain pure spit and polish. Berlin was a two-haircut-a-week town. We were never at ease. We were in an international spotlight and no "soldier things" were allowed. If we were off of the post we were required to be dressed either in dress uniforms or coat and tie.

Our duty there was continual joint maneuvers with the other three nations. The Russians kept pushing, trying to create incidents: one time the Russian tanks came cutting across our positions while we were on joint maneuvers. The maneuvers had started peacefully enough, but the U.S. troops were showing them up and they just went wild out there, breaking all the rules and daring anybody in their way to stop them.

If they had understood Spanish or we had understood Russian it might have caused some serious problems. There were generals yelling at each other out in those woods before everything calmed down and we apologized for being in the right of it. It used to really gripe us the way we were expected to take all that crap the Russians were dishing out to us. But, as in Korea, I was just a soldier following orders.

Maybe it was the constant pressure and discipline, but I thrived there, and I began to turn into a pretty good soldier. I started to think before I acted, and I developed a growing respect for the U.S. Army when I saw our troops in comparison to others.

I just hadn't developed a healthy respect for myself. I had always believed that if I screwed up, I would take whatever the consequences were and that was that. I was a tough guy, I was a loner, and who really cared anyhow?

In Berlin, I changed my mind. Any misstep of mine was a direct reflection on the entire U.S. Army and could launch World War III. I sure didn't want my temper to be the cause of a nuclear war. I realized the seriousness of the situation, and I decided to become a model soldier.

Maybe "model soldier" is a little bit of an exaggeration. There was that time when one of our guys wanted to know what the Scots wore under their kilts. That one's not really worth talking about. I woke up two days later with a broken nose and two black eyes. The lesson I learned from that is to never try to pull up a Scotsman's kilt.

I should have said that I had become a "good soldier."

All during my sixteen months in Germany I had been writing to Lala Coy, and we were carrying on a pretty hot love affair through the mail. I had less than one week to go in Germany, and all that I could think about was Lala. I wanted to get home, marry Lala if she'd have me, and try to decide if I was going to stay in the army or use my training to find a job in civilian life. I had taken a lot of courses and gotten a lot of training, and I felt that I had some marketable skills to offer an employer.

My last weekend in Germany I went out to celebrate with a couple of friends. We were walking out of a bar when we heard an argument, in English, going on at the curb.

The two men who were arguing were in civilian dress, as were we, but we recognized the two at the curb as a couple of new second lieutenants who were assigned to our unit. The most sober shavetail was trying to get the other one into a cab and back to the base. The intoxicated one wasn't having any of it. He was going back inside that bar to finish what he had started, whatever that was.

My buddies wanted to get the heck out of there before the MP's showed up, but I figured we could give them a hand and settle it before it really became a bad situation. For once in my life I was thinking about the people who depended upon me, the U.S. Army, and not myself.

My friends lagged back and I walked over and asked the most

sober one if I could give him a hand. He said that he'd appreci-
ate the help, but the drunk one said he didn't think he ought to
be getting manhandled by some "little Mexican noncom so and
so." One of my buddies yelled "Deck him," and before I could
think, I did it.

He fell back into the cab and the two of them took off for
the base.

Man, I was as mad at my buddies as I was at myself. I
thought that if they had come over to help me it never would
have happened. What kind of friends did I have anyway? Were
they looking to solve a problem or create one?

The next morning was Sunday and I was in church early.
Man, was I worried! I discussed it with a priest, and he told me
that he thought I was making too much of the incident. I don't
believe that he understood the situation fully. "Go in peace," he
said. I wish that priest had been my commanding officer.

Rank and discipline are the glue that holds the army together,
and I had struck an officer, in public, with witnesses. That was a
criminal offense. Especially in the Berlin theater.

If the army chose to make something of it, it would mean
stockade time, prison, and a dishonorable discharge after I had
served my time. What a way to go home! What a way to win the
heart of Lala!

Monday morning I was sweating it out, but I didn't have long
to wait. The word was passed on down that the top sergeant was
looking for me. When I walked into his office First Sergeant
Charlie Turner just looked at me, shook his head, and told me to
follow him. I tried to talk to him, but he wouldn't even look in
my direction while we marched into the captain's office.

The captain was a young man, not too long out of West Point.
He was a "right by the book" kind of officer. Nobody knew him
too well. I could only expect what I deserved, the worst. My file
was in front of him. He would read a while, then look up at me,
then go back to reading. I was at ease in front of him and I was
sweating. Perspiration was dripping off me.

I could see my life going straight down the tubes. Would Lala
be interested in me after I got out of prison? Would she even
write to me once I was in Fort Leavenworth? I had been making
big plans for our future together—considering whether to remain
in the military or get a civilian job. I had believed that I had

earned a promising future and that I was on my way toward it. Now I was one step from prison. The past three years had all been a sham. I was going to end up a bum, just like everybody always figured I would.

"Corporal, you know why you're here. I understand there was a little trouble in town Saturday night. I've read your file, and you've been a pretty good soldier up until now. I see, too, that you're rotating home in a few days. I'm going to ask you something. Think before you answer me. Corporal, did you or didn't you strike an officer Saturday night?"

Then he grew totally silent, folded his hands in front of him, and looked up at me.

Ah man, this was it. The sergeant, next to me, was expecting me to just say "No sir" and march back out of there. The captain had offered me my life and my future back again. And he was sitting there expecting an answer.

I just couldn't take the opportunity that I had been offered, no matter how much I desired to. All the time that I had been standing there, knowing what I had done to my life, I had also been staring at a plaque on the wall behind the captain's desk. It read "I do not lie, cheat or steal nor tolerate those that do," the honor code of West Point, and "Duty, Honor, Country," which was the West Point motto.

All the time I had been standing there I had been promising God that if I got out of this mess I would dedicate my life to that code. Now here I was with a chance to lie my way out of it. I just couldn't do it.

"Yes sir, I hit that officer." I said it fast and then I couldn't take it back.

The first sergeant looked at me as if I was crazy. The captain didn't say a word for what seemed like an hour; then he ordered the two of us to go out into the hall.

I figured the sergeant was there to keep track of me until the MP's came to get me. Boy, that sergeant was not at a loss for words then. He called me every name in the book. Mostly he called me stupid for not realizing what a chance the captain was giving me. He was wrong; I knew it. I just couldn't lie and take it.

Suddenly, the door opened and I, Corporal Benavidez, heard the captain say, "Sergeant, return the *PFC* to his duties."

Neither the sergeant nor I could believe it. I lost a stripe, one lousy stripe was all I had lost. All he did was demote me from corporal to private first class. My life, my plans, my future, they were still there. I could only thank God for guiding that captain while he decided my fate. And I swore that I would prove him right.

Later that day I was called back to the captain's office. He said that he had overheard me using a lot of foul names to describe him after I had left his office earlier. I had been using some rough language all right, but what I was doing was cussing out one of my buddies from the night of the incident that had gotten me into trouble. The captain acted as if he thought I had been talking about him. He really knew how shaken up I still was and was just joking with me, but I didn't realize it at first.

Finally, he put me at ease and asked me why I had answered him with the truth. It had stumped him, too. I told him about his plaque and how "I do not lie, cheat or steal nor tolerate those that do. Duty, Honor, Country" had made a sudden impression on me. I told him that someone I knew had been telling me the same thing in different words all of my life. I told him I wanted a career in the military, and I couldn't base it on a lie.

He stood up and shook my hand. He told me that I was the type of soldier they needed, and he told me to follow that advice and I would never go wrong. Maybe it seems a little hokey or a little dramatic, but that's the way it happened. All of a sudden I had made up my mind that a military career was what I wanted, and that throughout it I would honor Grandfather Salvador, Aunt Alexandria, Uncle Nicholas, and Mr. Haddock by matching my actions to the ideals of the West Point code of honor.

Something had just snapped in me. That situation had stripped me right down to the bone and put me back together again, as a soldier. Maybe it was more than that. Could it be that the West Point code of honor and motto that carried so many thousands of young officers to positions of greatness in the service of this country applied to a young enlisted man of no reputation as well?

That code and motto burned themselves into my soul that day.

I had made some important decisions about my conduct and my career. Now I would go home and find out what Lala had decided about another part of my life.

8

Courtship

I had heard the saying that some guys are fighters and some guys are lovers, and I clearly fit into the first category. I wanted to see if I could change that part of my life, too, when I returned to El Campo.

Even though Lala and I had known each other since we were about twelve years old, and I had begun taking a special interest in her before going to Germany, I had no idea that she had noticed me, too. It seemed that she had. I think that women may work those things out so that men never know who is pursuing whom.

While I had been home on that three-day leave, I had taken her to lunch at a nearby confectionery during her break from her job at Zlotnik's clothing store.

We met at my home in the company of my family. We met at her home in the company of her family. We did go out one evening for something to eat and we had to take only one chaperon with us.

These might have been the "happy days" of the 1950s to the Anglo community, but in our community, things were about the same as in the 1850s. One-on-one dating was a thing of the future.

Our feeling for each other was something special. I knew it, and when I gazed into her green eyes, a legacy of her German ancestors, I believed that she felt the same way. Three days just had not given us the time to know more than that. So we dated through the mail.

From the first letter I knew that she knew more about me than I knew about myself. She understood the hatred and bitterness that caused my fierce temper. Evidently she had spent a lot of time talking to my female cousins, because she knew things about me that I had never told her and that only my family would know. It was such a relief to be understood, really understood.

As the letters flew back and forth and I was getting more serious, I realized that I owed the respect to both our families to handle this situation correctly.

This required another series of letters to Uncle Nicholas, my grandfather, and Father Altamira, the parish priest. I had been an altar boy for the father at one time, and I hoped that he would remember my service and put in a good word for me with Lala's family. Eventually, Uncle Nicholas and Father Altamira made a well-announced and well-planned formal appearance at the home of Juan Coy, Lala's father, and asked permission for us to see each other when I returned from Germany.

I had sweated about the response they would get, much as I had in the captain's office. I thought about the reputation I had developed in my early days, none of it good, and I could just see Uncle Nicholas trying to explain the "new" me to old Señor Coy.

Lala doesn't recall that her family had the reservations about me as a suitor and husband that I imagined. She says that they liked me and my family and felt that I would give her a good life. I think that her recollection may be colored by her good nature and steadfastness, the qualities that have seen her through some difficult times.

Finally, according to Uncle Nicholas, Lala's father agreed out of respect to him (who took full credit for my good fortune) for us to continue to write to each other. He also agreed, with reservations, that we could see each other when I returned from Germany.

Although I was happy to be going home and eager to see my family, I returned from Germany with an eagerness I had never felt before. It felt so good to know that I was coming home to Lala. I believe that I had been a loner for so long that the normal loneliness and need just weren't as strong for me as for some people. But now I had Lala, the piece that had been missing in my life. So serious was I that I carried with me a music box that was more than one hundred years old. It had been given to me in Berlin by a German fellow I had helped when he had a stroke. The music box had a replica of an altar, before which the Holy Mother sat holding the Baby Jesus. It played "Ave Maria." I said that it was to be for Lala's and my first child.

Once I was home we started the formal dating procedure within the community. We first went out in chaperoned groups to parties and dances. Eventually we were granted the privilege of being allowed to talk privately on her front porch. However, her sister Minnie sat by the window watching us lest our hearts begin to rule our heads.

The year 1958 was a good one for me. I had a beautiful girl who loved me, a 1955 Chevrolet hardtop, and an assignment to Fort Benning, Georgia, to go to MP school. On my return from Germany I had learned that there was an opportunity to join the military police. This had always been part of my plans and I jumped at the chance. The army was starting to have quite a few Puerto Rican soldiers joining up. The need for bilingual non-coms of all specialties was growing.

Since I had decided to make the army my career, this looked like a good opportunity for me. I graduated second in my class while regaining my lost stripe and picking up one more to boot. No, I take that back, I was first in my class, but they dropped me down to second the day of graduation.

A couple of the guys graduating with us had done a little too much celebrating and never showed back up to clean out the barracks before the ceremony. I was in charge of that clean-up detail, and I just figured that if those soldiers didn't think enough of their clothes and things to come back and get them then they must have wanted me to have all of their stuff just thrown in the Dumpster. That's what I ordered my troops to do.

I guess the commanding officer didn't quite see things my way, and for "conduct not becoming a leader," I was dropped from first to second. I figured that the colonel should have taken up the slack for those two guys when it came to the work party if he felt that way. I was still working on that temper of mine.

I made frequent trips in the Chevy from Fort Benning to El Campo to see Lala. It's amazing how far you can travel on a three-day pass if your heart's in it, and mine sure was. During that year we really did get to know each other. When all you're allowed to do is talk, boy, do you talk.

I learned that Lala's perception of the bigotry and separatism within the community was very different from mine. I was short, dark, and very Hispanic looking. She was tall, almost my height, green eyed, light complexioned, light haired. If you didn't look twice, you'd think she was Anglo. And that's how she had been treated.

When I was ten years old and stuck up in the balcony of the movie theater with the other Mexicans, she had walked right in down below with the Anglos. Lala listened while I dredged up all of my old hates and all of my old problems. She helped me kill all of those old dragons.

We found ways to do a little more than talk during that year. Finally, we were allowed to go to the movies, and in the dark, we held hands and sneaked the occasional kiss. On December thirtieth, we became officially engaged.

At a nuptial mass held at six-thirty in the morning of June seventh, 1959, Lala and I took our wedding vows at St. Robert Bellarmine Church in El Campo. Father Altamira, who had interceded with her father in my behalf, conducted the mass. Lala came down the aisle on the arm of her father. She was wearing a long lace gown and carrying a bouquet of orange blossoms. Through the veil that covered her face, I could see that she was smiling shyly.

In the best tradition of our culture, we had many attendants—eighteen, including the flower girl and ring bearer—and we had more than one hundred and fifty guests. The bridesmaids wore orchid dresses and the men wore tuxedos. My cousin Leo Foisner, of the hamburger trick, and his wife placed our kneeling cushions before the altar. My cousin Mike and his wife presented the wedding *lazo*, a rope of flowers that signified our union. Alec Ruiz and his wife brought the silver coins, which Father said signified that Lala would manage the money, and Dora Garcia and Edward Martinez presented Lala with a prayer book and a rosary.

Our families and friends know how to celebrate a special event, and we had both a reception in the parish hall, complete with a four-tiered wedding cake, and a barbecue at noon.

When the festivities were over, Lala and I went first to her home to receive the traditional blessing from her parents. We knelt before them while her mother placed her hand first on Lala's head, then on mine. Then her father repeated the ritual.

We left the Coys' and went to the home of Aunt Alexandria and Uncle Nicholas, where we each were blessed twice more.

Feeling blessed indeed, we traveled to Monterrey, Mexico, for our honeymoon. We stayed at a hotel in the mountains outside Monterrey near the beautiful waterfall La Cola de Caballo— Horsetail Falls. At last we were husband and wife.

From Monterrey en route home, we stopped in San Juan, Texas, just across the Mexican border. We visited the Shrine of La Virgen de San Juan del Valle, which would be destroyed in 1970, apparently deliberately, by a pilot who crashed his airplane into the building. The wooden statue of Our Lady of San Juan before which Lala and I made our secret *promesas,* our promises for our married lives, was undamaged in the crash and the resulting fire.

After the wedding, Lala moved with me to Fort Gordon in Georgia, where I had been assigned to drive the post commander, General H. M. Hobson, the commanding general of Fort Gordon and the Military Police School.

I served as driver for several generals during my career, and it was never my favorite job. The designation "driver" is somewhat misleading, for anyone given that assignment is virtually a servant and bodyguard to the officer and his family. As "driver" I have baby-sat, prepared meals, and run errands.

In fact, I was stationed at Fort Bragg and returning from the cleaners with some of General Throckmorton's uniforms on the day that President John F. Kennedy was assassinated in Dallas. Mrs. Throckmorton told me the terrible news.

Driving for generals was not bad duty, but some things they did got on my nerves. One general carried a swagger stick, and when he wanted to get my attention, he would rap me on the shoulder with it. One day, he gave my shoulder a blow and said, "Stop." Because of the traffic conditions, I slowed but didn't come to a full stop. He rapped me again. "I said stop." I slammed on the brakes and nearly threw the general into the front seat headfirst. He growled at me, and I responded, "Sir, you said stop." The Benavidez temper was not yet fully under control.

While driving for another general, who had the secretary of the army as his guest, we passed a national cemetery. "What a beautiful, clean place," the secretary remarked. "I wonder how many are dead there."

"Why, all of them, Mr. Secretary, sir," I said. The general treated me coldly for days afterward. The Benavidez lip wasn't yet fully under control either.

Driving for officers had its annoyances, but driving for their wives was worse. Once when I was taking one general's wife to the officers' club for a coffee party, we neared the post's firehouse. The firemen had strung ten to fifteen hoses across the street, and I slowed the car. "Go straight," Mrs. General commanded. I turned right to take a short detour and avoid running over the hoses, and Mrs. General's makeup just came loose. When I delivered her to the door of the club, she jumped from the car and slammed the door.

Later in the day, I picked up the general to take him home, and he said, "You got the boss mad today, Sergeant."

"What did I do to upset the boss, sir?"

"I'll talk to you about it tomorrow," he said.

The next day, he told me that he was displeased because I had disobeyed an order from "the boss." I explained that I thought it would have been an embarrassment to the general if the firemen had seen his car drive over the water hoses when avoiding them was merely a matter of taking a one-block detour.

"Harrumph. Just try not to upset the boss."

I used the job driving for General Hobson to finally make my way into the Airborne.

General William Westmoreland was the commander of the 101st Airborne then. He was coming to make a speech at Fort Gordon, and I was assigned as his driver. I knew who he was, and I knew what I wanted. In my mind I planned out our conversation for two days before he arrived.

As it always turns out, I never was able to maneuver that conversation. The general beat me to it. He was there to recruit more soldiers for the Airborne, and the first thing he asked me was, "Sergeant, have you ever thought of going Airborne?"

"General, sir, that's all I have ever thought of. I'm due to re-up and I'd pay my own way if I had to," was what I blurted out.

He just sort of harrumphed and didn't say another word. But two months later, when my re-enlistment papers were coming in, there was my assignment to jump school along with them.

My new assignment didn't thrill Lala as much as I had expected. She was just learning about being a soldier's wife, and she couldn't figure out why I'd ever want to jump out of an airplane.

I look at the pictures that were taken of us then and realize how young and inexperienced we were. It's hard to realize that the fresh-faced young man in the pictures was me. I looked young and in love. I was young, and I still am in love.

The peacetime military is a hard enough life for a wife. Many can't take the constant moving and the instability that it causes the family. In wartime it's a million times harder. Living with that constant fear of a knock on the door or a phone call. It tears some women up.

Most of my old wartime buddies are married. They're just not married to the same woman they started with. It takes quite a woman to stay with a soldier who went where I went and did what I did for twenty-five years. Maybe those *promesas* we made helped us to stay together.

While I was lying in the hospital, or fighting in the jungle, Lala was raising our children. She was cutting the lawn, and fixing the washing machine, and crisscrossing the country following her husband. When I was home she added the humanity to my soul that was missing and healed me both physically and mentally. Lala never complained.

Lala was one in a million. What she ever saw, or still sees in me now, I will never figure out. I do know this: Military wives are every bit the patriots their husbands are. Any ribbons and medals that their husbands earn belong equally to them.

9

Airborne

After four years of service and reenlistment, I had finally made it to the Airborne. The year was 1959 and time was moving on. If I had kept my mouth shut when I was enlisting in the first place I might have been there four years earlier. If I hadn't started that fight in Augsburg, I might have had my Airborne wings two years earlier. *Quien sabe?* Who knows?

Until I became Airborne, I had often allowed my temper and my insecurities to control the direction of my life. Now I was a married man, and I wanted to fulfill my responsibilities to Lala. I was a sergeant with four years in and a career ahead of me. If I could really follow that motto of "Duty, Honor, Country," if I could keep it up, I felt that I had a promising future.

Uncle Nicholas had instilled several beliefs in his children, none more important than "Be the best, in whatever you do, be the best." He meant that to extend to chopping cotton, pulling beets, shining shoes, or fixing tires. I was determined to be the best. Being in Airborne was my next step toward that goal, and I planned on being the best trooper they ever had go through that jump school.

While I was in training for Airborne Lala and I lived in a small rental home about a half hour's drive from Fort Bragg, North Carolina. I left home before the sun came up each morning, and I dragged what was left of me back into our house after dark every night. That chauffeur's job had sure gotten me soft.

Because I was one of the few who were already sergeants, I was made a platoon sergeant the first day. I had men to lead, and when that was the case, I never could dog it a little and bring up the rear. I always had to be out front giving a good example for my men. Sometimes I would try to think of a way to lose a couple of those stripes so that I could get a little rest.

I never had been so tired in my whole life. Sometimes I thought I should have stayed in the MP's. Driving a general's car began to seem a better job than I had thought while I was doing it. Even the "Mrs. Generals" I had driven and baby-sat for began to seem much nicer than I had thought them at the time. For the months that I was in training such thoughts passed through my mind more than once.

I made up my mind that I would not let negative thoughts defeat me this time. This time I was pure Airborne—all the way. Those of us who were Airborne were trained to jump out of a plane or a helicopter. The first step toward that goal was to train at the tower. As any jumper knows, the easy part is the first thousand feet between him and the ground. The tough, dangerous part is the last thirty-four feet, where he prepares to rejoin earth, in this case hard-packed red North Carolina dirt.

Thirty-four feet may not sound too high, but when a person is strapped into the rig, looking down five stories, it looks like enough to kill. And it can. The first few times the trainers don't even count on the trainees jumping themselves. They know that most guys won't. A trainee just stands at the door of the tower platform, and some darn sergeant starts talking to him. All of a sudden the sergeant has got his foot in the trainee's back. If he ever thought of backing out, it's already too late.

First time off the tower I almost killed myself. The top of the tower is built with a roof like a little house. I could see the guys going off in front of me, but I couldn't see what happened to them after they got pushed out of the door. But I could hear the grunts and screams and moans when they hit the end of the line and their whole weight was caught by those two thin straps between their legs. That was followed in about six seconds by the sounds they made when they hit the ground.

Over eighty percent of the transfers out of Airborne training occur between the first time on the tower and the second. It's that bad.

Standing on the edge of the tower awaiting my first jump, I made a mental check of all the things I had been taught. Tight body position, elbows in, head down. When I felt that sergeant's foot in my back that all disappeared from my mind. I felt like a drunk puppet on a string. When it was over, the sergeant on the ground walked up to my crumpled body and told me get back up there and do it again. I couldn't believe that he really even expected me to get up without a medic to help me. He did, and I did get up. The second jump I remembered a little more that I had been taught, and I came down looking more like a soldier.

I don't even remember the drive home that night. Lala told me later that I just limped in the door, mumbled something to her, and went straight to bed. Next morning I remember waking up at four as usual. I had to wake Lala to help me get out of bed and get dressed. I hurt in more places than I knew I had.

"What did you do yesterday?" I asked as Lala helped me into my shirt.

"I prayed," she said. "I don't want to be a widow."

I had to be at the post by five. On the drive over I was trying to figure out which buddy of mine I should call back at Fort Gordon. I wanted to ask somebody to help me get my old job back. Then I met my men and saw what they looked like. Their faces were solemn, and some of them moved about in obvious pain. No doubt they had driven to the post trying to figure out how to return to the places they had been before coming to Fort Bragg.

I knew when I saw them that I couldn't quit, and I determined that none of my soldiers would quit either. I wouldn't let them.

Soon we were jumping from planes, which was nothing after the leap from that tower. Pretty soon we all had our wings and it was on to more schools, after which we would be assigned. I felt proud that I was now one of the elite. I was Airborne. The only unit more elite was the Special Forces. They had been around since 1952, but they were still a very small and very specialized unit. I needed more experience in the Airborne before I tried to make that step up.

I crisscrossed the United States from 1959 to 1965 while with the 82nd. I never had any permanent assignment, just one school and training maneuver after the other. During this period, Fort Bragg was home to Lala and me.

The Cuban Bay of Pigs disaster in April 1961 and the Cuban missile crisis in October 1962 drove us close to combat, and these tensions caused us to increase our combat readiness. The 82nd Airborne stayed prepared for any situation.

I loved the life I was leading so much that I was certain that the rigors of training had been worthwhile. In March 1965 I was given a six-month Airborne recruiting assignment at Fort Ord, California.

In October 1965 I was assigned to Vietnam. American military personnel served only as advisers then. Before shipping out, I was given another round of training, again at Fort Bragg. During that period, I was notified of Grandfather Salvador's death, but there was no possibility of my returning to El Campo for his funeral. I gave thanks that he had lived a long, full life, and I recalled his parables about helping people. Perhaps I was helping more where I was than I could in El Campo.

Included in the training for assignment to Vietnam was the issuance of a small card on which was printed the nine rules of conduct in Vietnam.

NINE RULES
For Personnel of US Military
Assistance Command, Vietnam

The Vietnamese have paid a heavy price in suffering for their long fight against the communists. We military men are in Vietnam now because their government has asked us to help its soldiers and people in winning their struggle. The Viet Cong will attempt to turn the Vietnamese people against you. You can defeat them at every turn by the strength, understanding, and generosity you display with the people. Here are nine simple rules:

1) Remember we are guests here: We make no demands and seek no special treatment.
2) Join with the people! Understand their life, use phrases from their language and honor their customs and laws.
3) Treat women with politeness and respect.
4) Make personal friends among the soldiers and common people.
5) Always give the Vietnamese the right of way.
6) Be alert to security and ready to react with your military skill.
7) Don't attract attention by loud, rude or unusual behavior.
8) Avoid separating yourself from the people by a display of wealth or privilege.

9) Above all else you are members of the US Military Forces on
a difficult mission, responsible for all your official and personal actions. Reflect honor upon yourself and the United
States of America.

Soon I would learn that the nine rules were not only "simple"
but also simplistic. I might have been a kid again, being told by
Aunt Alexandria how to behave at a birthday party.

I was given courses to learn basic conversational Vietnamese
so that I could "use phrases from their language": *Chào ông,*
Hello, sir; *Cám o'n ông,* Thank you, sir; and *Xin goi bác-si giùm
tôi,* Please send a doctor for me. I was given basic information
about the religions and customs so that I could "understand their
life." I was also taught that we were "nation building" in
Vietnam and that military advisers were expected to help distrib-
ute relief supplies, to build and repair roads and schools, and to
instruct the people about modern agricultural methods.

By this time I was into my third hitch in the army. I was a pro,
or at least I thought I was. I had been to Asia before. I had spent
quite a bit of time in several other third-world countries both
advising and training. I thought I had seen it all.

My fellow soldiers and I had been hearing the truth about the
situation there from the other advisers who were cycling back,
but we didn't believe them. We were also starting to see a slow
trickle of body bags and wounded. I don't really believe that
even our training personnel had any real idea about what we
were walking into.

10

Bloody 'Nam

"Say, mate, just keep eating, don't look up, we're not alone."

The rice turned to sand in my mouth. We were about six klicks out of Tam Ky, Vietnam (about one hundred and fifty kilometers northwest of Saigon), and I was on my first combat patrol in Vietnam. The quiet of the jungle was shattered by a short burst of rifle fire. I dove, headfirst, for a big tree about ten feet behind me. I rolled over and came up ready to fire. My eyes caught Dickey; he was looking straight up above me, into the tree. There was a crooked smile on his lips. I could hear something falling through the tree. I ducked when the AK-47 rifle came tumbling out of the branches. It was followed by a body cartwheeling to the ground at my feet. When it hit, I could hear the bones crunch.

"Sorry about that, mate, had to shoot a little early but he had bloody well sighted in on you. Have to keep your ears open out here, mate, if you want to stay alive."

I prodded the body with the toe of my boot. "Thanks, buddy, guess I've got a lot to learn."

"Learn it quick, mate, I'm getting tired of breaking in new advisers."

He walked back over to the trunk of the tree and squatted. His eyes were half closed as he puffed on a hand-rolled cigarette hanging out of the corner of his mouth.

I just stood there, sweating, not knowing what to do next. The squad of South Vietnamese soldiers we were assigned to as advisers were crawling back out of cover. They chattered and laughed over the incident as if they were school kids who had witnessed some playground shenanigans. They knew that they hadn't been in immediate danger because the sniper would go for the "round eyes" first.

A little voice inside me said, Roy, stay close to Dickey, he's gonna make it.

I was about two weeks "in country" and on my first trip into the bush. I was a ten-year soldier at the time, but I'd never been shot at before. This war was for real. I decided then that I'd better get with the program or I wasn't going to last out this patrol let alone the next eleven months.

The year was 1965 and I had been assigned as an adviser to a Vietnamese infantry unit, the 25th Infantry "Tigers." The U.S. involvement in this civil war was very limited back then. During my training I had been drilled daily on the limits of my "observing" and "advising," and how to be polite to my hosts in their country. I looked back through my notes, and I couldn't find anything that instructed me in the appropriate response when I almost got my butt shot off while the people I was trying to help watched and laughed.

Warrant Officer Dickey was a work of art. I never knew his full name. We all just called him Dickey. He was a tall, slim Aussie and had just come out of fighting Communists in the jungles of Malaysia. We were fortunate to have him with us. This was just another walk in the park to him. That's how it looked, but when I really began to watch him I started to learn things.

Every step Dickey took was planned. He never stepped on a branch, and he avoided the trails whenever possible. You couldn't hear him crunching through the leaves. Never a wasted motion. Eyes always moving about. Everything looked deceptively natural. Watching Dickey was like watching my Uncle Nicholas hunt squirrels in the Colorado river bottom. Both of them made actions that were very practiced look easy. If staying alive meant playing follow the leader, okay, this I could understand. Dickey knew the enemy and I didn't.

Staying alive in Vietnam meant blending in. In any sniper attack or any firefight, we were the main target. Every booby trap was designed for us. Again, Dickey helped me notice these things and learn how to blend in with the Vietnamese troops. It was easier for me than the others. My size; my skin color; my

Hispanic-Indian, almost Oriental, look became an advantage. All my life I had been fighting against the bigotry created by these differences. Now they were helping to keep me alive. I still had a lot to learn, but I was learning.

I learned that if the VC infiltrated your camp at night the first throat they cut would be the one of somebody who was snoring. They did that because most Vietnamese don't snore, and they wanted to get the "round eyes" first. I learned to sleep on my stomach so I wouldn't snore.

I learned that if you're walking through the jungle a sniper is going to nail the guy who's slapping at the mosquitoes. Vietnamese ignore them, and I learned to let them chew on me and keep going. I learned to walk like the Vietnamese, and squat like them, and eat my rice like them, and balance across those little levees dividing rice paddies just like them. I also wore black pajamas and conical hats just like the Vietcong did.

I remember another day when I didn't act like the Vietnamese, and Dickey jumped in and saved my bacon again. Just the two of us were out in front. We had walked into what looked like a deserted village. Hanging from a fence post was a bag with a little puppy inside. Its head was the only part sticking out of the bag, and it was squirming and whining. All I could think of was that poor puppy and how somebody must have left it there and forgotten it when they evacuated the village.

I was a lot closer to the fence than Dickey, and I started to reach for the bag. Suddenly shots popped around my feet. It was quicker for Dickey to fire a short burst near me than to yell at me. I jumped back and he came running up, pulled his knife, and slit the dog's throat.

"Say, mate, it's a trap, you know," he said as he cut down the side of the bag. Inside was a Russian-made hand grenade. It was attached to the bottom of the bag and the pin was tied to the dog's hind leg. "Sorry to kill the little pup, but I didn't know how they'd fixed it. Remember, chap, dogs are considered food here, not pets."

I was still learning. Clarence LaChance, a noncom like me, had tried to clue me in when I had first come in. LaChance picked me up at the chopper pad. It was almost dark when he got there. "I've never made this run at night before," he said. "Can't be predictable, they'll get you if you are. I figure they expected us to lay over here till first light. Heck, they own the night. They know it, we know it. Comin' back like this was unpredictable, gotta be unpredictable."

Clarence was a quiet, serious kind of guy. His East Coast staccato and my South Texas drawl must have sounded to the Vietnamese like we were speaking two different languages.

When I met our commander, Captain Creech, the following morning he said just about the same thing as LaChance. Paranoia was the order of the day. Nothing was what I had expected it to be. I had been real proud to be sent here. I had looked forward to serving with men who were all volunteers. No draftees, no first-timers, all experienced army veterans. I was a sergeant in the 82nd Airborne. Action was what I was trained for and I was itching for it.

Until I got there.

Nothing that I had been trained for had anything to do with what was really going down. For openers, the guys we were advising wouldn't fight. For them, this war was comparable to somebody's giving me a gun in my hometown of El Campo, Texas, and telling me to go shoot my cousin in San Antonio, Texas, or to sneak up to Waco, Texas, and blow up my uncle's tractor. Both sides were so interrelated that the war just didn't make any sense to them.

Democracy, communism, "domino theory," all those things made sense someplace. Maybe they made sense in conference rooms ten thousand miles from Vietnam, but they meant nothing there. What we had to work with were a bunch of farmers in one uniform with U.S. weapons on one side and a bunch of farmers in another uniform with Russian weapons on the other side. Our guys didn't want to shoot them; their guys weren't too crazy about the idea either. Killing the "round eyes" was the only thing they could both agree on.

On one patrol, there were four of us, including Captain Creech, who ran the show. I was out on patrol with the captain and a squad of our ARVN troops led by a Vietnamese sergeant. As advisers, U.S. captains could not tell ARVN sergeants what to do. All they could do was advise. The captain was a short, stubby little rooster, just a little bigger than I was. Besides the captain there were Dickey, LaChance, and me. By the time I got there the captain was near the end of his tour.

We were all pretty considerate of "short-timers." It always seemed worse when a "short-timer" got zapped. With me being the new guy, everybody figured if someone was gonna get it, it ought to be me. Sounds tough, but it's just the way it was. We were spread out, coming across a drainage ditch at the edge of a village, when we came under sniper fire. We all hit the side of the ditch. No one was hit by the fire, and we were standing in that waist-deep muck, leaning against the bank and waiting. Someone had to do something.

The sergeant was on my left and the captain on my right. Creech whispered past me to the sergeant to get some men moving to the left along the ditch. Maybe they could outflank the sniper. Maybe just draw some fire so we could spot the sniper's position. The ARVN (Army, Republic of Vietnam) sergeant turned his head away as if he hadn't heard a word. The man wouldn't even look us in the eye.

Finally the captain was so frustrated he said, "Sergeant, cover me, I'm gonna move out through the ditch, maybe draw some fire." All I could think of was that the captain had only three days left in country.

"No, Captain, I'll go," I said.

"Hold your position, just get the sniper," he said as he went running off through the water.

He didn't get ten feet before the sniper opened up. We spotted his position, and as soon as the ARVN opened fire I went running after the captain. I saw the rounds hitting around him and heard him groan and go down in the water. When I got to him he was more mad than hurt. He had tripped and fallen and just wanted to be left alone. Right then, all he wanted was out of there and that crazy war. The sniper had gotten away. I should have followed orders and gotten the sniper, and the captain told me so in no uncertain terms. I was still learning.

Our Vietnamese troops had an S2 intelligence officer named Tran. He spoke good English. Tran had gone through a lot of schooling and infantry training in the United States. He was one of President Diem's boys out of Saigon and a Roman Catholic like me.

When I first got there he had invited me to go with him and a few others to church on Sundays back in Tam Ky. A good while had passed since then, but one day, right after Division had approved a very unusual secret recon mission for me, he came by and once again invited me to go to church with him the following Sunday.

By this time Creech was gone and Captain Lewis was running the show. Lewis heard our exchange, and when Tran had gone he gave me a real strange look. Lewis wasn't just paranoid, he was an experienced paranoid. He knew an "intelligence" officer wasn't going to set up any established patterns like that.

On Sunday, a jeep pulled up to pick me up for church, but Tran was not in it. Lewis grabbed my arm and told me to stay back at camp. He saved my life. Later that day we found out the VC had blown up that jeep while it was crossing a bridge near town. Everybody was killed. We could never prove that Tran was a traitor, but I didn't need more proof than I already had. If I wasn't paranoid enough by then, I became so after Tran's kind invitation to attend "church." From that day on, I didn't trust anybody who wasn't an American.

Traitors, cowards, crazies, and only a few good fighters. If you could sort 'em out, that's how you'd divide the South Vietnamese troops. One of the craziest was ARVN Lieutenant Wag. I went on patrol with him only once. I would have killed him myself if I had gotten the chance after that patrol.

I found out how crazy Wag was.

A couple of weeks after the sniper incident when Captain Creech came close to getting hit, LaChance and I were starting out on another patrol in the same area and up walked Lieutenant Wag. Even Wag's own troops considered him a psycho. The day before had been LaChance's birthday, and we had done some serious celebrating. One sight of Wag cleared the cobwebs real quick. Wag had considered Captain Creech his friend, and the little skirmish a few weeks back was all Wag could chatter about as we walked through the brush. I knew where we were headed.

By mid-afternoon we were walking into the same village where we had lost the sniper. Wag was in the lead and in control. The place was almost empty. Most of the people were either still in the fields or hiding from us. We saw three villagers squatting about a hundred feet away in the late afternoon shade of a hooch. Wag yelled at them to come over to us. They sat there and ignored him. He pulled his thirty-eight pistol and popped a

couple of rounds at 'em. They came running over with their
hands in the air.

Within a few minutes Wag had the whole village, maybe thirty-five men, women, and children, bunched up in front of him.
He kept screaming that they were all VC and had tried to kill his
American friends. They just stood there with fear etched in their
faces. Anything they said, anything they did, they knew they
were going to lose.

Wag reached out and grabbed a woman from the back of the
group. She was big, maybe seven, eight months pregnant. He hit
her once and knocked her down. He started kicking her in the
stomach. He kept screaming that she was a VC whore and that
he was going to kill the baby before it was born so that it
couldn't grow up to kill any more of his men. The guy was
absolutely off his rocker. I looked at LaChance, and he looked at
me, and we both knew there was nothing we could do. I started
to reach for my knife. I could feel LaChance's hand on my arm.
Wag was glancing back at us. One wrong move and I think he
would have had his men open fire on us.

This was Wag's country, his war, and his squad of men surrounding both us and the villagers. We were just observers. He
got tired of kicking the pregnant woman and grabbed a man
from the crowd. He was one of the three who had been squatting in the shade when we had come up. Wag pulled out his
bayonet and started stabbing him. He stabbed him up and down
the arms. He kept yelling at him, demanding that he admit that
he was a VC while he stabbed him in the chest and the sides.
The more he cut him the crazier he got. That poor little pregnant woman was curled up on the ground moaning while Wag
danced around her and over her cutting and cutting. Man,
LaChance and I, we just started backing out—we couldn't do
anything to stop it, but we could get out. Finally, Wag left the
bayonet sticking in the guy and grabbed for his pistol. He just
stuck it up against the man's head and shot him. We saw the
man's blood and brains spray the crowd.

The look in the eyes of those villagers was chilling. Wag was
doing the killing. Wag was the crazy one, but they were looking
at us. American uniforms, American weapons, two big
American soldiers standing by doing nothing to stop it. To those
villagers we were doing the killing and the beating. They figured

we were in charge and had ordered Wag to do it. You could see those suspicions in their eyes.

I have killed a lot of men. I'm a soldier. Sometimes it's my job to kill. I've seen a lot of men die, too. Blown to bits near me or bleeding to death in my arms. With all I've seen, I will never forget the look in those villagers' eyes.

The horrifying thing was that Wag wasn't the worst of them. Such evils weren't one-sided either. The South Vietnamese, the North Vietnamese, and the Vietcong, they were all cut from the same cloth.

We got that message, loud and clear, a short time later.

Things were heating up in our sector in II Corps, and refugees were starting to become a problem. Both sides had taken to destroying whole villages as retaliation for anything and everything. Those poor farmers had nowhere to go and nothing to eat. Down the road from our camp, just outside of Tam Ky, the refugees had started to congregate and build temporary shelters. By this time there were over three hundred of them living there without roofs or latrines, just existing.

My mind raced back to the picking fields of Texas and Colorado. Back to my youth. We had lived well compared to the way those people were living.

We talked about the situation among ourselves and with other advisers in the outlying camps. Finally, we did something about it. We scrounged around, as only U.S. Army troops could, and came up with enough material to build three barracks and some sanitation facilities for them.

We were still feeling pretty proud of ourselves a couple of nights later when we heard all hell break loose down there. As we raced out of our hooch, all we could see were our gunships laying down fire around the camp. About that time all hell broke out around us, too. Two mortar rounds almost landed right on top of me. The latrine was one jump away and the only cover around. I stayed dry and took my chances above ground. Sniper fire was coming in pretty heavy. We knew it wasn't a full-blown attack. It was just a little holding action while the VC butchered the refugee camp.

They were making a point. Accept help from the Americans and see what's gonna happen to you.

LaChance, *Die Uy* (Captain) Lewis, and I made it over to the

camp at first light. There wasn't an ARVN soldier in sight.
These were their people lying there butchered and they could not
have cared less. The people who were still alive were wandering
around in a daze.

We heard a wailing coming from around the corner of one of
the barracks, and the captain rounded the corner first. I wish I
had never followed him around that corner. Three children were
nailed to the barracks wall. Nails through their little hands and
nails through their tiny feet. They had been crucified three feet
off the ground. The VC had used them for target practice and
they were pretty chewed up. All I could do was cross myself
over and over again. I have never experienced so many conflict-
ing emotions simultaneously before or since. There are no words
known to man that can express my feelings at that moment in
my life.

An old man was kneeling below a little naked girl who had
been crucified. His palms were turned up, and he was catching
the drops of blood as they slowly dripped off her toe. My worst
nightmares are the subconscious recollections of that father crying as he collected the child's lifeblood. We backed out of the
camp without a word. Each one of us knew that if we hadn't
tried to help those people they would still be alive, and the villagers knew it, too.

I never could see one lick of difference between the people
we were fighting for and the people we were fighting against.
Only by being there could anyone really absorb the impact of
what we witnessed. Civilized people don't do the things that the
Vietnamese did to each other. Even civilized warriors don't
expect to witness such atrocities. God has taught us the value of
each unique human life. Defending yourself, preventing criminal
conduct, and fighting in declared wars are the only justifications
for the taking of life. All other is murder.

Compared to what had been done to the people we had tried to
help, even Wag's actions seemed vaguely understandable. He was
crazy, and he acted alone. I could understand his actions as being
similar to those of a guy who goes berserk and kills his family, or
shoots at cars going by. People go crazy, it happens. Society pro-
tects itself from those few misguided souls who don't value the
single human life by locking them up or executing them.

But seeing what the Vietcong had done to their own countrymen—to the innocent children of their neighbors—made me realize that evil is real and that Satan is alive. That truth I bear witness to. The sight of those children crucified on that wall changed me forever.

11

Dress Code Black

The only chance we had to relax and be ourselves was back at Tam Ky, where there was a good-sized American compound. It was called the "Payne Compound" and was named after a U.S. Marine adviser who had been killed a few months earlier. Quite a few Americans were in Vietnam then, and a lot of them weren't in uniform. They were agricultural advisers, political consultants, industrial observers, and communications technicians. They were CIA, and they were running the show.

I'm a soldier. I follow orders. It just seemed strange to know that our senior officers were following CIA orders. Our battle plan was obviously political, not military.

Payne Compound was the only place where you could get some real news and hear what was going on outside of your little sector. It was a clearinghouse for information and a stopping-off point for guys coming into the interior. The conversation and camaraderie there kept us all sane. It kept everything in perspective, except, of course, when we heard news of something like what President Lyndon B. Johnson had said in a speech at Johns Hopkins University.

He had said that the goal of the United States in Vietnam was to allow the South Vietnamese "to guide their country in their own way." Some of us who had witnessed some of their "ways" wondered if that was such a good idea.

Tam Ky is located about twenty miles east of the Black Virgin mountain range. The famous north-south route known as the Ho

Chi Minh trail wound through those mountains. While we were building up the strength of our advisers in the south, the North Vietnamese were using the trail to build up their troop strength in the south to match it. This buildup was what a lot of the talk at the compound was about in those days.

One day, out of pure frustration, I decided to use some of that information in an attempt to finally do the job I was sent there for. "Captain Lewis," I said, "everybody knows those guys are building up troops over in the mountains. How about I take a few of our CIDG's or Saigon Cowboys over there and get the straight of it?" (CIDG's were members of the Civilian Irregular Defense Group, hired by the American troops for information and scouting purposes.)

"What are you talking about, Roy?" he said. "Our orders are to observe and advise the local troops, not go looking for trouble."

"Come on, *Die Uy*, you know what our duty's like. Take a walk in the brush till someone pops a cap at us. Then we go find the closest village and sit around while our troops try to torture someone into admitting they're VC. Cap, they trained me to gather intelligence; let me do my job."

I nagged him like a CIDG, or hired cowboy, who wanted an ice-cream cone. It worked. He passed the suggestion on up to Division and they filtered their go-ahead back down through Tran, the intelligence officer. Right after that was when the guys got killed on their way to church. Real interesting coincidence.

A few days later LaChance and I led our hand-picked squad out of camp, west toward the mountains. We were all dressed in black pajamas and those little conical hats peasants wear. South Vietnamese troops were known for not ranging too far from their fortified compounds. By the first night we were well into what we considered enemy territory and we needed to blend in. We carried a mix of U.S. and Russian weapons and looked like a bunch of VC on patrol.

By the second day out we were up in the low mountains. We walked along in a steady drizzle surrounded by clouds of mosquitoes. It seemed all uphill now. We fought the rock and the mud and the stinking jungle as we moved farther into enemy territory. Every second we expected to run into a bunch of VC or NVA regulars. The tension mounted as the hours crawled slowly by.

By the third day we had come across several old VC camps.

Some looked like they had just been abandoned. We had hand-picked our squad but still didn't really trust any of them. With Tran in on the planning of this mission, we didn't know if we might be walking into a trap.

On the fourth day out it was more of the same. We were all beat from the climb into the mountains and edgy from the tension. Around late morning we took a break and I went out to scout around.

One second I was cutting through the vines, the next I was sliding on my back downhill. I dug in my heels and grabbed for the trees as I slid past them, finally catching one of the trunks and stopping. I looked up and could see I was only ten or fifteen feet down off the ledge of the cliff. When I looked down I froze. The rest of the way down wasn't as steep. At the bottom of the hill, about three hundred yards away, camped along a riverbed, were between eight hundred and a thousand men.

I just lay there sweating while the insects chewed on me. After a few minutes of panic I realized that the troops below hadn't spotted me, and I slowly crawled back up the hill. I'd crawl a few feet, then look down, then crawl a few more. By the time I made it back to camp I thought I'd been gone an hour. LaChance said it had been only about ten minutes. I filled them in on what I had seen, and we went back and cut out a good observation post along the edge of the cliff.

At first glance it had looked like VC camped down there. When we got our field glasses on them we could tell the difference real quick. Uncle Ho Chi Minh, the Communist dictator of North Vietnam, had been telling the world that the civil war in South Vietnam was just that, a civil war between the South Vietnamese troops and the Vietcong rebels. The only outsiders, he said, were the American advisers.

To keep the lie alive Ho Chi Minh's troops would follow the trail out of North Vietnam into Laos and Cambodia rather than entering South Vietnam directly. In Laos or Cambodia they would change into the standard VC uniform of black pajamas and sandals cut from the rubber of old truck tires. All their personal things and all identification were left behind as they crossed from Laos or Cambodia back into South Vietnam. Even from three hundred yards away through the glasses you could see that their black pajamas were new and that the camp was run with a military precision that was not the ragtag VC style. This was a well-fed, well-equipped, well-disciplined North Vietnamese Army (NVA) battalion.

Now we needed more information. We had come a long way to find the North Vietnamese. The longer we stayed out, the shorter the odds were getting that we would make it back in one piece. We needed to make this "walk in the bush" worthwhile.

LaChance started joking with our squad about sending one of them down there to infiltrate when all of a sudden a kid by the name of Tho said "I go Sergeant" in his broken English. Tho was sixteen or seventeen, and he had become a favorite of the advisers. We had even talked of sending him back to the States for school. When he said he'd go to the camp we didn't know if it was bravery or the act of a traitor. Neither did the other ARVN soldiers with him. They knew they had traitors with them just as we did.

We swapped Tho's U.S.-made M-2 carbine for the Russian-made AK-47 that I was carrying, and within ten minutes we could see him walk past their sentries. They didn't have any better security than our ARVN troops did. Maybe it was a national trait. Before Tho walked out of camp I had a talk with him. I said, "Tho, if I ever prove you're a traitor, I'll cut your throat personally."

Every second we were sitting there we were waiting for the NVA troops to come pouring up that mountain like a mess of ants at a picnic.

While we were waiting, Clarence started joking with me. "Hey, Roy, if they come a-running up this here hill you gonna wait for Tho or hightail it for home?" He loved using his cowboy movie Texas slang with me. I probably sounded that way to him.

Then he got serious. "Roy, if they do come up after us, what do you think our odds are of getting out?" I didn't have time to answer. Through the glasses I could see one of them separate from the camp and start working his way up the hill about a hundred yards to our right. Pretty soon I could make out that it was Tho and that he was alone. LaChance kept an eye on the camp while I went out to meet him.

He was like a little kid who had been given a new toy. He couldn't stop laughing and grinning. He had accomplished his mission without creating suspicion, and we were there to prove it. When we debriefed him we really didn't get too much more than we already knew. He could tell they were NVA from their accents and what they were saying. They assumed he was from one of the small VC groups they were controlling. He told us that they were real proud of themselves. They were talking about how all the South Vietnamese troops were afraid of them and how the American advisers were scared to come out at night.

LaChance started joking around about how he was mad and told our boys to lock and load. We were going down there and give 'em a fight. Our boys thought he was serious and almost started home without us. It became obvious Tho was one of the standouts—although just a kid, he was a brave man compared to many of his countrymen.

From a pure military standpoint Tho didn't get much we could use. It was one of those acts of pure bravery that convinced us that we didn't understand these people and that we had to be careful about generalizing about them.

In two days we made it back to base camp. Captain Lewis was just starting to get nervous when we came trotting back through the gates. He was beginning to realize how much flak he'd have to take if he lost half of his advisers at one time, and so he was real glad to see us.

We were debriefed both by our own officers and by some U.S. "civilians" who were just "hanging around" when we got back. To tell you the truth, I never did find out if our information made any difference. In the months that followed I never heard a thing about any action in the area we had scouted. But I was just a grunt. I did my job.

Every time I thought I was getting a handle on what was going on and why, something else would pop up and convince me I knew no more than a flea on the backside of a dog. Wherever that hound decided to go, I was going along for the ride.

All our maps had the whole country divided into rough geometric sectors. You would use the topographical highlights of the area you were in to identify where you were, then cross-reference onto the map grids to put your location into perspective.

One day, we were out on patrol and I was on point. Now, point was the most dangerous spot to be in. You were the first in and the last out, and if the point man got killed it served as a warning to the rest of the patrol.

It was my own big mouth that had gotten me there. A few

days before, I had been jacking with the ARVN colonel about my being an Indian. I guess he had seen too many reruns of the Lone Ranger and figured "Tonto" was the guy he wanted out there scouting on his patrols.

I know that this was my last mission out of Tam Ky. The problem is, I don't remember it. I've tried to find out about it since then but the military files are sealed. Even after all this time, it is still considered classified information.

All that I've been told is that a squad of marines found a body near a jungle trail. No location, just a jungle trail.

The guy looked dead. He was dressed in black pajamas and Ho Chi Minh sandals. There was a Russian AK-47 near the body. They assumed the body was booby-trapped so they were real careful flipping it over. They needed to search the body. It looked like another dead VC who had stepped on a land mine. They found a set of dog tags sewn into the lapel of the pajamas. They cut them out.

BENAVIDEZ, SGT RP.

Yeah, they thought. That face could be Mexican, not Oriental. The corpsman found a weak pulse and they evacuated me. That's all I've been told, and to this day, that is all I know.

12

Dress Code White

Brooke Army Medical Center
Beach Pavilion
Fort Sam Houston
San Antonio, Texas

White.

The world is white, the people are white, the floor is white, the ceiling is white, everything is white.

White is the first thing I remember. The first thing I could put a word to. A word, finally words. Maybe it's been words I've been hearing. I don't know yet, I think white is all I know for now.

"Benavidez, how you doin' today? Time to go back."

"Doc, y'all got things messed up here, these pegs don't fit in those holes."

"Hey, Sarge, welcome to the real world, you wanna talk a little? Nurse, have Sergeant Benavidez brought into my office."

Over two months earlier I had been medevacked in from Vietnam. The year was 1966, and war wounds and trauma cases were still a new thing here. I was in the first wave of the flood to follow.

The only real external wound was a big *X*, like a brand, on my butt. The X rays showed the real damage. The best they could figure out was that I had stepped on a land mine. The mine, or a pretty big flat piece of it, had come flying out of the ground with thousands of pounds of pressure and hit me square in the butt end. It just didn't explode like it should and blow me and my butt into a thousand pieces.

What it did do was twist and telescope my spine like a corkscrew. Bone and cartilage were shattered, but the cord looked intact. The doctors said that they knew that I would never walk again. My brain had been rattled so violently in my skull that they never expected me to regain my senses either.

In two months of sitting there and staring at those blocks that covered the ceiling, this was the first responsive remark that I had made.

"Maybe he got lucky again," the doctor mused as Benavidez was being wheeled into his office.

"Sergeant, tell me your name."

"I don't care about my damn name. How do you expect me to do my job when you don't give me the right pegs for those holes?"

The sarge was back, and the doctor knew it. When he started to smile I got madder. "And why's everything white around here? What is this place, a damn hospital or something?"

By this time, the doctor was outright laughing and I was getting madder and madder. If I could have gotten out of that chair I would have done something about it, too. The more the doctor laughed, the madder I got, and the madder I got, the more memories began to come back to me.

Within hours everything had come back. No, not everything. To this day I can't tell you exactly what happened on that jungle trail. Why on this particular day I was dressed in Vietcong black pajamas is still a mystery to me. Where I was going and what my mission was are still drifting around in that fog. But, finally, I did know who I was, and where I was.

I knew, too, that it was my wife, Lala, who had been driving a hundred and fifty miles every weekend to sit and talk to a wooden Indian. And to tell you the truth, I wasn't real happy about any of the things I was remembering.

At first I was glad to be alive. I was glad to be home and to have Lala with me. Whenever I did begin to feel unhappy, I would tell myself to look around the ward. I'd try to feel blessed. At least I got all of my pieces still attached, I told myself. The kid next to me left a leg in 'Nam. The soldier next to him left two, and the GI across the aisle had two burned stumps where his hands used to be. I guess I am one blessed man, I would think for a while.

M. Sgt. Roy P. Benavidez,
USA SF (Ret.).

Roy as a sixteen-year-old
migrant worker in Colorado.

Roy and Lala's wedding reception, June 7, 1959. From left, Roy's Uncle Nicholas and Aunt Alexandra, and Maria and Juan Coy.

Korea, 1955.

Roy during airborne training in 1959 at Ft. Bragg, North Carolina.

During his second tour in Vietnam, Roy was with MACV SOF Sigma, a Special Forces reconnaissance unit. Its base was B-56, located near Ho Ngoc Tao, between Saigon and Long Binh on Highway One.

Fellow Green Berets Jerry Ledzinski and Rodolfo "Banzai" Mantalvo near Duc Hoa in May 1968.

Roy's friend from his early Army days, LeRoy Wright, and his sons. Wright saved Roy's life—and Roy did his best to return the favor. *Courtesy L. Wright Family*

Helicopter pilots Bill Darling, James D. Eisenhower (killed in August 1968), and Roger Waggie. Darling volunteered to replace Waggie's wounded door gunner on Waggie's second trip to save Roy on May 2, 1968. Waggie flew over a thousand combat hours and was awarded the Distinguished Flying Cross but was never recognized for his heroism that day.
Courtesy of R. Waggie

Lloyd "Frenchie" Mousseau, a member of the recon patrol killed on May 2, 1968.

Mike Craig (front), the nineteen-year-old door gunner who died in Roy's arms, and Bill Darling in Dong Tam, April 1968.
Courtesy of R. Waggie

Recovering from his thirty-seven wounds at Ft. Sam Houston in September 1968, Roy receives the Distinguished Service Cross from Gen. William C. Westmoreland.

President Ronald Reagan, Roy, Brian O'Connor, Jerry Cottingham, and Tom Carter.

Roy about to step on President Reagan's toe after receiving the Medal of Honor. Defense Secretary Caspar Weinberger is at left.

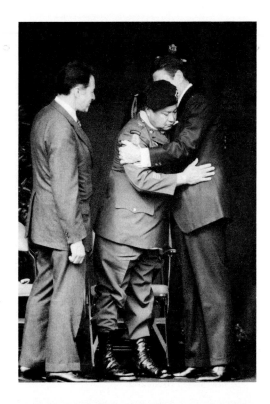

The Benavidez family at the White House following the Medal of Honor ceremony.

Roy and his family today. From left, son Noel, wife Lala, grandson Benjamin Prochazka, daughters Yvette and Denise, and son-in-law Stan Prochazka.

Soon, though, I would begin to have negative thoughts. The people back in El Campo would say I had been blessed. That lucky "Mezikin" boy, they'd probably say.

If I had to go home to recuperate, I imagined the comments of the biased residents of my town: "Look at that boy just sitting on that porch in that chair. That boy ain't got a care in the world. Only problem he got is if the mail comes late. We're working for that boy's welfare check. Bet he shot himself in the foot just so he could get that check. Heck, they're all the same, even too lazy to steal. Except from the gov'ment."

My thoughts were wild in many ways. If I could just figure out what happened, I would think, if I knew what happened, I know I could fix it. Man, I can't live like this. They shoulda just left me there, they shoulda just let me die. This is worse than dying. If my legs were gone, man, that's one thing, I mean, all right, they're gone, it's over, you live in the chair and you make the best of it. You go on. But they're not gone.

Man, those doctors are crazy. I'm not stupid, they said the spinal cord's not broken, just "traumatized." I know they can fix me, they just won't. I heard them talking about me. I know they're getting ready to discharge me on a total disability. I heard them saying there's nothing they can do for me. I just don't believe it.

I've spent eleven years in the army. This is my life. I've got respect here, I've got pride, and I'm good at what I do. What in God's name do they expect me to do? Quit a loser?

"Sergeant, you've got some visitors, let's get you into that chair."

The chair, the damned chair. For the rest of my life someone is gonna have to help me into the chair.

Rogelio, my brother, took the chair from the orderly and pushed me to the dayroom. He or my cousin Leo and his wife, Margaret, drove Lala up to San Antonio from El Campo every weekend. The dayroom where we sat and talked looked out over the parade ground at Fort Sam Houston. Actually, I sat and they talked, and talked, and talked. They talked about home and the family. Some relative had been ill. We had another new nephew. Someone had gotten married. Through it all, I wanted to scream. Down below, out the window, I could see the soldiers marching, and running, and walking, and standing. I just wanted to scream. "Help me, God, don't leave me like this, please, God, help me."

My memories of those days are still a little foggy. I kept going in and out of the fog, absorbed by my own problems. Only later did I realize that seeing me like that had to be a living hell for Lala. First the telegram telling her that I had been injured, how badly she didn't know. Then the wait until I was back in Texas. She never talked about it, but she must have gone through a nightmare of her own before I was returned and she learned that I was in one piece, one broken piece, but alive.

Our marriage, like our courtship, was more traditional than the marriages of today. In the 1990s, everybody's liberated, marriages are equal partnerships, and everybody's got a vote.

But that's not the way we were raised. Our arrangements were very formal, and our roles were fairly well defined. Lala was the wife; she took care of the house, and she would take care of the children when they were born. I was the husband; I earned the living and made the family decisions. Sounds simple, but it's a lot more complicated than that.

At the time that I was injured, we had no children, but Lala's life was all tied up in the woman's work of our big, extended Latin family. The men talked to the men and the women talked to the women. With me gone all the time it was not much of a life for her. But that's the way it was. For her to complain about it would have been unthinkable. I could have been the town drunk and she would have kept her grief to herself.

The women did have their ways of getting through to the men, but that open discussion that is taken for granted today just didn't exist in our culture then. At least for the women it didn't.

It was a long time before I began to wonder how Lala felt those first few weeks when I was really out in left field. I didn't even know who she was. Heck, I didn't even know who I was yet. When I began coming out of it, I'm sure I made life even worse for her. For a while, I didn't want to talk. I didn't want to listen. All I cared about were those two dead stumps hanging off the end of that chair. Everything else went in one ear and out the other. I really loved Lala for making that trip up to see me so many times, but I couldn't show it. I was so wrapped up in my problems I just couldn't realize anybody else existed. I was too busy holding my own personal "pity party."

When I finally did want to talk, all I wanted to talk about was what my life had become. My life was the bed and the chair. The days were broken up with little diversions like Lala's visits and therapy. The staff called it therapy. Most of it was made up of teaching me how to live in the bed and the chair. Suddenly, I realized they really believed the bed and the chair would be my way of life. They were convinced, but I wasn't.

Counting ceiling tiles was a big part of my day. I could see 327 of those little buggers from my bed. Every day, it was the same number.

One thing kept me going. I had always been religious. My belief had begun when I was a little kid. Just looking around in the big church taught me something about faith. I knew even then that there was something bigger than I was, bigger even than the adults I knew. I knew then, too, that God listens, even when nobody else listens or cares. From the time I was a child and I lost my parents I have always believed that.

Hispanic life was strongly tied to the Church when I was growing up. It still is today, and wherever in the world I was, I maintained my ties to the Church. I believe in Jesus Christ. I am a Christian.

While I was in the hospital, I spent a great deal of time in the little chapel, which was usually empty. When the doctors didn't listen, and the therapists didn't listen, and when Lala just couldn't listen anymore, I had someone to talk to. My faith grew stronger each day. Somehow I just knew that it was not my destiny to sit in a chair the rest of my life.

I began to believe that my life had been spared for some purpose. I remembered the first time I had awakened after getting blown up by the mine. I was staring into the eyes of a priest. I let out a scream that disturbed the entire ward. The priest was looking at me with a solemn expression on his face, and I thought he was giving me the last rites. He probably was until I started yelling. I demonstrated loudly that I was not ready to quit this life yet.

Sitting alone in the hospital chapel, I examined my beliefs. I came to believe that I was living proof that we have a loving Father. I began to look forward and to try to envision my future once more.

13

A New Enemy

The doctors had made up their minds. The army had no use for me. Like a misfired round from a 105-mm howitzer, I was useless to them. But they did have to dispose of me carefully. Sounds cold. It is cold, and it needs to be that way. When the business is death and destruction and their aftermath, the attitude toward the individual soldier must be cold.

My inability to soldier properly could cost other men their lives.

If a soldier is out in the field and there are casualties, he has to make decisions. If he doesn't think that he can save one man, he is trained to hit him with some morphine, if he can spare it, so the injured man will die without so much pain. Then he will go work on the guys he may be able to save. The same rules applied here. When the doctors first looked at my X rays they made decisions. The fact that I didn't like them didn't mean a whole lot to them.

The way I looked at it I had two goals that I had to reach. The first was to stall, buy some time so that they wouldn't discharge me immediately. I needed time. Things were moving too fast. My life was out of my control, and I was out of the loop.

The second goal was to walk again. To achieve that, I needed the time.

The doctors and nurses did care about me and their other patients, but, by necessity, they thought of us more as pieces of military equipment than as men. As a piece of machinery, I had to be removed from the rolls as a sergeant in the 82nd Airborne. A good inventory of equipment is necessary in the military. As a man, I would be discharged with a full disability pension and put into the Veterans Administration system of care. I had to slow down that process until I could convince somebody, anybody, in that hospital that I could recover and go back into the inventory again.

I tried begging. They were human, and it worked for a little while. But the decision had been made before I even got back to the real world. It almost had been chiseled in stone before I became able to argue my case. Every week, the staff would meet and discuss the status of the patients, and it was getting pretty hard for anybody to justify the reason that my papers hadn't been processed for discharge yet.

So, I prayed a lot. I also started to do the only thing that had ever gotten me anywhere in my whole life. I put my head down and I went to work.

During the night I used my arms and I rolled myself out of bed. The floor seemed as far away as the red clay at Fort Bragg had seemed when I had jumped from the tower. I hit with a crunch.

The guys in the ward heard me fall and started yelling for the nurses. "Shut up, you guys," I groaned. "This is my therapy, leave me alone."

The first night, I didn't even make the wall before Mrs. Smith, a black nurse, came in and chewed me out as only an army nurse can do. She got the orderlies to get me back into bed. From that moment on I just marked time during the days and worked on building up my arms and shoulders so I could work on my own therapy program at night.

The next night I made it to the wall and dragged myself around so that I was sitting against the wall. That's where the nurses found me. I got my butt chewed out again and was thrown back into my prison cell, the bed.

Before my next try, I had the guy next to me move his nightstand over so both stands were between our beds. That night I crawled all the way to the wall and managed to use my arms on the two nightstands to finally pull myself erect against it. My two hands were flat on top of the nightstands and I was just sort of hanging there. I tried to put weight on my legs and a burning pain shot through my back that felt like I'd been stabbed with a red-hot knife. I collapsed against the wall and slid to the floor. That's where the nurses found me that time.

Night after night, I bailed out of bed, crawled for the wall at the head of my bed, and pulled myself up. I pushed the night-stands ahead with my arms, pressed my feet against the cold tile floor, and dragged my dead body along until my arms were under me again. Then I'd start all over again. Finally, I was moving about two tiles at a time.

Mrs. Smith and Mrs. Rainey, another nurse on the ward, stayed on me for a while, but eventually they came to ignore me. They could either ignore me or tie me up. They were too full of humanity to tie me up, so they ignored me. They'd ask me if I needed help; if I said no, they'd just shake their heads, walk on, and leave me alone.

I had learned that if I got knocked down, I had to get up and keep fighting until I knocked my opponent down and he didn't get up. Every night, I got knocked down. Every night I got back up again.

For the guys in my ward, my nightly performance became the best show in town. In fact, it was about the only show in the ward at night. As soon as I rolled toward the floor, I heard them start placing their bets.

"Hey, look at that Mexican. I'll bet you a beer he falls."

"I'll bet you a drink he falls."

At first, not much money or beer changed hands after the nightly betting. I did fall at first. I fell down so many times that nobody was willing to bet that I would stay upright. Finally, I stood braced against the wall with my hands lifted six inches above those two nightstands. After that the betting got pretty even again that I would someday walk out of there.

The pain was like nothing I could have ever dreamed about. Every night it would suck the sweat and tears from my body and my soul. Every day I would go back to that little chapel and sit alone and restore my soul. I went through all the stages of blaming God, accusing, doubting, and arguing, but he never deserted me. He'd never let me leave that chapel until I was ready to try again. After chapel, I went to physical therapy to try to restore the rest of my body for my nightly battle.

Finally, I could stand. In unbearable pain, I could lock my dead limbs under me and they would hold my weight. The next step was moving. Night after night I would work my toes until I could move them. Then I worked on my ankles. Finally, I could angle the toes in one direction, then slide the heels along behind them and slowly shuffle along the wall. I did this myself, at night, alone except for the hoots and cheers of the guys betting on my success or my failure.

I feared the psychological pain I suffered during the day more than I dreaded my nightly therapy. I feared the trip in the chair to a doctor's office where he would tell me my papers had been processed and that I was history as far as the army was concerned. Every time they came to get me for therapy I was wound up like a spring.

"Where am I going, am I going to therapy? Do I have a visitor?" I'd whine.

"Yeah, Roy, I'm taking you to therapy again, just relax, you're going to therapy."

In therapy I'd sit with the guys with no legs, or the true paraplegics, and learn how to live in the chair. I was not a good student. I wouldn't give in to the chair. At night I was beginning to win my battle, and I wasn't going to let the therapists convince me that it was a lost cause.

When Lala came to visit me on weekends, I sometimes treated her coldly. When I was wheeled into the dayroom and I saw her waiting, I felt as if the brightest light in my life had just been turned on, but by the time I reached her side, I became sullen and silent. Every time, after she had left I had an urge as strong as my urge to walk again. I wanted to kick myself for being so cold to her. Time and again, I froze up during her visits because I hated to have her see me in that chair. I didn't want her to begin to believe that I would be in it for the rest of our lives.

The doctors had informed Lala of their prognosis that I would never be able to walk, and I was afraid she would believe them. I didn't feel too evenly matched with them—a shell of a man strapped in a chair against doctors in starched white coats with the authority of X rays and five-dollar words.

Because of my fear and pain, I put my sweetheart, the only woman I had ever wanted to have as my wife, through plenty of anguish, and at a time when she should have been happy, for she was expecting our first child.

I was living in constant fear of being presented with my discharge papers. If that happened, I feared the future. I could not envision my life without the pride that I had developed during eleven years in the army. Without the army, I felt that I had no future. The army was my home, and my job, and my future. A wheelchair out on the porch in El Campo and a few dollars a month wasn't a good trade.

I compared my situation to that of a concert pianist whose hands had been amputated. Someone might say to him, "Here's a few dollars every month. You can listen to that music all you want. You just can't play it anymore. No, we don't want to hear about your problems, to us you're just a number, so move on so we can get to the next number."

I was bitter. I was a soldier, I knew the rules, I understood the reasons for them, but I was bitter and mean to anybody who would listen to me. Even to Lala.

One day I had that confrontation I had been dreading. Instead of coming to take me to therapy in the morning the staff just left me in the bed. Pretty soon I could see a big man with a clipboard coming toward me. He was a full-bird colonel and a staff officer, the head of orthopedics.

"Well, Sergeant," he said, "they tell me that you have been making some progress on your own."

"Yes, sir," was all that I could say.

"You know, son, no matter what you do, I don't believe that you will ever walk again. We're processing your discharge papers. I think it's time for you to get serious about your therapy and rehabilitation and get on with the rest of your life. You'll learn that you can live a long and productive life in the chair. Don't you agree, Sergeant?"

"No sir, no sir," I stammered. "I can walk, I'm starting to walk already." I threw the covers off my legs and rolled them off the bed. I wouldn't let him speak until I could show him. I stood against the bed and shuffled along the floor, with that horrible fire in my spine, for three steps, keeping one hand on the bed for balance.

The ward was strangely quiet but for the shuffling of my feet on the floor. My ward mates could not have been more focused had they been standing at attention in the presence of an officer, something that many of them would never be able to do again. My nurses, Mrs. Smith and Mrs. Rainey, stood alongside me for support.

"That's real good, son. We just don't believe that you'll ever regain enough use to be qualified for active duty again. We have no choice but to discharge you."

Man, at that point I had nothing to lose. "No, Colonel, you can't do that. I know General Westmoreland personally; I used to be his driver. I'm going to call him and tell him to get me out of here. I'm going to tell him to get me someplace with doctors that want to help me, not kick me out." The guys in the ward were piping up, too. What did they have to lose either?

"Give the guy a break."

"Come on, Colonel, listen to him."

"Don't kick him out yet. I've got two beers bet on his walk tonight."

"Yeah, Colonel, fix him up so he can go back and get zapped the next time." There was no shutting those guys up. They were fighters, too, and I had given them something to fight for.

The colonel snapped his file shut and marched out of there. He never said another word to me and I never saw another senior officer again. But they didn't discharge me. At some point discharge procedures were dropped. I never knew when, and I never knew why, but I suspected that my daily talks in the chapel had been the reason.

In May 1966, when I had been at Beach Pavilion for five months, I began to be given therapy to walk again. As I started to walk again I started to become a whole person once more. I couldn't wait for Lala to get back each time so that she could see the progress I was making each day. She was seeing the change in me, too, and our visits became more and more normal.

As I healed, I quit feeling so sorry for myself and really started looking around the ward. I realized that I had been selfish and self-centered. A lot of the guys who had been cheering me on would have felt lucky to be able to live in a wheelchair.

One guy had two burned stumps where his hands used to be. He was having to learn to live that way for the rest of his life. I told myself that I would remember to be grateful every time I picked up a phone, or a pencil. Or when I held somebody's hand, or brushed my teeth, or wiped my butt.

My buddies didn't want pity; all they needed was a little understanding. I vowed that I would try to make other people aware of how such men feel. I would say, "When you see that guy on the street don't pity him. He doesn't want that. Don't help him either. He's a man and just as proud of what he can do as you are. Just treat him like a man and try to understand. Try and understand that he got that way fighting for you and for your way of life.

"Maybe it was ten thousand miles away, and maybe it was a stupid senseless war, but he was there. He didn't choose the time and place and the situation. When he was called, he served. And he sacrificed, without question, for you. If you've got a problem, blame the politicians who commanded him to go there. Better yet, blame yourself for electing those guys in the first place."

I looked around me and felt more and more blessed that I could walk. It hurt like hell, but I could walk.

Within a couple of months I was moving well enough to be declared fit for limited duty. I was in constant pain, but I wouldn't dare mention it or I figured they'd still want to discharge me.

Before the fourth of July, six months after I had been flown in, I walked out holding Lala's hand for support. The men in the ward cheered, but the orthopedist, who was there to see me off, complained, in reference to the betting that had gone on while I was trying to walk, "Sergeant, you've left me with a whole ward of alcoholics."

Lala and I went to El Campo to pack before going on to Fort Bragg, where I would be assigned to a desk job, the only one they figured I was fit enough for. The pain was still so bad that I was living in a Darvon fog. It was the only way that I could stand it.

I had crammed twelve to eighteen months of healing and therapy into six short months. I did it out of fear, and I was now paying the price.

14

Chasing the Silk

I was activated and on my way to Fort Bragg, North Carolina. My new duty was as "administrative assistant to the personnel sergeant at the headquarters of the 82nd Airborne, Headquarters, 2nd Battalion of the 325th Infantry." Quite a mouthful. Instead of tracking VC and NVA through the jungles of Vietnam, I was tracking paper through the jungles of bureaucracy. Boy, was I thrilled. At least, I told myself, I was active and in uniform again.

Before I got out of the hospital I had known what my new assignment would be. I reached an old buddy of mine from the 82nd. He was Special Forces now, and stationed at Fort Bragg, which was their headquarters, too. He arranged with the army to have my house trailer moved from El Campo, where Lala was living while I was in 'Nam and the hospital, to Bragg, and across the street from his.

I was almost a twelve-year veteran and a sergeant, and I had *amigos* all over the world. The army was my work, my life, and my home. The army and Lala, who during this period had exhibited the kind of bravery that is required of wives of career soldiers. Late in her pregnancy, she had gone with me thousands of miles from her family and would soon deliver our first child. Denise was born on July the thirty-first, shortly after our arrival in North Carolina. The trailer we lived in logged more miles going from post to post than most people travel in a lifetime. It came to represent home to me; no matter where we were, when I opened that door I was home.

The job went as I had expected it to go. Lousy. I was handling benefits and problems for the families of my buddies who were off fighting in Vietnam, acting as advisers in the Dominican Republic, and who knows where else. I knew it was an important job, and I was doing it.

At least I felt some satisfaction in knowing that I could help make things a little easier for the families. The idea of family had taken on special meaning for me after Denise's birth. I had been on the other side and I knew how it felt to be cut off from my loved ones, and I thought about how I would have felt to have missed seeing my daughter's first smiles. I quickly learned how to shuffle that paper and make it come out the way I wanted it.

What was lousy was that I felt as confined as I had in a hospital bed. I was a warrior, not a clerk. Sitting at that desk was like sitting in a prison for me.

Sergeants run the army. That verity had been proven to me over and over again. Starting with that recruiting sergeant in Houston, and including that personnel sergeant in Arkansas, I had been taught that lesson, sometimes painfully. Now it was my turn to manipulate matters. I became a master of the "magically appearing lost document" and the "illegible signature" and all of those other tricks it took to move paper down the pipeline.

Meanwhile, I was still living on Darvon and on stronger medication. It's really amazing I never killed myself on that short drive back from the NCO club where I went every night after work. Sometimes, I wouldn't even know how I got home. I just knew that I hurt like the fires of hell were being stoked in my back and legs and shoulders and that I had to get whatever relief I could.

I was seeing a doctor on the post who would see me on the sly. If he had required me to fill out sick call slips every time I saw him I would have been shipped back to the hospital, where I really still belonged.

"Benavidez, you're killing yourself," he said one day. "I know how much of that Darvon you've been taking. I also know how much you've been drinking. You can't live on that stuff like you've been doing."

"What am I supposed to do, Doc? It's the only thing that dulls the pain enough to allow me to make it through the day, and the booze is the only thing that gets me to sleep at night."

"Sarge, you've got to work it out. Exercise and hard work are the only things that might bring you any kind of relief. You've got to stretch those injured muscles and build them back up again. Right now your back and legs are cramped up tighter than a drum. The pills are just masking it. You've got to solve the real problem. I can't help you any more than that."

I left my bottle of Darvon sitting on his examination table and went cold turkey. I was up two hours early every morning. First I ran, then I went to the gym and worked out. I didn't feel any better at first, but I sure did want to stop living in a permanent fog as I had been.

After a few weeks, I began to see that the exercise was working. When I sneaked back into the doctor's office he was shocked at the change in me and said that I looked like a new man.

In the Airborne, you have to jump at least once every three months to be qualified to get "jump pay." I had no real plans for getting that qualification, but one Saturday I ran into my neighbor, Sergeant Tom Gloria, out in the carport. Tom and I, along with other Hispanic NCO's, had started Club Latino, which is a Hispanic-American group that organizes Hispanic Heritage month at military installations all over the world.

Once every couple of months, jumps were arranged on the weekend for those guys who were in desk jobs and either liked to jump or liked that extra fifty-five dollars per month they got for being "jump qualified."

"Come on, Hoss," he hollered. "I see you running every morning, you're in great shape. At least come along and keep me company."

Pretty soon we were down at the landing zone. There were over a hundred guys and a couple of hundred parachutes laid out on the ground. There were three choppers to jump from and two frantic sergeants trying to keep everything moving.

I stood off to the side of the group and watched. All the while, I was rocking on a mental seesaw. One side of my mind was figuring out how to land when I jumped. Most right-handed people are taught to hit and roll on the right side, their stronger and more agile side. My injuries were on the right side, so I was standing there figuring out if I could keep my mind clear enough to remember to hit and roll to my left. The other side of my mind was scared to death. As the fear set in I started to tighten up. I started to walk, and all of a sudden I could barely move as the pain started shooting through me. The fear and tension had locked me up like a rusty gate.

A hand on my shoulder jerked me back to reality.

"You jumpin' or what?" It was one of the sergeants who was handling the paperwork. "You've been on special duty, where's your slip?"

"It's in the car, Sarge. I'll give it to you before I load."

"You're group twelve, five is up now, you got about forty minutes. When I holler, you load. I ain't gonna holler twice."

My mind was made up. Now I had to make it happen. The slip, what I needed was a slip. The sarge knew there was some medical reason for my being at a desk. Thank goodness he didn't know the truth. What he wanted was a standard form, signed by some officer, which stated that I was medically and physically fit to jump. It also would state that I had gone through another round of prejump training. Including the dreaded tower. No way. There was no way I could produce a legitimate slip. If I even asked my commander to let me start training again he'd ship me back to the hospital, as a mental case this time.

Okay, I'm a sergeant, I told myself. I'm an expert on paperwork. What do I do now?

I looked at the guys milling around over at the chopper that had just landed. The other sergeant was loading the next group in. I strolled over to him as the bird was taking off. "Hey, Sarge, take a break. I've got some cold drinks over there in the car. I'll get the next group off."

"Hey thanks, buddy," he said as he flipped me his clipboard. I was just another sergeant, helping out a buddy.

As soon as his back was turned I started flipping through the papers on his clipboard. I hit pay dirt, a whole stack of blank "refresher slips." As I walked around, with my back to the other sergeants, I was filling in my slip. I dated it a few weeks back and scrawled the signature of an officer I knew who had been transferred out last week. I crumpled it up and shoved it in my pocket to "age" it a little.

A few minutes later I heard them yelling for group ten. The sergeant was leaning against Tom's car and sipping on a cold drink. "Man, I gotta find my chute, I'm up next," I said as I handed him back the clipboard with my slip on it and trotted away.

This was it. My hands were shaking while I strapped on my helmet and chute. I saw the last group landing, and they looked sharp. Everybody was laughing and joking around. I was in shock. Just a few months ago I had been told that I'd never walk again. Just a few weeks ago I couldn't even walk a block without the pain making me stop. Now I was going to jump out of a helicopter at one thousand feet. I told myself that I had to be crazy, that I was going to break my back this time. The chair. I saw that chair that I was going to live in for the rest of my life while I saw the ground pull away from us.

We jumped six at a time. Three each out of each side door. We were lined up, sitting in the doorway, our legs hanging out of the chopper. Just sitting there waiting for the pat on the back that told us to push off the floor and into the sky. This is the easiest jump that is ever made. I told myself that, too. It's like falling off a log. When a jumper comes out of a plane there is always prop blast and forward speed that makes him fight to get in the right position in the air and makes him fight the chute to get control. Hovering, almost stationary, in a chopper, all I had to worry about was my landing.

At least that's what I thought. As soon as I hit the sky I forgot everything that I had learned on my previous fifty-odd jumps. I started to spin, and I twisted my lines back and forth like a puppet being manipulated by an incompetent puppeteer. I did worse than I had done my first time off the tower. The only thing I did remember was to land on my left leg and roll left. The sound of the parachute silk popping in the air was still music to my ears. I was finally home.

When I was down, I was so happy to be in one piece I didn't even mind having the sergeant yell at me and call me a leg for my embarrassing-looking jump. I grabbed another chute, strapped it on, and signed up for another jump. About this time my neighbor, the instigator of this situation, had tracked me down.

Talk about a chewing-out. As far as he was concerned I was about the craziest thing he had seen this side of 'Nam. He thought I understood that all he'd wanted me to do was keep him company. And when he saw me strapping on a second chute he almost turned me in. He was my buddy, and he knew what my real physical situation was. He'd seen me living on strong medication and he'd run with me a lot of mornings when I was trying to "work it out." He thought I was crazy, and he said as much.

My second jump was better, but I landed wrong. I got up and limped away, and even with the pain I felt like a soldier again. It was amazing how much better I felt mentally. My third jump was picture perfect. Even that old sergeant thought so.

I was back, I was really back. All of the fear was gone. I still had the pain, but the fear was gone. I was jump-qualified Airborne again, and I wouldn't be riding a desk for long.

Before I was wounded in Vietnam I had applied for transfer into the Special Forces. If a soldier was a fighter in the army, that was where he wanted to be. They were the elite of the elite. They accepted only volunteers, only noncoms and above, and only Airborne-qualified troops. At one time, the training alone washed out over seventy percent of those who tried to be Green Berets. That transfer was the next step I wanted to take. I got to know the personnel sergeant and asked him about my transfer to Special Forces. I told him that the papers had been filed almost two years before and had, as usual, disappeared into that great paper pile in the sky.

No problem, he said, as long as you've got a copy of the originals we can get them back in the pile again. Sure, no problem, I said, but the truth was that I hadn't seen my copies for years either.

"Hey, Sarge," I said, "give me a set of blanks, just so I know which ones to look for."

"Sure, B," he said, laughing. "Let me show you how to fill 'em out, too, just so's you can spot 'em real easy." Sergeants run the army, and all sergeants—well, most sergeants—help each other out.

Within a couple of days my "old" set of papers reappeared and started moving back down the tubes for processing. Re-creating those papers and signatures from two years ago was no problem. In fact, it brought back a lot of good memories of those days when I had been on active duty that my wounds had forced to the back of my mind. The biggest problem was "aging" those documents properly. I ran them through the washer and dryer once or twice, and they looked about right. Actually, the third set of originals looked the best.

I broke a few rules back then, and it wasn't the right thing to do. It was wrong. I know that now and I knew it then, but my time was running out. I was over thirty and still pretty badly damaged. I wanted back into that war. That war was the most horrible experience of my life, but I was a soldier, a warrior, and it was payback time.

I felt my life had been spared for a reason, and I knew that I couldn't find that reason sitting behind a desk.

I felt confident that I would be accepted into Special Forces. The war was heating up, and my background made me the kind of soldier they needed. I continued to run every morning, and I kept working out every chance I got. I knew I had only one chance at fulfilling my goal and that I had better be ready when the call came.

About a month after my papers were submitted, my transfer came in. It was early summer of 1966. I was to remain at Fort Bragg, where I was assigned to Special Forces training. I was a proud soldier now that I was going to be part of that group.

The roots of the Special Forces are found in the Office of Strategic Services (OSS), formed during World War II. American military intelligence had just been caught with its pants down when Japanese forces bombed Pearl Harbor on December 7, 1941. No viable system of intelligence data sharing existed until Congress passed the War Powers Act, giving President Roosevelt the authority to conduct not only open war but secret war as well.

Roosevelt gave World War I hero and Wall Street lawyer William (Wild Bill) Donovan the authority to proceed with the creation of a centralized intelligence system. Under Donovan's direction during World War II, OSS teams were highly successful in infiltrating behind enemy lines via parachute into occupied France, Belgium, and Holland.

The most famous of these missions occurred just before D day. It was called the Jedburgh mission. Three-man teams organized guerrilla elements for all-out attacks on German personnel positions and supply lines. Their assignment was to disrupt communications; destroy railroads, roads, bridges, train trestles, and culverts; ambush convoys; and delay troop reinforcements headed for Normandy Beach. They were highly successful, and their work helped to shorten the war.

One of the heroes of the Jedburgh mission was Colonel Aaron Bank. In 1952, he was charged with the formation of an army unit known as Special Forces. Colonel Bank's vision of Special

Forces was of highly trained personnel capable of organizing friendly forces into large paramilitary groups.

This was Special Forces. My new assignment. I had been chosen to compete for a position in this elite force. The question remained: Was I capable of completing the challenge?

15

The Elite

Physically, training for Special Forces was rugged. Most of us were experienced Airborne. We were considered the elite and we were all in good shape. But the training was tough.

We ran five miles a day carrying seventy-pound backpacks and winding down with calisthenics. We also ran obstacle courses and made parachute jumps. We were left alone in the wilderness for twelve days with a limited supply of food and water, expected to survive on that and whatever roots and berries we could forage and then to make our way back to camp by using our compass and maps or by studying the positions of the sun and stars, a true test of our navigational skills.

Many of us in training had already been to 'Nam. Those who hadn't might have thought physical training was bad, but the veterans knew the truth: Nothing can compare to the physical abuse a soldier takes in combat. But even the pain endured there was never as bad as knowing there could be a VC with an AK-47 waiting for you behind any tree. For some of the men, Special Forces physical training seemed like a cakewalk compared to their tour in 'Nam.

But not to me. I was in pain, a lot of pain. My back ached constantly. The truth was, I should have still been in physical therapy in a hospital, not physical training for Special Forces. My back wasn't ready to jump from an airplane or to make that exhausting twelve-day trek with only five days' supply of food and water. I forced myself to finish, trying to ignore the nagging pain and hide it from my buddies. I think they knew how much I was hurting, but they didn't say anything. Some of them probably thought I was crazy for going through with training, and they may have been right. The truth was, I had wanted to be a Green Beret for so long, I didn't want to let anything stop me, including the pain. But it was tough.

Throughout the training, I kept thinking of that cliché: Winners never quit and quitters never win. Clichés come into being precisely because they do hold some truth. I kept thinking of myself as a winner, because of my faith, my determination, and my attitude. I knew that a positive mental attitude would carry me further than any other ability I possessed. I knew that even though I had no control over circumstances, I was the only person in this world who controlled my mental attitude.

The mental training that we were required to have caused me anguish that surpassed the physical pain I was having. Besides paratrooper experience, expertise was developed in one of five specialties: communications, weapons, intelligence, demolitions, or medicine.

Communications experts completed a minimum of four months of specialized training. Weapons experts began with a two-month course and advanced to the study of allied and enemy weapons. Intelligence specialists traveled to Fort Meade, Maryland, to develop their skills in intelligence gathering, evaluation, and dissemination. Demolition specialists trained to use every explosive device known to man, which allowed them to destroy targets with the skill of an engineer. The medical experts completed a thirty-nine-week program that was so intensive that they could actually perform quality field surgery under the most difficult of circumstances.

Facing such intensive training, I was, after all, a school dropout who had never been much in the classroom. Early on, I qualified for both operations/intelligence and light and heavy weapons. I opted for O and I, figuring it was probably best for my army career since NCO's were usually promoted faster in that area.

My commanders expected me to study like a college student. I could grit my teeth against the pain and handle jumping out of airplanes, but I had no idea how to study. I was expected to learn underground organizations, escape and evasion tactics, counterintelligence, fingerprinting, and analysis of air drop and landing zones. All that on top of meteorology and oceanography was tough on a guy who had never made it past the seventh grade.

I had other responsibilities, too. I was the highest ranking noncom in my training class, which meant I was charged with supervising the men in addition to keeping up with my own studies. I was grateful when LeRoy Wright showed up.

LeRoy was a sergeant first class, and he had already finished his course in light and heavy weapons. I had known him in the 82nd. I knew that he had served two tours of duty in Korea, and had, in fact, requested the second, for during the first he had fallen in love with a Korean woman but had been unable to untangle all of the bureaucratic red tape and marry her before rotating back to the States. So, he had actually requested a second tour and had welcomed all of its discomforts in order to return to his beloved HeJa.

LeRoy succeeded in marrying HeJa, and by the time we were in Special Forces training, they had two sons, Dorian and Darryl. He had shown me their photographs, and now I could show him mine of Denise.

LeRoy and I liked each other from our first meeting, in spite of our differences, some obvious and some less so. LeRoy was a black man who had grown up in New Jersey. He had graduated from high school in his state, at the Bordentown Manual Training School, an institution that emphasized military discipline. He was, as he had always been, highly self-controlled and serious.

The contrasts between LeRoy and me were apparent; yet we had more in common than not. I had reformed from most of my wild ways some time before. LeRoy and I learned that while we had grown up thousands of miles apart, similarities existed in our backgrounds. While he was growing up, he, too, had been required to help out at home, baby-sitting for his younger sister, Marjorie, whom he had been given the privilege of naming at her birth, and holding jobs to make additional money for the family. Like me, LeRoy had seen in the military the opportunity to get an education.

In 1966, it was unusual for a black man to be in LeRoy's position in the military. Yet a better choice could hardly have been made than this quiet and competent man who would rarely let someone know that he liked him with words. Instead, an appealing smile would brighten his broad, handsome face, indicating that he was a friend.

Not only did I have complete confidence in LeRoy, he out-ranked me, so I turned over much of my leadership responsibility to him. I was left with no excuse to avoid studying.

I asked for and received permission to switch from operations and intelligence to light and heavy weapons. We studied every firearm imaginable, regardless of how basic or how lethal it was. The idea behind the training was to prepare Green Berets to use any weapon necessary, and to learn every tactic available. If Airborne was the elite, then the Green Berets were the elite of the elite.

When I finished light and heavy weapons training, I gave operations and intelligence, my first interest, another try. We trained constantly, and during that time I not only trained myself, I taught my skills to newcomers, learning even more in the process.

I might not have made it if it hadn't been for Pappy. Already a Special Forces soldier, Stefan "Pappy" Mazak joined our class to continue his training, which is required of a Green Beret. Pappy was a Czechoslovakian who had entered the Special Forces at a time when many of the Green Berets were foreigners. He had been a French resistance fighter in World War II, and as a Special Forces member was well-known for his gallantry.

One of the military stories about Mazak concerned his actions in the Belgian Congo. A surge of violence swept over this huge expanse of land, and most of it was directed against the white settlers, many of them American. Pappy was chosen from among the ranks of the Special Forces to help those settlers in remote areas who were without any security.

Lieutenant Frank Fontaine led a team that was attempting to rescue a priest and twelve refugees, of which six were nuns. To reach them, Fontaine's team walked to a village near an airstrip in Gwendje. The refugees' condition was shocking; the nuns had been brutally raped and were in desperate need of medical attention. Fontaine reached Mazak by portable radio and told him to locate a platoon of Belgian paratroopers and get to Gwendje fast.

As Fontaine approached the field, he was surrounded by a screaming band of about fifty threatening, gun-toting rebels. He singled out the most likely leader and invited him outside the circle for a private conversation. The self-styled leader informed Fontaine that "all whites were to die."

Fontaine produced a grenade, pulled the pin, and handed it to the leader. "Okay, boss, shoot me. I will die but we will die together." For two hours the stare-down continued, with Fontaine acutely aware that he could not hold the grenade firing lever forever.

Mazak had been notified by the circling planes about the situation on the ground, and he instructed his pilot to make an emergency bush landing outside the sight line of the landing strip. On the ground, Mazak emerged from the bush holding two submachine guns.

Across the runway ran Mazak, all five feet two inches and one hundred eighty pounds of charging rhinoceros. He fired wildly into the air as he screamed French Legionnaire profanities at the top of his lungs. Fontaine saw fear in the eyes of his chief opponent and tossed the grenade into the midst of his captors.

The remaining live rebels ran screaming into the bush, abandoning not only the refugees but their arms as well. Within minutes the refugees were airborne and headed for safety. Later the normally subdued Mazak apologized to Fontaine for his outburst of theatrics but stated, "I just couldn't think of anything else to do at that moment."

When Fontaine asked Mazak about the Belgian paratroopers he had requested, Mazak stated that he couldn't wait for the slowpokes to effect the rescue, that he knew that he was the only one available at the time.

As our instructor relayed the details of Mazak's action in class that day, my eyes became fixed on Mazak. A man shorter in stature than even I. I observed his humility as the story was recounted. As the instructor completed the story, all of us in the room rose to attention almost simultaneously without being ordered. Our instructor offered Pappy the greatest compliment he could muster when he said, "Detail face Sergeant Mazak. Present arms! Order arms!"

Our instructor asked Mazak if he would honor the group with some comments or reflections. It was extremely difficult to coax him to his feet, but we all insisted that we wanted him to speak. He slowly rose, and every eye in the room was glued to him. Pappy apologized profusely about his poor English and made it clear that he was a man of few words. What words they were! I shall never forget them.

Pappy reflected: "We in this room are all men who believe that actions speak louder than words. If I can impart anything from my life as a soldier it is this: There are only two types of warriors in this world. Those that serve tyrants and those that serve free men. I have chosen to serve free men, and if we as warriors serve free men, we must love freedom more than we love our own lives. It is a simple philosophy but one that has served me well in life."

At that moment in time I was drawn to this aging gladiator like metal to a magnet. Here was a man that I could identify with, and here was a man that I could learn from.

Since Pappy didn't speak English very well, studying was hard for him. I approached him and suggested that we pair up as study partners, and he liked the idea. My own lack of formal education made us a perfect team. We struggled, but we made it through.

During 1967 my Special Forces training carried me on numerous missions to Panama, Honduras, and Ecuador. These missions are still classified but I do feel free to state that the indigenous forces we worked with were designated by the U.S. government as "Freedom Fighters" and supporters of democratic rule.

By the time I completed the training, I felt prepared to fulfill the basic, general missions of Special Forces, which were and remain:

To seek out, train, and support men capable of becoming
effective, friendly guerrillas.
To seek out, engage, and neutralize unfriendly guerrillas.

Since I was bilingual, I expected to be sent to a Spanish-speaking country. I thought I had hit pay dirt when I learned that another Hispanic soldier who was prepared to go to Venezuela as a military adviser had been injured in a parachute jump and wouldn't be going anywhere for a while.

I knew Herrera, and I was sorry he had been hurt, but I saw my chance, so I asked if he would mind if I went to Venezuela in his place. He assured me he didn't mind at all, and I immediately spread the news that I was going to Venezuela—even before I talked to Special Assignments in Washington. I was so sure of myself, I even told Lala, but she, unlike me, was smart enough not to get her hopes up even though I knew deep down inside she wanted to go. Man, I would have loved to have taken her to live in Venezuela.

The latter part of 1967 had seen a dramatic increase in activities on both sides of the Pacific. Over 5,500 enemy casualties were reported between October and the end of the year. The United States was taking the war to the enemy, and our aggressive pursuit had stirred a hornets' nest in Vietnam.

Unrest of a different kind was being played out stateside. Opposition to U.S. involvement in Vietnam had reached new highs since the early days of 1965 when antiwar sentiment went public through the efforts of activist groups such as the Students for a Democratic Society (SDS). Their initial march on Washington with five thousand people was diminutive compared to the twenty thousand plus that participated in the March on the Pentagon on October 21, 1967.

Public outcry over U.S. policy ranged from moral and religious issues to a hunger for peace and an end to the nightly body count presented by the television networks. Although the media had from the onset supported the government's stand on the war, the tide of discontent was beginning to raise more eyebrows and questions. People who had previously not given any thought to the issues of war and government policy were being sucked in by the media for a number of reasons, including the high price of the war package, paid for with hard-earned tax dollars. Such sentiment was inevitable. The topic was very much alive and evident wherever people went. Those who opposed the war and U.S. policy were now in the majority.

Nonetheless, President Johnson was able to rally enough support for his war effort to justify an increase in troops. By year's end, U.S. forces would number 485,600. The South Vietnamese commitment was at 79,800, with remaining free world military personnel at 59,300. The downside to having such a massive contingent was that there was a comparably large casualty list. The United States had already paid considerably with over 16,000 killed in action. South Vietnamese KIA's numbered over 60,000.

My hopes were shattered about going to Venezuela very quickly in December 1967. I had a friend, a Special Forces personnel sergeant, whom I talked into calling Washington to request my transfer to Venezuela. I even waited around while he made the call, ticking off the list of things I needed to do before we left. I mentally packed my bags while he dialed the phone.

I listened while my friend explained about Herrera's accident, adding that I wanted to go in his place. Neither of us foresaw a problem, but alarm bells went off in my head when I saw my friend's face change. He even asked the Special Assignments person on the other end of the line to repeat herself, and he spelled my name a couple of times just to make sure the information he was getting was right. Finally he hung up. I didn't like the look on my friend's face when he told me I wouldn't be going to Venezuela.

I knew that Lala would be as disappointed as I was. Desperately, I hoped that I would be going somewhere that she and Denise could go.

"Well, then, where am I going?" I asked impatiently, angry because I thought I deserved a pleasant assignment.

My friend had the unfortunate duty of breaking the news.

My assignment was a far cry from Venezuela: I was headed back to Vietnam.

16

Second Tour

The stage had been set by American foreign policy years before that would necessitate my return, and that of many other soldiers, to Vietnam in January 1968. Because since 1941 there had been two major wars in the region, policy was dictating that the Pacific Rim would not, under any circumstances, be encumbered by Communist domination.

The military command for the area was known as the U.S. Pacific Command, and the area was absolutely vast. It extended from the U.S. West Coast to Indochina and from the Arctic to the Antarctic. America had staked out this area as being of strategic importance, and policies from the White House amply reflected our desire to control this entire area.

The United States Army Special Forces had begun playing a major role in the region in 1956. New post–World War II policies were being developed for this section of the world as emphasis on military strategy cycled into nuclear strategy. A need for *unconventional warfare* was thought to be needed in case any of the Pacific Rim nations were overrun and the immediate need arose to organize, train, and supervise indigenous populations as resistance movements. Such organization would buy time for military planners to develop nuclear strike responses to major enemy actions.

I was among those so trained for action in this enormous and complex world. In my smaller and more personal world, Lala was disappointed, not only about not getting to live in Venezuela but also because I was going back to 'Nam. I had been naive to dream of an exotic tour there with my family to go home to at night.

Nor was the general public aware of how massive the military plan was for the Pacific.

Lala didn't complain, in spite of her disappointment. She just prepared to move back to El Campo with Denise. It couldn't have been easy on her, watching her husband return to the war in Asia that was dominating the headlines on the national news every night. But in spite of the media reports, neither of us knew how much it had really changed since I was last there.

I was proud to wear the green beret with my uniform. I really believed, and I still do, in the West Point creed of "Duty, Honor, Country." I thought that other people who saw my uniform should be proud, too, not only of me but of all the men and women who were serving their country. But Vietnam was a different war, not only in Asia but in America as well.

I had been somewhat sheltered at Fort Bragg. We had seen the protest marches on television and knew what many people were saying about the soldiers in 'Nam, but we hadn't been close to many protests and had no real idea how much public opinion had changed.

I had to spend three days in San Francisco waiting for a flight out. Eight other Special Forces soldiers were with me, and we were all heading for South Vietnam, where we would use the skills we had spent months learning at Fort Bragg. At San Francisco International I got my first real taste of negative public opinion against Vietnam. There my childhood prank of sneaking into bull pens and "grabbing them by the balls" also came in handy.

We hadn't been at the airport long when a group of hippies walked up and started staring at us. We must have made quite an interesting picture—an entourage of long-haired flower children and nine closely shaven United States Green Berets. To us, the hippies were the ones who looked odd; to them, we were "baby killers." In fact, one of them even called us that, among other things.

I was mad. Here I was, prepared to go halfway around the world to fight for a country I believed in and was proud of, and they were criticizing us for it. It didn't seem right, and I wanted them to know it.

I told another Green Beret, Dan Chapa, about my plan. He was more than happy to go along with it and set about telling the others what we were going to do.

We blocked one of the hippies—a guy wearing a headband who had been one of the loudest mouths in the group—and his attitude changed pretty quickly when he realized he was surrounded by several angry Green Berets. He started to step back, but before he could I reached down and grabbed him by the balls, stopping him in his tracks.

We created quite a scene. While he stood there, frozen, I pretended he was a friend who was begging me not to go off to Vietnam.

"But I have to go!" I yelled loudly, attracting stares from passersby, who must have been very confused.

He moaned and begged me to let go, but I continued the charade, much to the amusement of my friends, who couldn't help getting involved.

"He doesn't want you to go," they added. My hippie friend, meanwhile, was still pleading with me to let go of him. When a big enough crowd had gathered, I finally did release my grip on him and he limped to the door, no doubt in great pain. He was followed by his friends, who didn't look like they wanted any trouble even though just a few moments earlier they had been calling us names.

We all got a good laugh out of it until a policeman walked up to us. He looked at us sternly, and for a minute I was afraid I was back in trouble again. But he looked me square in the eye and said, "Sergeant, what you did was wrong. But I don't give a damn: I served in 'Nam, too." Then he walked away. That's how the Vietnam War was—people just couldn't understand unless they had been there.

President John F. Kennedy had shown amazing foresight about the changes in warfare that were occurring when in his 1962 address to the graduating class at West Point he had given the following advice:

This is another type of war, new in its intensity, ancient in its origins—war by guerrillas, subversives, insurgents, assassins; war by ambush instead of by combat; by infiltration instead of aggression, seeking victory by eroding and exhausting the enemy instead of engaging him. It requires—

in those situations where we must encounter it—a whole new
kind of strategy, a wholly different kind of force, and there-
fore, a new and wholly different kind of military training.

Finally, we were flown to South Vietnam. We landed in mid-January 1968 at the American Air Force base at Cam Ranh Bay, where I would join a Special Forces team in the Vietnamese countryside. I didn't know what my assignment would be yet.

If the incident in San Francisco wasn't enough, my second clue that the war was very different from the one I had left only two years earlier came almost the second I stepped off the plane into the stifling Asian heat.

Even some of the soldiers were different. On my first tour, they had been dedicated, professional soldiers determined to do their job. But the first men I saw when I got off the plane were young, and they didn't look anything like the soldiers I was used to. Gone were the short military haircuts; they had been replaced by long hair and sideburns on men who looked much younger than the men I served with on my first tour. These were just boys. They were mostly draftees who had no real military experience, but I was determined to have them look like professional soldiers and not like the hippies I had encountered in the airport.

Fortunately, another Green Beret, a fellow Texan, felt the same as I did. Together, we walked through the tents and issued orders for the long-haired men to get their manes shaved off, and fast. Most of them didn't protest too much—they at least knew better than to argue with two Green Berets—but at least one man argued too long and too loud. We lifted him off the ground and carried him like a baby to his sergeant.

"I told this soldier to cut his hair," I explained to the sergeant, "and he damn well better do it."

The sergeant agreed wholeheartedly, and the soldier got his hair cut. I wonder how many feet of hair were shaved during my first couple of days back in 'Nam. The fault for the lack of discipline in the ranks did not lie so much in the men themselves but in their backgrounds and in the circumstances of their being where they were. Many had been underprivileged kids, kids who hadn't been able to go to college to escape being drafted to fight a war that they neither supported nor had the skills to endure.

After a while, I was sent to Nha Trang for my assignment. It was there that I learned that my study partner and buddy Pappy had "bought the farm" (been killed) only a few days before I arrived. The army had lost a great patriot in Pappy as well as a fine warrior. I had lost a great friend as well as a valuable mentor. I walked outside the office and offered a silent prayer in Pappy's memory. I reflected on his admonishment to our Special Forces class, and I couldn't help wondering what type of war Vietnam had become to claim such a soldier.

Due to the secrecy of many of their missions, the conditions surrounding a Green Beret's death were usually shrouded in mystery, sealed shut by a "Classified" stamp. Such was the case with Pappy's death. I was never to know many details about how he died, but I did know he had been with B-56, a recon unit northwest of Saigon. I had little time to grieve the loss of my comrade, a soldier who had survived the dangers of the Belgian Congo but who was brought down in Vietnam. We never did have time to mourn the loss of friends, but I made up my mind that I would heed Pappy's advice as my tribute to his memory.

At the local NCO club I got another opportunity to catch up on the changing war. The men always had news, and I found out that Special Forces men were being used for more than gathering information.

In the past Special Forces members had studied the rules that Mao Tse-tung had given to his Chinese Red Army soldiers. The rules set forth clear guidelines, and unconventional ones, for the treatment of the peasantry. They were to be treated courteously and fairly—this in contrast to the treatment they usually received from conventional soldiers. Further, they were to be helped.

Special Forces members had heeded the tenets that had contributed to Mao's success, and helped villagers with their basic enterprises—well digging, bridge building, and agriculture. Further, they had participated in their social lives and built a foundation for training them to resist attacks from the enemy.

Now I was told that Green Berets were being sent into combat. The casualties in the field were so high that the command needed men as fast as it could get them, and Special Forces men were also seeing action. From my limited experience earlier in Vietnam coupled with my SF training I felt certain that the current conflict in Indochina could best be served by SF and advisory roles.

I was told, too, that there was growing animosity between conventional warfare officers and SF forces, which was resulting in SF intelligence reports' being "deep-sixed" before reaching the right decision makers.

In addition, a tenuous relationship existed between the CIA operatives and Special Forces because of the secretiveness in both organizations. What was really happening between those two groups was a far cry from what had been intended when an alliance between them had seemed essential to develop foreign contact points. The effort had begun in Indochina in 1956, when Lieutenant Colonel Albert "Scott" Manning had commanded a sixteen-man unit that was deployed to Military Assistance Advisory Groups (MAAG) operating in South Vietnam, Laos, Thailand, and Taiwan. The decision to divide a mere sixteen men in such a vast arena of lands, cultures, and political agendas was justified by the success of the Jedburgh Mission. Now, some thought that the alliance of the CIA and Special Forces had become a dangerous and expensive experiment with the lives of individuals in both organizations.

Strange battle lines were being drawn around me that I did not fully understand. Nor did I have the proper frame of reference to evaluate the consequences of these circumstances. In fact, I became one of the Green Berets who was sent into combat to replenish the dying troops.

My unit, B-56, was smack in the middle of it. They had been hit with a lot of casualties, and I made up my mind that B-56 was the unit I wanted to join. Of course, my buddies thought I was crazy. Why would somebody volunteer to get involved in something that heated? Most men prayed that they could avoid units like B-56. Ed Stys, the sergeant major in charge of personnel at the Fifth Special Forces Headquarters Personnel Center at Na Trang, refused to help me when I told him where I wanted to go.

It didn't occur to me then that Stys knew more about the action B-56 was seeing than I did, or that he was concerned about seeing me go home to Lala and Denise in a casket. My stubborn streak told me I wanted to go to B-56, and I intended to do so one way or the other. I was really mad at Stys when he said he wouldn't let me go.

Later that day, I saw my chance to do what I wanted when I ran into the team commander, Colonel Ralph Drake. I announced to him my intentions to join the unit. I figured it was worth a shot. The colonel didn't say yes, but he didn't say no either, and I knew I was one step closer to joining the unit.

I really didn't want to go to B-56 to be a hero. I knew what it felt like to be an NVA target, and I was just as afraid as everybody else. But I had friends in that unit, and besides, no Special Forces group was guaranteed safety. I figured I might as well be among friends.

Finally, Stys gave in, and my assignment was official. We flew to Saigon in a C-47, a plane usually reserved for CIA transportation in Vietnam. In only a few minutes, I was at the B-56 camp near the village of Ho Ngoc Tao, in the II Corps area, ready to start my second tour.

I had no idea what I was in for.

17

Unconventional Warfare

When we first arrived at the camp, we started training immediately. Even though we had trained heavily for almost a year to be in Vietnam, Green Berets are always training. When they get through, if there is no immediate assignment, they train some more. They are expected to be prepared for anything at any time.

B-56 was a unit devoted to gathering intelligence about the NVA. The mission's name was SIGMA, and even to this day I feel compelled to refrain from discussing the details of this effort for fear of revealing information that is still classified. To do so could compromise the Special Forces in future operations. Mainly, our unit worked on insertion and extraction tactics, since we never knew when a team from B-56 would walk up on an entire enemy camp. If that happened, we had to be prepared to insert more soldiers or extract them if they were heavily outnumbered.

The National Security Act still regulates much about the projects I was involved with in Vietnam during my second tour. Most of the operations taking place at B-56 can be located and traced through index numbers listed in the Military Assistance Command Vietnam (MACV) historical records in the Pentagon.

I can say that I was assigned to the Fifth Special Forces Military Assistance Command Vietnam Studies and Observation Group (MACV-SOG). SOG was an acronym that officially stood for Studies and Observation Group but was unofficially known as Special Operations Group.

SOG was organized in February 1964 by General Paul D. Harkins, commander of MACV. The general mission consisted of conducting covert operations behind enemy lines in areas of Vietnam, Laos, and Cambodia, though our presence there was sometimes denied by officials. The missions included but were not limited to sabotage, subversion, guerrilla warfare, escape and evasion, capture of prisoners, psychological operations, and general unconventional warfare.

Troops participating in SOG operations came from the army, the Marine Corps (FORCE Recon), the navy (SEALS), and the air force (Air Commandos and Air Crews). These units formed by technical definition a Joint Unconventional Warfare Task Force. Joining the standard U.S. military components were Vietnamese units, Central Intelligence Agency (CIA) and United States Information Agency (USIA) personnel, and civilians from a number of companies.

SOG operations spread over the entire Indochina area. Their goal was to assemble unfiltered intelligence information directly for the president of the United States. According to protocol, our orders were supposed to come directly from the White House, and all actions were to be sanctioned by "The Man" himself. That's what SOG was told, and based on that information, SOG responded in kind.

B-56 Special Forces reconnaissance projects were customized for regional employment by the field force commanders (II Field Force Vietnam) to give them long-range patrol capability in extremely remote areas of their corps' tactical zones. Since SF did not want to have anything to do with the South Vietnamese military establishment, three Mike Force companies were assigned to SIGMA to provide reinforcing capability. Mike Force companies were units that were prepared to respond at the last minute to commands for either strike or reaction.

Project SIGMA had eight reconnaissance teams. There were also four roadrunner teams consisting of CIDG personnel who were infiltrated into Vietcong–held territories. These teams were dressing in regional NVA/VC uniforms, and they carried appropriate armaments and forged ID papers. The four Mike Force companies were composed of specially trained Airborne CIDG soldiers who could work in various areas, but only for limited periods.

SIGMA headquarters was located at Camp Ho Ngoc Tao, near Tu Duc, between Saigon and Long Binh on Highway One. Assigned there were a 160-man defense company, one commando company of Chinese, Cambodians who were utilized as roadrunners and on reconnaissance missions, and two commando companies. On November 1, 1967, SIGMA's assets there were transferred to Project Daniel Boone.

To train for insertion, we rappeled out of a helicopter into the underbrush. Or, if the chopper could land, we scurried out as fast as possible. The whole procedure took no longer than ten seconds. In heavy combat, there wouldn't be more time. If the soldiers on the ground needed more men, they needed them immediately.

But we had to be prepared to extract men, too, so we practiced the maneuver backward. The chopper came to pick us up, and we had to load as fast as we could. Sometimes, though, the terrain made it impossible for the pilot to land. That's where the McGuire rig came in.

The McGuire rig was really no more than lines (one line per man on the ground) dangled from the open doorway of the chopper. A "bellyman" inside the chopper, so called because he laid on his belly to operate the rig, made sure the lines didn't become twisted or tangled. It was a pretty important job because a rig foul-up could kill a man. The man on the ground slipped a loop at the bottom of the rig over his neck and shoulders, and the chopper lifted him off the ground to carry him to safety.

Coming out of a jungle in a McGuire rig is like going from night to day in a few minutes. First, there's the darkness and dankness of the jungle, then as tree limbs snap as the soldier is pulled through them, day appears.

One day, a pilot must have decided that our training needed some livening up, and he came up with a plan that no doubt gave him a good, long laugh. I sure hope he enjoyed it, because none of the men of B-56 were amused.

Five of us had been inserted that day near a small village, and we were waiting to be extracted. Our instructions were to wait near a large pit the villagers used to store their human waste, where the pilot would pick us up.

When the pilot showed up, he didn't land as we expected, even though there was plenty of room for him to do so. Instead, we saw the McGuire rig being lowered. A new recruit stepped up, attached himself to the rig, and was lifted off the ground.

But not for long. The pilot dipped the chopper, and the training team member was dragged, kicking and screaming, up to his knees through the huge brown lake while we watched in horror.

When the chopper returned, the remaining four of us stared at the McGuire rig and then at each other. For a long time, none of us spoke. No one wanted to volunteer to go next after the practical joke the pilot had played.

Finally, Jerry Cottingham swallowed hard and stepped up to the rig. We all breathed a sigh of relief when he was carried over the pit without being dipped.

No one else suffered the fate of that first team member that day. No one, that is, except for me. I was the last to go, and that meant I was the pilot's last chance to have a little fun.

Almost as soon as I was lifted, I felt the chopper descend and I knew I was going down. I braced myself for the dip, but my preparation was not sufficient, the smell was so sickening. I was dragged through the pit at waist level before the pilot lifted me again and I was carried back to camp, dripping excrement all the way.

Naturally, I hit the showers as soon as I arrived. I never did find out who the pilot was, and he better be glad I didn't. It's hard to fly a chopper with broken arms and legs. I figured out that pilot might have wanted us to find him so that his tour in 'Nam would be short. We had the last laugh. We didn't report the incident so that he could serve out his sentence in hell.

The pilot wasn't the only man to have a little fun. In spite of my bad back, Colonel Drake had chosen me to serve as belly-man on my first assignment when we inserted and extracted teams. I was joined by Brian O'Connor, a young radioman; Lloyd Mousseau; Jerry Cottingham; Jerry Fields; and a few others. We had formed our own small NCO club, which was nothing more than a small space in one corner of the barracks where we sat and watched television broadcasts from Saigon.

One night, Fields and I went to Bein Hoa, where there was a large army camp. Together with some ravenous A-team members, we raided the mess hall, pirating all kinds of groceries and even a small refrigerator. We all got a good laugh out of the stunt—in the best tradition of "midnight requisitions"—and we all enjoyed the groceries.

Also included in our group were several CIDGs—civilians who were part of the Civilians Irregular Defense Group program. They joined us in our fight against the VC. When the CIDGs were created in 1961 by the U.S. Mission in Saigon, their ranks were mostly made up of Montagnards, members of the tribes who lived in the highlands of Vietnam.

The CIDGs often got a bad rap, both from the ethnic Vietnamese, who considered them barbaric and wanted nothing to do with them, and the American press, who referred to them as "cowboys" or "mercenaries." Discrimination, it seemed, existed the world over.

In reality, the CIDGs were fiercely loyal people, and they could be a lot of fun. In fact, it was during one playful argument with one of the CIDGs that I earned yet another nickname, "Tango Mike/Mike."

One of the CIDGs in our group was a pretty big guy, and he was proud of it. One day he told the interpreter that he thought he looked like me, and the interpreter relayed the message.

I was only kidding, but I said, "I'd rather have a bowlegged sister than look like him."

He was understandably insulted, even though I tried to explain that I was just joking. Still, he wouldn't calm down, so I suggested that we have a wrestling match to settle our differences. He liked the idea, and we prepared to wrestle.

A crowd gathered to watch our match. I didn't want to take him out too soon, but when he reached out and knocked the green beret off my head, I ended it quickly. I did feel bad about beating him so fast in front of all the men, but he had knocked my beret off. Later, I went to some effort to make up with him.

Still, O'Connor couldn't help teasing me, calling me "Tango Mike/Mike," which was radio lingo for "The Mean Mexican." At that time, no one on our team was offended by the tasteless jokes we made. We knew everything we said was in fun. Besides, we were all prepared to lay down our lives for each other. O'Connor's nickname, "Big Team," stuck with him, too. Tango Mike/Mike became a name of recognition from the very men I had grown to love as brothers. It became my second family name, given to me by the men I fought to the death with. That bond cannot be described to anyone outside that loop. It's real, though, and it becomes part of your personality.

Mousseau, we called "Frenchy" or "Cajun." Mousseau's own father had been seriously disabled during World War II, and because he was often unable to work, the "Cajun" had grown up in a family that had its financial problems just as mine had. Mousseau grew up in southern California, not Louisiana, as his nickname might imply. He had been a Fonzy character there, but his low-rider, car club days were over by the time I knew him. The relatively innocent "rumbles" he and his club members had engaged in were over, too, and he had shed the ducktails and pompadour that he had worn during his youth. Like me, he had liked a fight when he was younger, but he was known to his family and friends as a tough guy on the outside and a marshmallow on the inside.

Now we had serious "rumbles" that required our attention. We lightened the load whenever we could by reminiscing and joking with each other. Fun and games never went on for long, however.

The mood sobered up quite a bit one night when two teams joined to form a reconnaissance operation. We met at an A-team outpost, and we sure showed up at a bad time. One of their men had been "sniped" only the day before. The whole team was shook up about it. It was hard to lose a brother, and all of us saw friends die from time to time. It never got easy.

Not long after we got there, the two teams separated ourselves from the camp and started a fire with small chunks of C-4 explosive. Normally we would've been talking nonstop, thrilled to see unfamiliar faces and trying to gather as much information as possible. But man, the news at the camp had us all depressed and none of us felt much like talking.

We were feeling pretty discouraged but started to heat our rations when we were suddenly jolted into action by the sound of bullets whizzing overhead and hitting the ground around us. Instantly, we hit the ground. Lucky for us the sniper wasn't a very good shot, but he did manage to make one of the pilots hopping mad.

Actually, the pilot, Roger Waggie, was furious. He hadn't had time to eat much in the last few days, and he had gotten to the point that even his C rations looked good. He jumped into his chopper and took off, hanging just above the trees where the sniper was. He fired rockets into the foliage below at our uninvited guest for several minutes before finally returning to our fire. Slowly, we got to our feet and watched as the pilot sat down and calmly started to eat once again.

That was Waggie. He had been in Special Forces before he started flying choppers. Waggie had direct experience about what we were going through on the ground and it caused him to be exceptionally good at his job. Actually he was a legend in his outfit, the 240th Helicopter Assault Company, "The Greyhounds."

Waggie's ancestors were the McCutcheons, Scotch-Irish emigrants who were recruited into the Shenandoah Valley during the 1700s to protect the settlers from Indians. I figured that McCutcheon blood ran in his veins like Yaqui blood flowed in mine. For that reason I told Waggie that I always slept with one eye open, and my instincts told me to always keep that eye on him. Roger laughed about my joke, but I swear he always had an evil little grin on his lips when he did.

We weren't bothered by snipers any more that night, but there were worse things to come.

One of my nightmares about Vietnam concerned an incident that occurred during April 1968. Two of the Special Forces troops that I served with worked as a special team within the First Reaction Company. Their names were Captain Jerome "Jerry" Ledzinski and Sergeant Rodolfo "Banzai" Montalvo.

The nickname given to Captain Ledzinski was "*Die Uy* Ski." *Die Uy* means "captain" in Vietnamese, and since they couldn't pronounce Ledzinski they shortened his last name to Ski. Ski was a '65 West Point graduate and a Ranger-trained commander, and was the best trained combat SF officer I had ever worked with.

His training had begun early, and it had been thorough. He earned the Eagle Scout Merit Badge while a member of the Boy Scouts of America. He graduated from Linsly Military Institute in West Virginia, where he grew up, and he went on to West Point, where he graduated with honors.

Montalvo was a Cuban freedom fighter before he joined Special Forces and became an SF Jumper, Ranger. He and Ski made the best team we had in MACV-SOG.

Security prohibits me from developing many of these topics, but I can relate that Ski and Banzai were absolute masters of their craft. When these two disappeared in enemy territory, their mission completions were almost one hundred percent. What was required of them is the material that great war stories are made of. Ski spent a total of four years in RVN and how he survived is truly a miracle, for no "Special Ops" teams in the history of the conflict did more to inflict damage to VC and NVA forces.

One day I was given orders to board a slick (helicopter) and make an emergency run into Cambodia to resupply a ground team with ammo and water. Once on board I could pick up ground communications with the team, and I learned that Ski was on the ground and in bad straits. His team was surrounded by the NVA and his escape route had been cut off.

Ski kept calling out, "I need extraction! I need extraction."

Command and Control kept denying his request. All they would say was, "Continue your mission. Request to evacuate denied."

As I viewed the situation from above I couldn't believe what I was hearing. That ass at C&C was condemning Ski to certain death. The chopper pilot and I debated and debated. Should we break orders and extract? My heart broke and tears filled my eyes as I observed their desperate situation.

The pilot and I both knew that even if we tried to extract them Ski would refuse to come out. He was the kind of soldier who would not disobey orders. As we descended to drop the rubber water cans and ammo, the ground fire became intense. As I dropped the supplies we laid down as much suppressive fire as we had with our .50-caliber machine guns. As our ammo ran out I said a prayer for those guys below. I believed that their situation was hopeless. We broke from the area and I returned to B-56 in a somber mood. I was mad and I just wanted to be left alone.

Many years later Ski and I were reunited. After we located each other, he and his wife, Tina, sent me a ticket inviting me to visit them and their two sons at their home in California. When we met at the airport we embraced each other and just held on as we were both "ghosts from the past."

Men shed tears in these situations because combat makes us so very close to each other. I can't explain the bond, but our lives were so fragile in war, and death was such a constant presence, that emotions became very intense. We were both so happy to have lived because we had known so many who had died.

During the early hours of the morning, Ski and I were alone in his den, still reflecting on the war. I think Tina just excused herself so Ski and I could be left alone with our memories. The subject of that mission came up as Ski reflected, "Roy, I think back on that day and realize that I could have gotten out of that situation a lot easier if those guys in that chopper had not dropped that water canister on my interpreter's head. It broke his neck."

Up to that point I had obviously not mentioned that I was on that chopper. "Yeah," Ski said, "They killed the only guy there that could get me out of there."

After an eternity of time I finally got up the courage to confess. "Ski, I'm the guy who dropped that water can on your interpreter. I'm so sorry." In a desperate effort to redeem myself I added "but I did pray a lot for you."

My eyes watched his for a sign of quick forgiveness.

Finally it came. "Roy, I'm sure the prayers did it."

"Well, Ski," I responded, "you got to realize that's why I joined the army. Can you just imagine the damage this Mexican would do as a bombardier in the air force?"

In April 1968, my work as a bellyman had declined. That was a busy time for B-56, and I was needed on more of the missions. On one of these missions I had instructions to return with a prisoner who could give us information about the VC in the area.

The team slept on their stomachs holding hands in order to be able to give silent signals to each other and to assure that we would not be separated. Night in the jungle was a terrifying time. We built no fires and used no lights, lest they be seen by the enemy. The tigers, four-hundred-pound monsters, roared. The sound never failed to raise goose bumps on my arms and to make my crew-cut hair stand up straighter than any hair dressing could make it. And the snakes, long and poisonous, crawled.

Varmints of one kind or another plagued us constantly. Yet we had to remain still and quiet. On one patrol during my first tour the CIDG sleeping next to me had begun to pound the ground and pull my hand. He repeatedly grabbed my finger and stuck it into his ear. I couldn't imagine what kind of signal he was giving me, but I had some odd thoughts. Finally, he began to moan. I reached for my knife. The guy was crazy, I thought, and he was going to cause us to be detected.

Just in time, Clarence LaChance whispered, "What's going

on?" He came to where we were, and even in the dark was able to discover the CIDG's problem. "Give me your canteen," LaChance whispered.

I fished in my rucksack and brought out my canteen. LaChance opened it and poured water into the CIDG's ear, and his moaning stopped. "Bug," LaChance whispered.

The poor guy had gotten a bug in his ear, and it was driving him crazy. The bug had nearly caused him to die suddenly from a knife wound.

On the mission to take a prisoner who could give us information, we spent the day hidden in the underbrush along a small path, unable even to talk. Our mission began before sunup, so we sat like that for a while, tormented by the nagging insects and communicating with hand signals. Even though several villagers walked along the path, we couldn't find anyone who looked like they'd be of much use to us. It was boring.

After numerous hours of no activity, we finally saw a peasant walking down the path carrying a rifle. He didn't look too concerned about anything, but then again, he didn't know there were two Green Berets waiting to ambush him. I gave the hand signal "one walking," and as soon as he passed, I pounced on him, knocking him unconscious.

We took our prisoner into the trees and waited for him to wake up. When he did, our interpreter interrogated him, but he swore he knew nothing. He said he was carrying the rifle to protect himself from VC in the area. We didn't believe him, but we did figure he was telling the truth about not knowing anything to tell us. After all, if we had been taken captive, we wouldn't have known anything to tell either. In any case, it wasn't our job to get him to talk, we were just supposed to pick him up.

On the other hand, it had been a long, hot day hiding in the bushes and I was more than a little irritated. Some of my Tabasco sauce convinced the prisoner that I had poisoned him and he "got right" with us soon. He didn't realize how truly wonderful that Louisiana sauce was. My men, meanwhile, were getting nervous. The chopper was on its way to get us, but we had been there a long time, perhaps too long. If there was one VC strolling down a path, there could be a hundred more right behind him.

Just about the time we first heard the sound of rotors in the distance and realized the chopper was nearby, the prisoner decided to make a run for it, even though his hands and feet were tightly bound. His decision was a mistake.

One of my men automatically whirled around at the sound of the cracking branches beneath the prisoner's feet as he tried to escape. As he raised his gun, I realized I was smack in the middle of his line of fire, and I hit the ground face first. The bullets he fired into the prisoner's stomach rang in my ears.

We were all stunned. The interpreter watched, wide-eyed. He was probably wondering if he should try to make a run for it, too. I was scared to death and furious with my troop, but there wasn't time to react. The chopper landed and we loaded the prisoner. We administered what little medical help we could. He was still alive when we reached the camp, but I never knew if he made it or not.

I gave the soldier who had fired a good cussing out. He was embarrassed, I could tell. During the middle of my tirade, the realization that one of my buddies had almost shot my head off hit me, and I threw up all over him.

During these insertion and extraction maneuvers, we had little sense of security, very little comfort, but one day I ran into LeRoy Wright, my buddy from Special Forces training. LeRoy was one of the best soldiers I had ever served with and he was gaining recognition as one of the best soldiers in our group. He was disciplined, had nerves of steel, and everyone who worked with him trusted his abilities.

LeRoy and I were growing very close to each other. He loved his family, and he showed me the pictures drawn by his two boys that they sent to him. Sometimes he showed me the cartoons that he drew to send to them, pictures of soldiers and planes and tanks, the things he had been interested in since he was a little boy and played with his metal soldiers. LeRoy was a good artist, and he said he wanted to be a professional cartoonist when he retired.

We always talked about our families at home. His family had begged him not to re-up and return to Vietnam. His father had asked him before he left what he would do if he ever found himself surrounded behind enemy lines. "I would fight my best to the end," he had responded. "Then someone else would know that I had done my best."

There was no racial distinction between us. We were a

Mexican-American Indian and an African-American, and he was married to a Korean woman. LeRoy often said that he thought that people were people no matter what color. We were all Americans and that's the reason we were there fighting together.

We were in the middle of some pretty heavy gunfire on one of our missions, and we had to be extracted. One of my men was badly wounded and the chopper could not land so McGuire rigs were dropped out of the chopper for us.

I harnessed the wounded soldier and then myself into the rig. The ropes had become entangled and were rubbing together— soon, if this continued, my injured man and I would plunge about three hundred feet to our deaths. I observed the bellyman being hit by ground fire and retreating back inside the chopper.

As I prayed for help, I looked up and saw a real angel appear as the replacement for the wounded bellyman.

Don't ever let anyone tell you all angels are white. I found out later that my buddy LeRoy Wright was strapping on the belly belt and hanging out the door to separate our nylon ropes. You could hear the supersonic crack of incoming bullets pass us as the situation worsened. Finally the ropes cleared each other and we were extracted from the hot spot and set down safely at a designated extraction area near Quan Loi. I looked up at that big, beautiful chopper and we exchanged mutual thumbs-ups.

That evening one of the chopper's crew members remarked, "Roy, you must be a Catholic all right."

"Sure am," I replied.

"How's that?"

A big grin broke wide open as he gave a large belly laugh and said, "I think that's the reason you got back here alive. That was a close one."

Our nervous laughter was short-lived as a medic brought the news to us that the young soldier who had been wounded on the patrol had just "bought the farm."

A silence fell on the room as the laughter was replaced with a whole new range of emotions.

18

Tango Mike/Mike

The name Tango Mike/Mike had become synonymous with my given name, Roy P. Benavidez. Apparently it was much easier for the Cambodian mercenaries to pronounce and remember than the name Benavidez. The name definitely had become my alter ego. Our alphabetical code names, which we called our Alpha names, were used exclusively on all radio transmissions to confuse the enemy who were monitoring us. If you were captured the enemy wouldn't know that Benavidez, R.P., was also Tango Mike/Mike.

Our heavy training and our missions continued. One morning at the end of April 1968, a chopper landed at the camp, and Mac, the bellyman, jumped out. He was accompanied by the rest of the team and a prisoner—an NVA officer.

LeRoy Wright, Brian O'Connor, and Lloyd Mousseau, the American contingent of the team, had been on their way to the briefing room, where they were to learn about an important, highly secretive mission they would be going on, but when they heard Mac yelling, they couldn't resist going to investigate.

Man, he was excited. A bullet had come a little too close, tearing a hole through his shirt and destroying the McGuire rig. But he was alive, and that was cause enough for celebration.

That's how it was. When the choppers took off to take team members on some mission, you never knew if you'd ever see them again. So when they came back alive, you felt like celebrating a little.

After we listened to Mac's close-call story, Wright, O'Connor, and Mousseau went on to their meeting. I didn't know what their mission was, but I sure found out later.

Colonel Drake told the men that they would be joining two Vietnamese Special Forces warrant officers and seven CIDGs on a special mission inside Cambodia to learn more about enemy activity. An NVA unit was suspected of moving south, and it would be the team's job to discover what paths they were using and to map unmarked trails. They were also instructed to steal an enemy truck and drive it back to B-56 so that intelligence officers could see firsthand what its contents were. Intel was expecting a major Tet offensive and they wanted that truck. Wright would be team leader, and they had a week to train for the mission.

The men were scheduled to meet at Quon Loi, near the Cambodian border, but they would leave early the morning of the mission and fly to Loc Ninh, the Special Forces camp near Quon Loi. They would leave for their mission from there.

During the week before they left, the men had stepped up their training. I continued my own training, too, especially after I was told that I would also be going to Quon Loi and then to Loc Ninh as support for a special assignment. I didn't know what the mission was, and I didn't need to know. But I trained for it.

Even though we went separately to Quon Loi, we managed to meet up the night before the mission. We sat around and played cards with several other men, insulting each other and having a good time. Wright won most of the hands, walking away with our money. It was like any other night, hanging out in the barracks at our makeshift NCO club back at the B-56 camp. There was no way to know what would happen the next day.

Wright's team bedded off early the evening of May 1. I flew on to Loc Ninh, where I spent the night and planned to sleep in. But while I slept that next morning, Wright's team flew into Loc Ninh before dawn and waited for their orders. When they finally came, the team was flown into enemy territory by Warrant Officer (WO) Bill Armstrong of the 240th Helicopter Assault Company. On board Armstrong's aircraft was a full helicopter crew, the three-man Special Forces team, and nine Cambodian mercenaries. The operation was being directed by Special Forces Lieutenant Fred Jones, who was on board the command and control aircraft piloted by Major Jesse James.

Armstrong zigzagged, dipped, and changed directions during the flight, a tactic that prevented the enemy from knowing his exact destination. When the chopper finally did land, it was in a thick jungle area. In a matter of seconds, the team was out and the chopper was gone, leaving no trace that it had ever been there at all. The team instinctively moved to the treeline for cover. They quietly listened for signs that they had been detected. It was O'Connor who later gave me the details of what took place.

The men studied the landing zone for a while, making sure they hadn't been detected. When they were certain, Wright showed them the path they would take on a map. He went first, and O'Connor brought up the rear, carrying the radio. All of the men carried special equipment—cameras, submachine guns with silencers, and a lot of ammunition, food, and water—and their load combined with the sticky heat was more than a little uncomfortable. They hacked away at the dense leaves, clearing a tunnel until suddenly Wright accidentally stepped right in the middle of a well-hidden trail that ran right through the jungle. Quickly, he stepped back into the overgrowth and, using hand signals, let the others know that they had found a path.

Mousseau took over, making his way down the trail, his weapon ready for fire. He returned in only a few minutes and told Wright he had seen a few enemy soldiers coming down the trail.

Wright ordered his men back to their positions. Since O'Connor was in the back, he told him to be prepared to lead the men out if they had to backtrack in a hurry.

O'Connor returned to his position and waited. There was nothing for him to do but sit, sweat, and stare. The jungle was eerily quiet—for a while.

But suddenly there was a small scream that got O'Connor's heart racing. He heard a short burst of gunfire, which he recognized immediately as an AK-47. He wanted to know what happened, but he, too, was a good soldier. He knew to wait for his orders.

He didn't wait too long before the signal came. They were backtracking. O'Connor led the team through the path they had cleared earlier, ignoring the vines that clawed at their faces and reached up to trip them. They carried their weapons ready to fire and ran at top speed until O'Connor led them into a gully.

"What was it?" O'Connor asked when he caught his breath.

Wright answered that they had run into some woodcutters. Mousseau had been forced to slit their throats, but one of them managed to fire off a few rounds before he died.

"They weren't just chopping firewood," Wright said. The team knew what he meant; the "woodcutters" had probably been clearing a path for more NVA.

Wright radioed Lieutenant Jones (Command and Control). Lieutenant Jones tried repeatedly to obtain permission from headquarters for an emergency extract for the team but was denied. They were ordered to return to the landing zone, which surprised the whole team. That was a great risk. If the NVA had heard the shots, they'd be looking for them.

Back near the LZ, Wright ordered his men to stop and listen. They could hear the voices of the NVA, hacking their way through the foliage. They were too far away for the interpreter to pick up what they were saying, but they were getting closer. Wright tried to make contact with C&C again, but he had no luck.

When the men listened closely, they could tell the enemy soldiers were not excited or angry. That meant that maybe they hadn't heard the gunfire. In any case, Wright's team had not been discovered. He decided not to try to make contact with C&C again, assuming they were probably safe.

The men stopped to study a map, trying to find a new way to reach their objective. A few minutes later, they could hear the machetes chopping at the foliage again. The voices were louder now, and they were coming closer to the Green Berets. This time, Wright managed to make contact with C&C to request extraction. But he received the same orders as before: Continue your mission. Lieutenant Jones desperately sought permission again to extract the team before it was too late but was again denied.

Wright relayed the orders to his team, and the men left the LZ area. They came across a small field and a small road. Beyond both was more jungle; they would have to cross the field and the road to get to the security of the dense trees. One by one they made their way across the field—and ran smack into at least twelve NVA troops.

The NVA and the Green Berets were equally stunned. Quickly, O'Connor and Mousseau turned to study a map so their faces would be hidden. A CIDG point man, thinking fast on his feet, approached the enemy soldiers, talking rapidly and waving his hands.

The interpreter walked up to O'Connor and Mousseau and quietly told them the quick-thinking CIDG point was trying to convince the NVA soldiers that the group was looking for a downed American helicopter. He turned to shout orders to the team, instructing them to search the jungle. O'Connor thanked God for the CIDG, and they all turned to obey the orders of their new leader.

The CIDG started to follow them, but he was called back by the NVA soldiers. Still barking orders at his men, the CIDG returned, and the Green Berets prepared to set up a defense perimeter.

Suddenly, the interpreter, who had been listening to the exchange of words between the NVA and the CIDG, cried out, "They know!"

Instantly, the small road burst into gunfire. Many of the NVAs fell in seconds, but they managed to launch a grenade into the treetops. Like a flare it went up, and O'Connor knew that there would be more enemy soldiers on their tails now.

Wright called C&C for emergency extraction. This time his request was granted, and he told his team that help was on the way.

Back at Loc Ninh, the pilots sprang into action when Wright's emergency call came through. No less than eight choppers flew in to assist.

The 240th had a fire team in orbit. It consisted of four gunships divided into two groups. The primary group was commanded by WO William Curry and his wingman, WO Michael Grant. The secondary group was commanded by WO Lou Wilson. They moved in immediately to lay down suppressive fire.

Larry McKibben was the designated pickup chopper. He was sitting on the pad monitoring the radio but was unable to start his bird due to a weak battery.

Armstrong's crew was the number two extraction unit and they contacted Command and Control to vector them into the pickup zone.

C&C vectored Armstrong into the far end of the PZ and he immediately began taking heavy fire. It was obvious to Armstrong that the troops on the ground were not VC but highly trained NVA regulars.

Armstrong could feel his controls "kick" as his hydraulics

were shot out. His aircraft was receiving intense enemy fire and his radio and navigational equipment were destroyed. From that point on he had no radio contact with anyone.

Below, O'Connor watched first in relief as he saw a chopper appear and then in horror when he realized it was landing a few hundred feet away. There was no chance of the men slipping through the NVA gunfire to the chopper. His nervousness further increased when he watched several men walk out of the wood-line, waving the pilot down. He panicked, knowing that the pilot thought they were his comrades.

Gary Land, the crew chief, and Robert Wassell were laying a steady stream of gunfire from both sides, killing numerous enemy. The co-pilot, WO James C. Fussell, joined Armstrong in using their thirty-eight revolvers in shooting enemy soldiers as they charged the chopper. Several were killed as they tried to bayonet the pilots through their shot-out windshield. Land received numerous wounds to his legs, shattering bones and severing an artery. Robert Wassell was struck in the throat. Special Forces medic James Calvey was treating the wounded as he continued to fire at the enemy with his rifle. Calvey was shot in the elbow and the round exited his shoulder.

An enemy round struck the control stick and as Armstrong bent down to examine the stick, a round struck him in the neck, exiting his head and causing a depressed skull fracture.

Gary Land continued to lay down fire until an enemy round struck his ammo belt, causing his gun to jam.

The Green Berets shot at the enemy near the chopper, and in return, a door gunner fired a few rounds at them, thinking they were the enemy. There was no way to let the chopper know they were firing at the wrong men, until one of the enemy fell dead and the NVA sniped at the helicopter. Suddenly, the door gunners realized their mistake.

From their position, the team could see a large group of NVA sneaking up on the chopper that hovered only a few feet from the ground. The enemy soldiers, realizing they had been detected, attacked the chopper with full force.

Armstrong's helicopter was being destroyed as it sat in the PZ. He realized that there was limited space for another helicopter in the PZ, so he attempted to extract his chopper, in order for another relief chopper to land.

Even though he was suffering from double vision, he was

able to fly the craft out of the PZ, taking out the tops of trees for a hundred yards. He safely returned his craft to An Loc and was medevacked to the 93rd Evacuation Hospital, near the B-56 camp. Armstrong and his crew were to live.

WO Jerry Ewing and WO Roger Waggie were piloting back-ups. After escorting Armstrong safely home, Ewing returned to the PZ as Waggie was trying to get in. As Waggie went down, Mike Craig, his crew chief, was hit bad with a chest wound and Waggie mede-vacked him.

The team on the ground was now almost out of ammo, so a chopper made a quick dive into the LZ and threw out some ammo, but the team could not get to it.

Wright gathered his men together for one last extraction attempt. They knew this would be their last chance. They planned to move near a clump of trees and an anthill, which would leave only about fifteen meters between them and the next chopper that made it in. But as they ran toward their objective, the foliage around them suddenly came alive.

Wright took a hit and fell back onto O'Connor, who was shot in the left arm as he fell. Wright was up again in a flash, but he only made it a few feet farther before he fell again, moaning that he had no use of his legs. Somehow, O'Connor and the CIDGs managed to drag him to the trees and the anthill.

Ten NVA soldiers crashed through a nearby treeline. They seemed to be coming from every direction. Mousseau called out that he, too, was hit. The men fired at the NVA, trying to drive out their attackers. Gunships flew overhead, firing at the enemy and setting fire to the jungle.

Two hand grenades were lobbed into the air. They landed next to Wright, and he screamed at his men to get down as he threw one of them back. It exploded in midair, but there was no time to get rid of the second grenade. Wright did the only thing he could do: he rolled to his side and shielded his men from the blow with his own body.

O'Connor thought his team leader had to be dead, but as he reached for the radio, Wright whispered, "Give me a rifle."

Another grenade sailed over O'Connor's head. The explosion was deafening. Next to him, Wright fired continuously.

O'Connor got on the radio and, screaming and cursing, called for help. He turned his head to tell Wright help was on the way, but before he could complete the sentence, a final, fatal shot caught Wright in the forehead.

O'Connor took two more shots to the ankle and thigh. He was becoming disoriented and could barely focus when the gunships flew overhead, providing support that gave O'Connor enough time to dress his wounds, inject himself with morphine, and tie a tourniquet to the interpreter's arm. From several feet away, he could see Mousseau dressing a head wound of his own.

Suddenly, O'Connor took another shot in the stomach. He crawled weakly next to Wright's body for a shield and continued firing, certain he would die there.

While the men were facing hot combat, I was at a church service. A chaplain was using the hood of a jeep as the altar. The first I knew that anyone was in trouble, I heard the clattering of weapons over the radio and a voice begging for help.

I ran for the airstrip, knowing they would need all the help they could get. Everyone was gathered around the radio, listening for news. We learned that one of the choppers, piloted by WO Curry, had gone down, but that a second pilot had stopped to pick up the crew and they were headed back.

One chopper returned. It was badly shot up, but no one seemed to be injured. The second chopper to come in, though, was a whole different story. The pilots flew in, landing as fast as they could with their beat-up chopper. For a moment I stood there, staring at the chopper. I didn't see how it could still fly.

That's when I saw Michael Craig, the door gunner for that chopper. He had taken a couple of hits, and I knew that he was going to die. He was only nineteen years old. We had celebrated his birthday just two months earlier.

I helped them take Michael out of the helicopter, then I sat with him on the ground. I put my arms around him and called for help. His pilot was Roger Waggie and he joined me. Michael was still conscious and in great pain, gasping for breath.

Michael was like our son or little brother. We all loved him, but he had been a real favorite of Waggie, for whom the experience of losing him was pure hell. Michael had always been so eager to serve. Full of life and happiness, Michael couldn't do enough to please other people, and in spite of his youth he was known as the best crew chief in the 240th. I wished that I could hear him say again as a mission began, "Let's go get 'em now."

"Oh, my God, my mother and father . . ." he said as I held him. Then he died, right there in my arms, his parents' only child. I lowered Craig's body and turned to the co-pilot of the chopper. "Who's in trouble down there?"

Waggie told me it was Wright's team and I felt my heart sink. Those were my brothers, and there wasn't much anyone could do to help them. My mind seemed to explode.

No one was giving up. After changing out a few parts, one of the pilots, Larry McKibben, announced he was going back in. While they were working on the chopper, members of the different crews compared notes about what they had seen. Each of them claimed there were more NVA down there than the man before him had.

I had to go with McKibben. When I heard his chopper start, I jumped in and buckled up. "You're going to need a bellyman," I told him. "I'm it."

Midway there, I wondered what I was really doing. I hadn't really thought my actions through before I got on the chopper. But once I could hear the cracking of guns below me, I began to think. I needed a plan.

"I don't think I can get down there," McKibben said. "It's just too hot."

That's when I really made up my mind. I couldn't leave them down there. We had to do something. Everyone had been trying and trying hard, of course, but there had to be a way. I just couldn't sit there and listen to my buddies die on the radio.

"I'll get down there," I promised McKibben. "Just get me as close as you can." My fear was gone. I can't explain what happened inside me. The best way to express my actions is "autopilot." It seemed that all I had been taught in my entire lifetime just kicked in and my body went on autopilot.

McKibben flew straight into the gunfire, zigzagging the chopper and making every attempt to dodge the bullets that were being fired at the aircraft. I crossed myself one last time, threw a bag of medical supplies out the doorway, and rolled out with nothing but my buddies on my mind.

Gunships above us were diving and firing in a desperate effort to draw enemy fire away from us.

I managed to get safely to a treeline, but I hadn't been on the ground more than a few seconds when the first bullet hit my leg. To be honest, I thought it was a thorn until I took a good look at it. That's how pumped up I was.

The gunships overhead were now out of ammo and were almost out of fuel. They headed back to Loc Ninh to rearm and refuel.

I found Mousseau first, and even though I knew the team was in trouble, I was shocked by what I saw. Mousseau had taken a round in the eye and in the shoulder. His right eye had been blown out of its socket, and his eyeball was hanging down on his cheek. He had dragged himself to a tree and propped himself up against it, running out of energy. But he was a good soldier, and he could still fire his weapon. He was determined to keep going. The CIDGs were in what seemed to be a pool of blood, but everyone seemed to be patched up as well as could be expected.

I used Mousseau's radio to call McKibben. "You better come get us fast," I said. "We're in real bad shape."

The firing had died down some. I couldn't see any of the enemy, and I figured that the gunship strikes might have slowed them down. But I did see O'Connor, and he indicated that two of them were still alive.

I told O'Connor that we were going to get out. "We're going to live. We don't have permission to die yet. Not here." He and the other survivor, his interpreter, half dragged themselves toward us, but suddenly the firing started up again, and I motioned them back.

That's when I took another round, in my thigh. I wondered how I was going to be able to walk back to the chopper, but I sent green smoke up to signal McKibben anyway, and yelled for everyone to run for the chopper.

Everyone who could make it got in. The crew inside dragged the men into the chopper, but O'Connor and the interpreter were still out there. I ran along the treeline, spraying it with an AK-47 until I reached O'Connor. McKibben and the chopper were right behind me.

"What does Wright still have on him?" I asked O'Connor. He told me Wright had been carrying the Standard Operating Instructions (SOI), some maps, and the intelligence-gathering device. I knew the documents were classified, and if I left them on his body, they would fall into enemy hands. I would have to get them. There was no choice.

I tried to get the interpreter to his feet, but he couldn't make it. He begged me not to leave him, and I promised I wouldn't. I told him to crawl toward O'Connor, and for both of them to get to the chopper. Then I went looking for the SOI.

I needed the documents, but I also needed Wright. I had no intention of leaving him there like that. But as I was crying and dragging him toward the chopper, a third shot caught me square in the back. I dropped my friend's body and fell forward.

I guess I was knocked unconscious. When I woke up, I rolled onto my stomach and got to my knees. I had a hard time breathing and I was soaked in blood. I knew I was going to have to leave Wright. I didn't have the strength to carry him.

But when I turned to run to the chopper, I saw that it was nothing more than a smoking mess. It had crashed to the ground just before I had passed out.

McKibben was dead, I knew that much. The co-pilot, Fernan, ran from around the nose. He had a blood-covered tree branch sticking out of his ear. He was waving a gun, dazed and in pain.

O'Connor and the interpreter were lying about ten feet from the crash. They hadn't made it all the way there. A CIDG, who seemed to be only mildly wounded, also lay on the ground. I sent him to get O'Connor's radio, certain he was dead, but I was mistaken. He called that he was okay.

Five men, including Mousseau, had survived the crash. They were hanging out of the chopper's tail, returning enemy fire. I knew I had to get them out of there. The NVA could have easily blown up the whole chopper with them inside. When we got the men out, I shot out the radio so it could no longer transmit.

We tried to set up a perimeter around a small clump of trees. We divided into two groups, and I followed Mousseau's team. I called for heavy air support, and when it came, I dispensed morphine shots. One of the CIDGs who was badly wounded pleaded with me to kill him. The poor guy's guts were hanging out, and with the sun and wind, they were drying up. Man, that's a tough thing to take.

Our air force forward air controller was Lieutenant Robin Tornow, who was now overhead. He had located two F-100s, with ordnance on board, in the area being flown by Captains Howard "Howie" Hanson and Robert Knopoka. He was calling them as the ground battle kept getting worse.

Tornow called out, "This is a Daniel Boone tactical emergency. I say again. This is a Daniel Boone tactical emergency."

Captains Hanson and Knopoka had taken off from Phan Rang Airbase, Republic of South Vietnam, on a preplanned strike mission targeted somewhere north of Saigon. Their call signs were "Bobcat" followed by two numerical digits.

Their mission was uneventful until they were about to drop their ordnance on the preplanned target.

Just before they received clearance to drop, they heard Tornow on the UHF "guard channel" requesting immediate assistance for "U.S. troops in heavy contact." That was the highest priority request and always brought U.S. fighters to those in contact.

"Howie" Hanson, as flight lead, contacted the forward air controller and was told to vector north into an area where they were generally not permitted to fly.

That area was Cambodia.

With FAC clearance they "screamed" across the border from South Vietnam into Cambodia and were the first fighters on the scene. Tornow, at great personal risk, "hung tight" and vectored the F-100s to the target.

Both planes were loaded with two napalm each, which they dropped first. Followed by two CBU-29s each. These were delayed-fuse cluster bomblets in clamshell containers and were dropped from approximately three thousand feet above ground level.

The CBU containers opened at a preselected altitude and scattered the bomblets over the entire area.

Each baseball-size bomblet (of which there were about two hundred and fifty in each canister—times two canisters carried by each plane) had several hundred ball bearings in it. When the bomblet fuse detonated, it sprayed the ball bearings in all directions.

Tornow was excitedly transmitting a message to the F-100s about how much the ordnance was helping. The bomblets were going off like "popcorn," which was giving us some immediate relief.

The following minutes belonged to TAC AIR and gunship strike after strike after strike. They were pouring it on the PZ and back into the woodlines and the clearing in front of us that intersected with the small road.

Branches, slivers of wood, metal, dirt, and body parts were stinging us from the percussion caused by the bombing. We could feel the tremendous heat of the afterburners of the F-100s. That's how low they were flying.

Gunships were diving and diving between the passes of the jets. The air support was like a swarm of killer bees attacking us. It later reminded me of that passage of scripture from the Book of Revelations about the sky turning black with locusts.

Through the middle of this moment of hell came a lone slick that touched down about twenty to thirty meters away. We knew that this was our last hope to leave alive.

We loaded the last of our ammunition.

This was it. Now or never.

I learned later that the fighters had run their fuel down to a level which would not allow them to return to Phan Rang, so they diverted to Bien Hoa, near Saigon, where they refueled and flew back to Phan Rang.

I got to O'Connor and gave him his third shot of morphine. I also took another shot in the leg. We were under heavy fire again, and I wasn't sure what was going to happen to us, even though I tried to reassure O'Connor. He must've thought I was losing it because I don't think any of us really thought we were going to get out of there.

We were surrounded. There was no way we could fire back at the NVA because it was impossible to tell where their shots were coming from. They seemed to be coming from everywhere. We had no way of knowing until later that our LZ was surrounded by over three hundred and fifty NVA and thirty crew-served weapons (machine guns).

The air attack managed to stop the assault for a few moments, but it was long enough for that single chopper to lower right in front of us, and a Special Forces medic, Sergeant Sammons, ran to us from the aircraft. Roger Waggie and his newly formed crew of volunteers, WO Bill Darling as crew chief and WO Smith as door gunner, came to our rescue. Everyone had come to the rescue. What I saw was the American fighting man at his best.

The two of us carried or dragged as many of the men as we could. But the NVA were firing directly at the chopper, shooting the men as they were lifted aboard. Two of the men were shot in the back as they tried to crawl to safety inside the chopper. I could barely see through the matted blood in my eyes due to shrapnel wounds on my face and head. Waggie's chopper was badly shot up. He and his co-pilot were shooting through their front windshield with their thirty-eight pistols, while Darling and the door gunner and Smith were firing the M-60s at separate groups of NVA charging from the sides. Darling and Smith had volunteered to man a gun because they knew we were running out of men, and as officers they didn't have to volunteer for this situation. All I know is that because they did, soldiers would live.

I made another trip to find Mousseau. He was lying in the grass. I tried to carry him to the chopper. I didn't even notice when one of the NVA soldiers, lying on the ground, got to his feet. I also didn't notice when he slammed his rifle butt into the back of my head. I turned to look at him. Both of us were surprised, I because I hadn't seen him and he because I had turned around after he had delivered the blow, but he reacted quickly and hit me again. I fell, my head swimming in pain.

I now had only one weapon with me, my Special Forces knife. I reached for it, and when I did he pointed his bayonet at the front of my belly. Fortunately, he hesitated, and it gave me enough time to get to my feet. He sliced my left arm with the bayonet, and I shouted to O'Connor to shoot him. But he was too drugged to move, so I did the only thing I could. I stabbed him with every bit of strength I had left, and when he died, I left my S.F. knife in him. The last round in my stomach had exposed my intestines and I was trying to hold them in my hands. I could see Mousseau lying on the floor, staring at me with his one good eye. I reached down and clasped his hand and prayed that he would make it until we reached Saigon, where the medics could help him. Sadly, he would be among the approximately two hundred men who died on both sides during that battle.

I hoped that LeRoy was with us, that at least his body was going home to his family. I had loaded some bodies on the chopper, and I prayed that his was among them. The problem was that I couldn't always see what I was doing because I was bleeding profusely, and the blood obscured my vision.

How Waggie flew that chopper is a miracle itself. No instruments left, badly shot up, the cabin floor ankle-deep in blood, and we were headed in the wrong direction. Some air force jets showed up and turned us around for home.

Later, I learned that LeRoy did make it out of the jungle.

Sergeant Rodolfo "Banzai" Montalvo led a platoon of Chinese Nung mercenaries into the area the next day on a body recovery mission. He located LeRoy and the other dead CIDGs.

Banzai told me that the NVA had been "waiting" for us that day. He said that he counted approximately thirty foxholes with crew-served weapons around the LZ and more dead NVAs than he had time to count. As they were attacked by NVAs and had to leave the area, he observed that the entire area was a carnage of dead bodies.

My next semiconscious memory was that of lying on the ground outside the chopper. I couldn't move or speak. I was in deep shock, but I knew that the medics were placing me in a body bag.

They thought I was dead and I couldn't respond. To this day I can still hear the sound of the snaps being closed on that green bag.

My eyes were blinded. My jaws were broken. I had over thirty-seven puncture wounds. My intestines were exposed. Jerry Cottingham recognized my face in the body bag before it was closed. I remember Jerry screaming, "That's Benavidez. Get a doc!" When the doctor placed his hand on my chest to feel for a heartbeat, I spat into his face. He quickly reversed my condition from dead to "He won't make it but we'll try."

I was truly once again totally in God's hands.

19

A Long Journey

I spent many days after I arrived back in Saigon on heavy doses of narcotics. When I first awoke, there was a nurse down on her knees screaming and asking God, "Why do you keep doing this to these men?" There was a young soldier on the next operating table without arms or legs. She had broken under the heavy load of casualties that surrounded her. I faded in and out while the doctors, nurses, and medics fought to save my life with surgery after surgery.

But one morning I was finally able to open my eyes and I looked around at the other wounded soldiers. Across the ward I saw O'Connor, and I was thrilled to see that he was alive. Neither of us could move or speak, so every morning we wiggled our toes at each other to say, "Look, I'm alive. I made it another night."

Colonel Drake came to visit me and O'Connor several times. He touched my shoulder until I was able to talk. When that day finally came, I asked if they had recovered the documents I had found on Wright's body. He couldn't believe that practically the first words out of my mouth were spent asking him about the documents, but I had been worrying about them for a while. He promised that everything had been taken care of and I relaxed.

Sadly, one morning O'Connor died, or so I thought. There was a chance that he had been moved to another ward, but no one told me. I just knew I woke up one morning and he wasn't there to wiggle his toes at me. After what he went through, I expected the worst.

I couldn't write to Lala, but I was worried because I knew she had probably gotten a telegram telling her I was injured. Man, I didn't want her to know how bad I was beat up, so a kind lady Red Cross volunteer wrote a letter telling her that I would be home as soon as possible.

One day I was told I was headed for Japan for more intensive surgery. From there, they told me, I would be processed and could eventually return home. I was taken to a Tokyo hospital and I spent quite a while there. But I was grateful to be alive. For a while there, I had not thought that I was going to make it, either.

Finally, I was going back to Texas, but not home by any means. I was allowed to walk to the helicopter that was waiting to transport me, and when I managed to shuffle up to it, a nice young medic decided to lend a helping hand.

He tried to lift me around the middle, which sent shock waves of pain through my entire body. He was squeezing a foot-long incision and all the stitches I had in my side from the wound a bullet had caused when it had exited my body. I squirmed, trying to get away from the man, but the more I struggled, the more he tried to help.

He left me with no choice. I drew my arm back and punched with every last bit of strength I had. Both of us were shocked, but when he saw the bandages on my stomach, he felt terrible. He spent several minutes apologizing while I grimaced in pain. But soon I forgot all about it as I drifted off to sleep for the long flight home.

They took me to Brooke Army Medical Center, Beach Pavilion, Fort Sam Houston, in San Antonio, which became my home again for almost a year. Lala came to see me regularly, and many of my friends and relatives also stopped by. I knew the drill by memory. There was no complaining this time. All I had to do was look around and see the carnage that surrounded me.

The surgeons had a few procedures to perform to get me back in shape for duty. I had shrapnel in my head, scalp, shoulder, buttocks, feet, and legs, some that they removed and some that they left to work its way out. Shrapnel had also destroyed my right lung. My mouth and the back of my head had been hit with a rifle butt. AK-47 bullets had entered my back, one exiting just beneath my heart, and another bullet had entered my lower right back. Both of my arms had been slashed by the NVA soldier's bayonet.

One day I was resting when a second lieutenant came in and started calling out names. He was delivering medals to the men, and needless to say, most of them were Purple Hearts. I was pretty disgusted with the way he handed the men their awards, one after the other without saying a word. It didn't seem appropriate considering what most of these men had given up.

He called my name, then gave me two Purple Hearts. He turned to go and then, remembering something, handed me a small black box.

"Oh, this is yours, too," he said. "I almost forgot."

I was stunned when I opened the box. Inside was a Distinguished Service Cross. I didn't even know I had been nominated. That was the second highest award given by the United States military. Only the Congressional Medal of Honor was higher.

"Congratulations, Sergeant," the lieutenant said, smiling down at me.

I appreciated the medal, but there was some protocol that was being ignored. Only a general can present a DSC.

"Excuse me," I said. "With all due respect, sir, it takes more than a second lieutenant to hand out this award."

He glared at me. I knew he was busy and he had things to do, but I knew what the regulations were.

A male nurse—a sergeant—in the ward backed me up. He took the medal from me and led the lieutenant out of the ward, explaining that it could be embarrassing for everyone if it were not presented properly.

Once they were gone, I panicked a little. For one blessed moment I had actually held that medal in my hands, and now I wondered if I would get it back. What if they changed their minds?

They didn't, of course. In fact, General Westmoreland himself arrived to present the medal to me. By now he was chief of staff of the U.S. Army. He even surprised me by remembering that I had driven for him and that he had suggested that I should go Airborne. For those of us who had served under him, there was a general feeling of respect and admiration for the man. He was a fine commander as far as I was concerned, and he loved his men. No one could have done a better job in such a trying situation as the general. Many politicians and civilians attempted to dump the war problems on him, as a scapegoat. Those of us who knew him and fought this bloody war knew better. I only hope he knows how much I respect him.

My family, friends, and the press gathered beside my bed while the general talked about my spirit and bravery. And I was proud of myself, not only for receiving the medal, but also for sticking up for myself when it hadn't been presented correctly.

That night, I lay in bed and I stared at the medal for a long time. I thought about what an honor it was to have received it. I didn't think I could be more proud that the army, at least, recognized the sacrifices that were made that day. My mind drifted off into a tear-clouded fog as I remembered those brave men who had died.

What a privilege it was to have known them in this life.

In the hospital, my fellow soldiers and I watched television and learned of developments that had occurred in the United States while we were in Vietnam. Much of what we learned concerned the change in attitudes in the country. In 1968, on the third day of January, Senator Eugene McCarthy from Minnesota had announced that he was seeking the Democratic presidential nomination. He, along with Robert Kennedy, an early supporter of the war, promoted themselves as "peace" candidates. The list of government leaders opposed to the war was growing rapidly. Every war that the United States had ever been involved in had been opposed by some; however, the opposition had always been a minority of the population. Vietnam was changing that dramatically.

I learned that Cambodia's Prince Norodom Sihanouk had tried to patch up relations with the United States. He had sought the alliance of China after the United States had committed its support to the South Vietnamese. Counting on North Vietnam's being the victor in the war, he had permitted transit of their supplies along South Vietnam's border. Now China had become involved with its own "Cultural Revolution," and Sihanouk was vulnerable to the South Vietnamese.

Jacqueline Kennedy had gone to Cambodia on a state visit, and Chester Bowles, U.S. ambassador to India, paid Sihanouk a private visit. Sihanouk offered to open his country's border to U.S. troops in "hot pursuit" of the enemy, provided that his people were not put in harm's way.

President Johnson refused the offer. He probably feared that taking it would look like an escalation posture. Those of us who had been in Vietnam knew that at the time there were growing numbers of enemy across the border. Some of us knew all about the "Daniel Boone" raids, highly dangerous operations conducted by volunteers and mercenaries who ventured into Cambodia wearing customary black pajamas or unidentifiable uniforms and no identification. They went in search of intelligence and to sabotage the enemy whenever possible.

Turmoil on another front had erupted when the U.S.S. *Pueblo,* an intelligence ship, was captured in open seas by North Korean gunboats on January 23.

More fireworks were about to explode. These explosions, however, were not intended to bring harm to anyone. The occasion was Tet. The Vietnamese lunar new year was about to begin. My ward mates and I remembered that forces on both sides anxiously anticipated the coming of January 30, when the holiday would begin, because it was customary to call a cease-fire during Tet. Our expectations had been high because the National Liberation Front had called for adherence to the cease-fire by the United States and its allies.

The cease-fire never had a chance. An hour into the holiday, the NVA had hit a number of cities in the I Corps and II Corps. All forces in South Vietnam were put on "red alert" by noon of the same day.

The initial attacks were like the rumblings a wildcatter feels before the well explodes. The first explosion took place at three in the morning on January 31. Attacks took place simultaneously on all major installations and cities in South Vietnam. The enemy had launched the Tet Offensive. It had been planned for months.

In some ways the most hurtful attack was the one on the U.S. embassy—it went right to the heart of our country. It was mid-morning before the compound was finally declared safe and under full control of U.S. troops.

Of course many Americans, as well as millions of people worldwide, had seen the war we were fighting as they had never seen war before. Enormous television coverage had poured into homes all across the country. No event was more traumatic for them to see than the horrible street execution of a captive by General Nguyen Ngoc Loan, South Vietnam's national police chief.

Tet changed the opinions of many people, most importantly some in influential positions. Walter Cronkite, who had once supported the war, broke ranks and reported that it appeared that the United States might have to consider a "stalemate" position. Opposition to the war was intensifying.

Richard M. Nixon announced his candidacy for president on the first day of February. His platform was based on a so-called secret plan to end the war in Vietnam, a ploy that gained him immediate support.

Throughout February, a bloody month all around, we heard that the enemy massacred 2,800 in Hue. The week of the tenth was an all-time high casualty week. The United States suffered 543 killed and 2,547 wounded in action. The enemy suffered as well. On February 25, U.S. and South Vietnamese troops recaptured Hue with 5,113 enemy casualties reported.

Some of the news had come from stateside. President Johnson narrowly edged out Eugene McCarthy in the New Hampshire Democratic primary, and Robert Kennedy seized the advantage and announced his candidacy on March 16.

On March 31, President Johnson went before America and declared a unilateral halt to air and naval bombardment of North Vietnam. We, like the rest of the nation, were stunned by his closing statement. He announced that he would not seek re-election. On April 3, North Vietnam gave its commitment to peace negotiations in Paris.

On April 4, Dr. Martin Luther King, Jr., was assassinated in Memphis, Tennessee, deepening the country's racial wound. On April 27, Vice President Hubert Humphrey threw his hat into the ring, announcing his candidacy for the presidency.

On May 2, 1968, I lost many friends, and I was badly injured. When Robert Kennedy was assassinated in a downtown Los Angeles hotel on June 6, I was in no condition to absorb the news.

At that year's end, there were over 536,000 U.S. troops in Vietnam; more than 30,600 had been killed in action. The free world forces numbered over 65,000, and the South Vietnamese forces 820,000, with over 88,300 losses.

On January 22, 1969, when Richard Nixon was sworn in as president, I was once again able to get the news as it occurred, and I had plenty of time to watch television. On May 14, President Nixon proposed a simultaneous withdrawal of U.S and North Vietnamese forces from South Vietnam as part of his eight-point peace plan. Initially he dubbed the plan "de-Americanization," but Defense Secretary Melvin Laird semantically polished up his choice of words and changed the term to "Vietnamization."

In May 1969, elements of the 101st Airborne division were entrenched in the famed battle of Hamburger Hill, so named because of the carnage that resulted from the fierce fighting.

In that same month, I was finally released from the hospital, and I looked forward to getting back to work. I was almost as beaten up as our poor country and somewhat limited as to what I could do physically.

I was first assigned to temporary duty at Fort Devens in Ayer, Massachusetts. I was assigned to the 10th Special Forces Group Headquarters, working in the S-3 (operations) section. I even made a jump while I was there, but that was the last one. The pain was so great that it just wasn't worth it.

I did hear some pretty interesting things while I was there. Occasionally I would bump into an old Special Forces buddy, and we would spend some time reminiscing in the NCO club. Several of them referred to the Congressional Medal of Honor— some of them thought I had received it, and others said they heard I was recommended for it. I never thought too much about it.

My break from the bitterly cold weather came in 1969 when I found out that General Robert Linville, for whom I had been a driver in the 82nd Airborne, would be needing a driver. I put in a phone call to him, and I was transferred to Kansas, where I spent three years.

Our second daughter, Yvette, was born on November 20, 1969, at Fort Riley, Kansas. Family life was finally a reality. I enjoyed every minute of it.

I got another break when I met up with General Patrick Cassidy, who was touring Fort Riley in 1972. He noticed I was wearing the DSC, and he asked if I would like to come to Fort Sam Houston in Texas to serve as his driver. Naturally, I accepted. Lala and I could hardly wait to take our children back to Texas, where they would be near our families.

General Cassidy thought he remembered me, too. Actually, he

did, but I fibbed a little so he could not be sure. One day he remarked that he had almost court-martialed a soldier named Benavidez for kicking an NCO in the groin in Augsburg, Germany.

"You wouldn't happen to know him, would you?" he asked, staring closely at me.

"No sir," I said, gulping. "There are a lot of men with my last name in the army now. Did that Benavidez spell his name with a z or an s? He must have spelled it with an s."

He seemed to buy it, and I let out a sigh. The subject never came up again, but my past almost returned to haunt me. It was a close call. Here I was breaking my own rule with a lie. Perfection was still avoiding me.

On August 26, 1972, my son, Noel, was born and our family was complete.

While I was serving at Fort Sam Houston, Uncle Nicholas died, and I was able to go to El Campo for his funeral. The respect in which the citizens held him was evident, for many people gathered to pay tribute to his memory. He had been held in such high esteem that he had one year been named Citizen of the Year by the Police Officers Association. For me, he had been the uncle of a lifetime. I could only be grateful that he had enjoyed a long life and that he had taken Rogelio, who had come to be called Roger, and me in and treated us as his sons.

After a couple of years, General Cassidy decided to retire. He let me choose my next assignment, and I chose a position that allowed me to stay in San Antonio and work with the Special Forces reserves as an adviser. I was there when the last American troops left Vietnam in 1973 and when Saigon fell in 1975. My thoughts and those of the other servicemen were of the MIA's and POW's still there. We only hoped that they could be gotten out. My mind was not able to absorb the impact of Vietnam at that time. My emotions and reasoning ability about this subject were in deep conflict.

Some other advisers working with me at Fort Sam Houston repeated to me the earlier rumors I had heard at Fort Devens. Many of them, too, seemed to think I had received the Medal of Honor. I asked General Cassidy about it, but he seemed skeptical, explaining that the process by which the medal is awarded is difficult: There have to be written eyewitness accounts and all kinds of bureaucratic paperwork. I knew the MOH wasn't an easy thing to come by, but I had no idea that there was so much to it. I didn't even know how many of the men were there May 2, 1968, and I sure didn't know how to track them down.

I did assume, though, that if anyone had recommended me, it was Colonel Drake. So General Cassidy requested the original recommendation by the colonel for my DSC, just to see if he had by any chance suggested the higher award for me instead. Not surprisingly, when the general's request came back, it said only that the army couldn't find the recommendation. That didn't surprise me, considering the time I spent behind a desk after my first tour in 'Nam. I knew what strange routes paperwork took in the military.

But my Green Beret buddies seemed sure I had been recommended.

I worked with Colonel Jim Dandridge, a former SF intelligence officer in South Vietnam. One day he brought up the subject of the MOH. "I know Drake recommended you," he said, very sure of himself. What's more, he knew where Drake was and offered to call him.

When we called Colonel Drake, I couldn't help but remember how good he had been to me while I was fighting for my life in Saigon. He was there with his hand on my shoulder, which definitely had made me feel better since I wasn't sure if I was going to live or die and my family was across the ocean. Apparently, Colonel Drake hadn't been so sure I would make it either.

"I thought you were dead," he said when I finally got him on the telephone. He went on to say that he had only recommended me for the Distinguished Service Cross and not the Medal of Honor as Colonel Dandridge said. He didn't even know I had been awarded the DSC. He admitted that with the sketchy details he had provided for my DSC recommendation, it was surprising I had received the medal at all. The nature of the mission was secretive, so there wasn't much information Drake could give about me.

Colonel Drake and Colonel Dandridge decided to give it a shot anyway. Colonel Dandridge was going to mail a copy of the citation I received accompanying the DSC and Colonel Drake would review it. Then, he said, he would determine whether or not to resubmit his earlier recommendation, but this time it would be for the highest award—the Congressional Medal of Honor.

As it turned out, Colonel Drake did resubmit his recommendation in a letter to the awards and decorations board at Fort Sam Houston. In his letter, he used words like *valor* and *heroism*—words that make a soldier proud. He rewrote the recommendation when he discovered that I had voluntarily boarded the extraction helicopter to aid my fellow soldiers, recovered the classified material, and destroyed the communications system on the downed helicopter. He further stated that I had refused to board the extraction helicopter until all were on board.

Now there seemed a real possibility that I would be awarded the MOH, but soon it came to seem unlikely once again. Colonel Drake wrote another letter, this one to me, telling me about the two-year time limit for submitting recommendations for awards. However, I learned that the air force was sponsoring legislation to expand the time limit for making recommendations.

I had the opportunity to visit with Larry McKibben's parents in Houston, Texas. Larry was the pilot who had crashed while trying to help us out. They had lost their only son, and the memories were very painful for them. Even though I tried to convey the valor Larry had shown, the look in their eyes was far, far away. I left the meeting very saddened for their loss. Larry had given his life to rescue those men that day, and I just wanted them to know what kind of soldier he was. I think they already knew.

Finally, Colonel Dandridge got a letter from Ronald Radke, who had been a warrant officer in Vietnam. Radke had flown one of the gunships that flew overhead the day of the big battle, providing some relief for those of us on the ground. That letter motivated the colonel to keep investigating my eligibility for the MOH. Some of the men he contacted didn't want to help, not because they were being cruel but because, for them, the war had become a painful, private thing they were fighting to forget, not relive through some letters.

In all, Colonel Dandridge managed to collect five letters, even though all of them weren't direct eyewitnesses. He figured that was about the best he could do, and Colonel Drake, once again, resubmitted his recommendation. Two additional letters came in, and Colonel Dandridge forwarded those to the board, too.

His request was denied. The board still didn't see there was enough evidence to warrant presenting me with the MOH. I assumed that the subject was closed. Two eyewitnesses of the battle did not exist. Wright and Mousseau were dead, and I assumed that O'Connor was, too.

Waggie, the pilot who eventually got us all out of there—and who, incidentally, was never decorated for his heroism on that mission—was living in Virginia. But like so many other men, he was greatly affected by the war. He certainly didn't want to write about it, but generously, he did write a letter. Parts of it described action that had become somewhat blurred to me. Waggie wrote:

On the last desperate attempt to extract the team, SSG Benavidez made three trips to load the wounded soldiers on the aircraft. I saw SSG Benavidez kill two of the enemy as they attempted to rush our helicopter. He was in serious condition and covered with blood. He carried a radio and other equipment to the aircraft as he helped the wounded. On his third trip SSG Benavidez carried a South Vietnamese member of the team who appeared dead to me. SSG Benavidez fell between WO Hoffman and myself. I gave him a "thumbs-up" sign as we left.

William Darling was located in 1977. He had been a member of Waggie's crew, and he agreed to write a letter on my behalf. Darling wrote:

I saw SSG Benavidez make trips to the aircraft carrying radio equipment, and carrying a very badly wounded interpreter under his arm. On one of his trips (the second) he shot two enemy who were behind our helicopter and whom I couldn't get with my machine gun. On his final trip he was holding his intestines in his arms—I didn't think he would make it back; he was very badly wounded.

Once again, Drake resubmitted his recommendation and waited. But the upgrade was still denied.

I retired on total disability in 1976 and moved home to El Campo. Art Haddock died after my retirement, and I served as an honorary pallbearer at his funeral. I gave thanks that I had known him and that as a wild young man I had enough sense to absorb some of the lessons he had tried to teach me.

My beloved Aunt Alexandria also died shortly after my retirement, and I was at her bedside. When my cousins and I knew she was gone, we talked about all of the little things she had done for us through the years. "We lost a great soldier," I said.

She had worked in the fields beside her family members. She had provided physical and spiritual nourishment to her family. In addition, she, who never learned to speak English, had taught my brother, my cousins, and me to read and write Spanish. Her foresight was unusual in a time and place where children who speak Spanish in their homes never learn to read and write the language because their instruction at school is in English. When I imagine the difficulty she had in settling us down for her own school after our regular classes, I wonder at her strength—in this as in so much else.

Still there were rumors that I was a candidate for the MOH. No one knew what the board wanted, but Fred Barbee, the publisher and editor of the *El Campo Leader News,* thought he did.

"It's politics," he said. "The mission was a secret. You were in Cambodia, for God's sake. The army doesn't want to admit that. If they decorate you with the highest medal there is, they'll have to acknowledge where you were."

Barbee wrote the editorial that literally went around the world. Barbee suggested that the action I was in "actually took place outside the boundaries of Vietnam, perhaps in an area where U.S. forces were not supposed to be." He continued: "After all, at about that time the American public was being fed information downgrading the amount of U.S. participation in the actual combat operations."

When he wrote the editorial, Barbee had no idea what it would become.

My son and I were watching television one summer day in 1980 when the phone rang. It took me a second to gather my wits when I heard the caller say, "Hello. Is this Tango Mike/Mike?"

"Who is this?" I asked, wondering which of my SF buddies was calling.

"This is Big Team," the caller said. I think my heart stopped for a second. "Big Team" was the nickname given to Brian O'Connor. But I had thought that he was dead.

"O'Connor? Is that you?" I asked, unable to believe it. We were both overwhelmed. We cried. After all, it had been more than a dozen years since we had last seen each other, and at that time we were both unsure of our fates. In fact, each of us thought that the other had died.

O'Connor, it turned out, had read the editorial. He was living in the Fiji Islands. He had taken a trip to Australia and checked into a hotel. The hotel was a regular hangout for O'Connor on his frequent trips to Australia. The desk clerk immediately recognized him when he checked in.

"Hey, mate, there's an article about you in the newspaper here. Saved it for you. Thought you might be interested in it," said the desk clerk.

O'Connor was shocked when he read the newspaper account that had traveled around the world from El Campo, Texas, to Australia via Associated Press.

He vowed to write a statement. He did, too. That same month the Department of the Army received his ten-page, very detailed letter, and suddenly the army changed its ruling. And Congress announced I was to be notified that I would be receiving the Medal of Honor. I couldn't believe it was actually going to happen after all this time.

Many people had spoken in my interest. A few whom I knew about were General Edward C. Meyer, who was the army chief of staff at the time; Lieutenant General Robert G. Yerks, who was then army deputy chief of staff, personnel; Major General Joseph P. Franklin, who was commandant of cadets, U.S. Military Academy; and then Congressman Joe Wyatt from the Fourteenth District of Texas. Another who had acted in my behalf was my friend Ab Webber, a Houston businessman and a 1951 graduate of West Point.

I was going to be awarded the Medal of Honor, but there was one small problem.

At the time, the hostages were still being held in Iran. President Jimmy Carter's term was drawing to a close, and the official word from the White House was that he had signed my MOH orders and wanted to give me my medal before he left office. It was decided that I was to wait for President Ronald Reagan to be inaugurated and get settled before I could receive the MOH.

Finally, in February 1981, I took forty-three members of my family, including Lala and my three children, to the nation's capital to receive the Medal of Honor.

I had lunch the first day with Secretary of Defense Caspar Weinberger and Secretary of the Army John Marsh. We had a good time, and even convinced Weinberger to try some hot *pico de gallo,* which set his mouth on fire and gave Marsh and me something to laugh about for a while. I'll never forget the look on his face when the heat set in.

That afternoon, I got to see several of my old buddies, including Cottingham and Colonel Drake. I was glad to see them, and I was especially glad they were there. I thought they deserved the award as much as me.

But the biggest treat of the day came when Drake brought me a "surprise": Brian O'Connor.

We spent several minutes hugging and just getting used to the fact that we were both alive and in the same room and safely away from gunfire. Neither of us could believe it. We spent the whole night talking about our friends—Wright, McKibben, Mousseau, Craig—the list was endless. It was hard to talk about our buddies being gone, even though many years had passed. But O'Connor and I had something in common; we each knew that the other had been through hell.

The next day I found myself in the Oval Office. We were greeted there by President and Mrs. Reagan. I still couldn't get over it all, but my son, Noel, had no problem. He walked straight over to a jar of jelly beans on the president's desk and stared at it, wide-eyed. The president offered the jar of candy to Noel, saying, "I have another one." Noel readily accepted the gift, and the incident put all of us more at ease. The ice was broken and I felt ready for anything that might follow, perhaps too ready.

A military aide to the president informed us that it was time to board the presidential limousine for the short ride to the Pentagon, where the awards ceremony was to take place. As the president, first lady, Lala, and I stepped inside that grand vehicle, I had to hold back tears, thinking about how far this black taxi was from that little "jitney" cab in El Campo.

I almost cussed in front of the president, and I probably would have if it hadn't been for Lala. I had gotten so used to calling the NVA who tried to kill me with his bayonet a "son of a bitch" that I wasn't really prepared when President Reagan asked what had gone through my mind that day.

"I got mad and I had to kill the son of a bi—" Lala managed to kick me swiftly before I finished my sentence, but the president got my drift, and he laughed. Lala didn't. She was pretty embarrassed.

Upon arriving at the Pentagon courtyard I immediately realized I couldn't recognize all of the crowd. Along with my extended family, others attending the ceremony at the Pentagon were: Ab Webber, who was instrumental in my receiving the Medal of Honor; Fred Barbee; Steve Sucker, a reporter for Fred Barbee; Lieutenant Colonel Charles Kettles, whose assignment it was to collect the eyewitness statements; Brian O'Connor; Bill Armstrong; Jerry Cottingham; and Tom Carter, one of the helicopter pilots.

Many important men were missing—those who had saved me. Roger Waggie wasn't there. He, LeRoy Wright, Lloyd Mousseau, and Larry McKibben should have been there, too, receiving their own medals.

The president made quite a speech. He talked for what seemed like a long time about sacrifice and gratitude, about humanitarians and acts of kindness. I was grateful he included the part about how we helped build hospitals and schools while we were over there. It gave a picture that we were there to help the Vietnamese improve their life-style, not just to kill the NVA.

After he finished talking about me, President Reagan read the citation himself, which, to the best of my knowledge, a president had never done before. He told the audience the details about May 2, 1968, and why I was receiving the Medal of Honor. While he spoke, I relived that day in my mind.

Then he read:

On May 2, 1968, Master Sergeant (Staff Sergeant) Roy P. Benavidez distinguished himself by a series of daring and extremely valorous actions while assigned to Detachment B-56, 5th Special Forces Group (Airborne), 1st Special Forces, Republic of Vietnam. On the morning of May 2, 1968, a 12 man Special Forces Reconnaissance Team was inserted by helicopters in a dense jungle area west of Loc Ninh, Vietnam, to gather intelligence information about confirmed large-scale enemy activity. This area was controlled and routinely patrolled by the North Vietnamese Army. After a short period of time on the ground, the team met heavy enemy resistance, and requested emergency extraction.

Three helicopters attempted extraction, but were unable to land due to intense enemy small arms, and anti-aircraft fire. Sergeant Benavidez was in the Forward Operating Base in Loc Ninh monitoring the operation by radio when these helicopters returned to off-load wounded crew members and to assess aircraft damage. Sergeant Benavidez voluntarily boarded a returning aircraft to assist in another extraction attempt. Realizing that all the team members were either dead or wounded and unable to move to the pickup zone, he directed the aircraft to a nearby clearing where he jumped from the hovering helicopter, and ran approximately 75 meters under withering small arms fire to the crippled team. Prior to reaching the team's position, he was wounded in his right leg, face, and head. Despite these painful injuries, he took charge, repositioned the team members and directed their fire to facilitate the landing of an extraction aircraft, and the loading of wounded and dead team members. He then threw smoke canisters to direct aircraft to the team's position. Despite his severe wounds and under intense enemy fire, he carried and dragged half of the wounded team members to the waiting aircraft. He then provided protective fire by running alongside the aircraft as it moved to pick up classified documents on the dead team leader. When he reached the team leader's body, Sergeant Benavidez was severely wounded by small arms fire in the abdomen and grenade fragments in his back. At nearly the same moment, the aircraft pilot was mortally wounded and his helicopter crashed. Although in extremely critical condition due to his wounds, Sergeant Benavidez secured the classified documents and made his way back to the wreckage, where he aided the wounded out of the overturned aircraft, and gathered the stunned survivors into a defensive perimeter. Under increasing automatic weapons and grenade fire, he moved around the perimeter distributing water and ammunition to his weary men, reinstilling in them a will to live and fight. Facing a buildup of enemy opposition with a beleaguered team, Sergeant Benavidez mustered his strength, began calling in tactical air strikes and directed the fire from supporting gunships to suppress the enemy fire and so permit another extraction attempt. He was wounded again in his thigh by small arms fire while administering first aid to a wounded team member just before another extraction helicopter was able to land. His indomitable spirit kept him going as he began to ferry his comrades to the craft. On his second trip with the wounded, he was clubbed from behind by an enemy soldier. In the ensuing hand-to-hand combat, he sustained additional wounds to his head and arms before killing his adversary. He then continued under devastating fire to carry the wounded to the helicopter. Upon reaching the aircraft, he spotted and killed two enemy soldiers who were rushing the craft from an angle that prevented the aircraft door gunner from firing upon them. With little strength remaining he made one last trip to the perimeter to ensure that all classified material had been collected or destroyed, and to bring in the remaining wounded. Only then, in extremely serious condition from numerous wounds and loss of blood, did he allow himself to be pulled into the extraction aircraft. Sergeant Benavidez's gallant choice to join voluntarily his comrades who were in critical straits, to expose himself constantly to withering fire, and his refusal to be stopped despite numerous severe wounds, saved the lives of at least eight men. His fearless personal leadership, tenacious devotion to duty, and extremely valorous actions in the face of overwhelming odds were in keeping with the highest traditions of the military service, and reflect the utmost credit on him and the United States Army.

Finally, while I stood at attention, the president fastened the medal around my neck. That was the proudest moment of my life, and I thought of the words of another president, John F. Kennedy, who had said, "The Green Beret is the symbol of excellence, mark of distinction, badge of courage in the fight for freedom." Perhaps I really had lived up to those standards. I also thought of President Harry S. Truman's statement: "I would rather be a recipient of the Congressional Medal of Honor than be president." I felt that I had come a very long way from the picking fields of Colorado and Texas. I wished with all my heart that all of the men—Mousseau, Wright, McKibben, Craig; all of them—could have come home from the jungle and experienced the same thing. They deserved it just as much as I did.

After the medal was finally around my neck, I stepped back to salute President Reagan. But as I did, he stepped forward to embrace me, and I was so surprised that I accidentally stepped on his shoe. If Lala hadn't wanted to crawl under a rock when I almost cussed in front of the commander-in-chief, I'm sure she did when I crunched his toe in front of the whole country. Naturally a photographer from the *Washington Post* captured the moment, and the photo made the front page.

I did get to spend a little more time with my buddies. We talked some more about the old times. One of the hardest parts was saying good-bye to O'Connor after finding out he was alive after all these years. He and one CIDG were the only survivors of that mission. Knowing he was alive and well definitely made all of my efforts of that day worthwhile.

When we arrived back home that night, there was a huge party for us in El Campo at the high school gymnasium, complete with a phone call from the governor. Coming home to that was just as special as the time I had spent in Washington. Two El Campo police officers, Robin Taylor and Jesse Juariz, escorted our bus to and from Houston Intercontinental Airport. My days of quiet retirement were soon to come to an abrupt end. Battles remained to be fought.

20

Fair Treatment

A great sense of shock and betrayal ran through my thoughts as I finished reading a letter I had just received from the Social Security Administration on February 22, 1983. After receiving disability benefits for seven years due to my war injuries I was being asked to be retested by a Social Security doctor and one of their psychiatrists in order to determine if I was faking the extent of my injuries.

Initially I was emotionally crushed that my country would question my integrity in this manner. After all, my disability had been determined by the United States Army Medical Corps upon my medical discharge. The very medical unit which had so painstakingly saved my life was now being challenged by other government officials to reprove my injuries.

The letter further stated that if it was determined that I had falsified my medical condition I could be required to reimburse the government for all the Social Security funds I had received in the last seven years.

After regaining my composure I went to see my doctor in El Campo, and he assured me that I was unable to work. The Social Security Administration then required me to appear before its doctor and psychiatrist in Houston. Their extensive exams determined that I was one hundred percent disabled.

One test I failed was that of lifting a fifty-pound weight. I could not. My hands were gnarled but functional, and I thanked God every day that Dr. Hugh Ratliff had been able to save my two arms. He had painstakingly performed four operations on my arms and had taken tendons from my wrists and thumbs to make them mobile. Blood vessels had been rerouted for circulation. Not that I had any complaints, especially when I thought of the multitude of amputees and paraplegics who had surrounded me in the hospitals or of the 58,191 dead men who had given everything in Indochina.

I was also required to take a pulmonary volume test. Presumably, someone thought that I might pass it. There was a slight problem, since my right lung had been totally destroyed by an enemy bullet.

I couldn't believe that my country was humiliating me like this. At first I took the situation personally, then I decided to start checking around with veterans' organizations in an effort to see if others were going through this inquisition.

I wrote a letter to my senator, John Tower. Instead of relief I received another letter two weeks later ordering me to appear before another psychiatrist and an administrative judge. For two and one half hours I recounted the Cambodian battle. I stripped so that they might examine my multiple holes, scars, and stitch marks; yet these two men remained skeptical that I was disabled. They even asked me repeatedly about my fellow soldiers who had died. I began to feel that they were trying to prove me mentally unstable.

I hoped that this examination would settle the issue once and for all. However, the judge wrote directing me to appear once again in Victoria, Texas. I was shocked when I read the last paragraph of the letter; present at the meeting would be yet another psychiatrist, who, after this meeting, would decide my status. That was the final straw!

I have never felt so humiliated and angry in all my life. The bureaucrats were just about to meet a guy named Tango Mike/Mike, and it was going to be their turn to apply for disability.

Before I appeared before the "shrink," some interesting things occurred almost simultaneously. I was contacted by William A. Lowtheir, a writer for *Reader's Digest*. He wanted to write a story about me. I quickly accepted the offer but decided against using the article for any personal gain concerning the Social Security problem.

The TV show "Real People" picked up the article and wanted

me to allow them to do a special to be aired on Memorial Day, May 31, 1983. I agreed to the interview.

Next, a reporter with the *Dallas Morning News* called me for a quote on the national problem about the wholesale discontinuance of Social Security benefits for several hundred thousand recipients, many of whom were veterans, their widows and children. This was the first I had known of the magnitude of the cuts.

I unloaded on the Dallas reporter. He may have thought he was interviewing a "madman" whose Social Security psychiatrists were trying to get into a straitjacket. As soon as those stories were printed, I was flooded with calls, letters, and telegrams from reporters. More messages came from disabled veterans and their families who were experiencing the same humiliations that I had been going through.

I had never encountered so many desperate people. Almost every letter and phone call was a plea for me to intercede in their behalf with the administration. Most of the letters addressed me personally, referring to me as Roy. Most referred to me as a hero and indicated that I was the only person they knew of who could help them. Many stated a feeling of hopelessness: If the government could do this to a Medal of Honor recipient, what chance could they have? The letters were heartbreaking.

Carloads of people began searching out my house in an effort to persuade me to help them. Each time I read a letter or talked with people, I felt a sense of impotence. I wondered how I could help them when I couldn't even help myself. I was honored that these wonderful Americans thought that much of me, but I felt totally unqualified to speak in their behalf.

My position came to seem increasingly complex as I pondered it. I wondered how I could go public and criticize a country that meant so much to me. I wondered how I could criticize the commander-in-chief who had placed the Medal of Honor around my neck. My mind was in a turmoil.

One thing was certain. I had not gone out and created this fight; it had come to me. I had not asked these people to make me their spokesperson, and I felt poorly qualified to fill that role. Yet I felt that I could not retreat a coward in the face of controversy just because I wished to continue my simple life. I felt that it had fallen my lot to voice a common injustice to the nation's leaders. It was time for me to put up or shut up.

Perhaps the real reason I had received the Medal of Honor was to try to right this wrong. I wished for a forum in which I could plead this just cause. I found help from a former Green Beret, the Washington attorney Tom Burch. Tom had knowledge of Washington, the bureaucracy, and the military, and he shepherded me through the biggest battle of my life. I was invited to address a special hearing before the Select Committee on Aging in the House of Representatives.

While my anger remained strong at the treatment that I and others had received at the hands of our government, I felt a sense of reassurance. Only in America, I thought, could someone with my background be given the sacred opportunity to stand before representatives in Congress and state a grievance that adversely affected so many people. I had thought no day could eclipse the day that I received the MOH, but I was wrong. This day became the most important day in my life because so many people were counting on me to represent them, and I prayed earnestly that I would not fail them.

On June 20, 1983, I was in the Cannon House Office Building to address and respond to questions from the U.S House of Representatives Select Committee on Aging.

Representative Edward Roybal from California, chairman of the committee, said in his opening remarks that state government officials had begun to go public with strong objections to the policy and administrative guidelines forced on state disability examiners by the federal government. He also spoke of the "shabby, un-American treatment" of me and thousands of other veterans and nonveterans.

I was called to testify, and after giving my prepared statement, in which I explained my position, I answered questions from the committee members. Congressman Roybal asked me if I had been examined by two medical experts who had concluded that I was completely disabled. I told him that was correct; then I continued: "If, sir, if my comrades and I are denied the benefits that we deserve, then I ask one last favor—to please kneel and join me in prayer to God to save this republic from bureaucratic bungling, there is just no hope. Thank you very much."

Congressman Wise of West Virginia spoke of the losses we were still having—people dying from the trauma caused them by the "continuing disability investigations" that caused them to wonder how they would get by. He said that I might help some of those people.

"Thank you very much," I said. "I am sorry that we have lost so many lives, them committing suicide because of the running around that they are given. Someone has to put a stop to this nonsense."

Congressman Shumway of California asked if the full description of my injuries had been placed on file with the Social Security Administration.

I responded: "Sir, if it has been, no one knows the terminology of the medical wording. I don't think that the people in the Department of Human Resources, that read my medical records, made or read or interpreted the medical terminology because if they had done so, they would still be reading those records. They are about as thick as two Bibles, sir."

Congresswoman Oakar of Ohio asked me about my thoughts about the administration's proposal for further study on changes in Social Security for people with physical problems such as those inflicted on people in Vietnam.

I told her that I just happened to be in Vietnam and that I hoped that the benefits of all veterans, their widows, and their children would be given a close look.

Congressman Lantos of California said that he was disturbed that much of the questioning had focused on what was clearly an "outrageous instance." He said, "We are looking at a man of obvious integrity and commitment and intelligence, a recipient of the Congressional Medal of Honor, a heavily decorated combat veteran, who has been abused by his own government." He also thanked me for testifying and said, "You have taught us again the lesson of duty, honor, and country."

Congressman Richardson of New Mexico asked me whether, if I had known that I would be treated so poorly by my own government, I would have chosen to serve in the armed forces.

I said, "There will never be enough paper to print the money nor enough gold in the vaults of Fort Knox for me to keep me from serving my country or helping my fellow comrades, my brothers in arms, because I live for duty, honor, and country."

The committee members stood and applauded as my testimony ended. Then Congressman Roybal introduced the next witness, the governor from Arkansas, Mr. Bill Clinton.

About three weeks after I appeared before the committee, I received a telephone call from Congressman Roybal. He thanked me for my testimony and said that he thought it had made a difference in the committee's decision. He told me that all benefits to those then receiving them would remain intact, and that any cuts would be restored. The congressman also apologized to me for what I had been through.

The congressman said that I should not be discouraged by what had happened but heartened, for I had been fortunate enough to see the checks and balances of our system of government at work. He told me that I had helped to make the process work.

The experience of having my eligibility for Social Security benefits questioned had caused me sorrow that had compounded my feeling of disappointment in the results of some of my service to my country as a soldier. In my retirement I had felt dissatisfied that most of the SOG units' efforts in Vietnam had been wasted.

I knew that for four years Special Forces, via SOG units, had done extensive intelligence gathering behind enemy lines. We had discovered that the North Vietnamese were working like termites to build underground cities and to stock them with necessities in Laos and Cambodia. The data that we compiled was supposed to be going unfiltered to the White House.

I also knew that General Westmoreland had pleaded with his commanders to be allowed to pursue the NVA into Laos and Cambodia, where they were establishing their sanctuaries. Many of us who were serving in Vietnam had felt that the general was right, that we needed to go into those countries and crush the NVA.

By the time of the Tet Offensive in 1968, the crushing defeats of 1969 and 1970, and the fall of Saigon in 1975, it was too late. The NVA could not be bombed out of their refuges. They had literally dug in and had waited for the United States to grow tired of the war.

A great deal of the work that my buddies and I did was lost. Many of them were lost as well. Bearing that knowledge had been difficult enough, and the questioning of my eligibility for Social Security benefits, added to my other concerns, nearly brought me to my knees.

Several times before, though, I had gotten up and walked

when doing so had seemed impossible. I determined that I would do so once again. I had given to my country, but it had given to me as well. I felt that payback time for that gift had come. I would not sit on my butt and feel sorry for myself. I had, after all, adopted a credo long ago in Berlin, and I vowed that it would guide me for the remainder of my life.

Epilogue

I have been retired from military active duty since 1976, and I live in El Campo. I have time to spend with Lala, my children, and my grandson. But I haven't been sitting in a rocking chair on the front porch. Too much needs to be done in this country, and I try in my way to do some of it. I now help with LifeSupport, Inc. in Houston, Texas. It is a nonprofit organization that helps young people throughout the nation. I travel the country speaking to various groups. I tell them that freedom has a price. That price is often human flesh and blood.

When a free nation such as the United States of America commits its military to war on foreign soil, the objectives of that war must be clearly defined, and the majority of the host nation must be committed to the doctrine of individual and national freedom. The Vietnam conflict was a tragedy that should not have happened because in my opinion the majority of the South Vietnamese did not understand or support individual freedom. They were ill prepared as fighters to wage war, and many, it seemed, hoped only for a benevolent dictator. The rules of engagement with the enemy were wrong. These rules were not military rules, but civilian rules. As it was in Korea, the military was told to fight with one arm tied behind its back.

Between 1958 and 1975, over three million military personnel responded to the orders of the various presidents and went dutifully to battle. The American citizen/soldier always responds to the battle cry of freedom. This leaves him vulnerable to false prophets who disguise ulterior motives with the honorable quest for freedom.

Soldiers don't pick their wars; they respond to orders from their commander-in-chief. During the period of the Vietnam conflict, the lessons previously learned by our leaders were forgotten, and as a result, 47,356 American soldiers died in combat and 10,795 died in noncombat situations. Eight women are included in these statistics. The number of wounded totaled 201,324, and thousands of others returned emotionally damaged by the terror of combat inflicted on them. There are 2,490 still missing in action. Over 2 million South Vietnamese died.

The young soldiers who were sent to me by their parents and wives were entrusted to me to train and protect to the best of my ability. As an NCO, I took this responsibility seriously. Many times that burden was almost unbearable. Especially when intelligence reports were estimating high casualty rates. Those of us who were acting as advisers to the Vietnamese in 1965 knew that a tragic mistake had been made when, on the eighth of March of that year, combat troops of the 3rd Marine Division (Battalion Landing Team 3/9) landed on Red Beach, just north of the port city of Da Nang. They arrived prepared for a conventional war that was not to be. Even NCOs such as myself realized that this conflict could best be assisted by our observer duties because green recruits from the States were destined for slaughter in such a military action.

My mind was filled with disbelief as the war kept escalating and the number of casualties grew. My rage toward the Washington politicians swelled inside me, but I felt compelled to contribute my skills to a nation I loved more than life itself. The United States of America had given me freedom and an opportunity to succeed as a young Hispanic-Indian American, and I was determined as a soldier to pay my dues. I was determined, as Uncle Nicholas had so impressed upon me, that the name Benavidez would not be disgraced by me.

In any military action, this country must be united behind the act of war because the price to pay is the sacrifice of its most valuable possessions—its sons and daughters. When I returned to my homeland in bits and pieces after my first tour of duty in Vietnam, I encountered the war protestors who were targeting their confused bitterness against the military rather than toward the politicians, where it belonged. All I could understand was that the true peacemakers were wearing military uniforms or body bags or steel-gray military-issue coffins, and that these flag burners were using their freedom to protest against people who had fought and died for their country. More than ever, I was determined to keep my life focused and disciplined so that I could continue to serve my country and honor all those soldiers who had died that others might be free.

My return to Vietnam in 1968 as a Special Forces soldier placed me in an even more dangerous situation. We were the intelligence-gathering arm of DELTA, WHITE STAR, OMEGA, PHOENIX, and SIGMA (operations I am not at liberty to discuss). What I can say is that most of our operations were largely behind enemy lines in Laos and Cambodia. We recruited Cambodian mercenaries to travel with us because they were fierce fighters and we could trust them more than the Vietnamese. The Vietnamese did not have the will to fight. The yearning for freedom in the hearts of men must be galvanized in a democracy or its government will collapse. Nations without the will to fight and die for that lone principal—freedom—are doomed to history as pagan totalitarians. Time and time again American soldiers have shown that they have the will to fight. All the American fighting men ask is that they not be killed for anything short of freedom.

I was honored by the National Security Agency by being inducted into the Intelligence Hall of Fame for my efforts on May 2, 1968. I also work with our veterans' organizations, encourage veterans to tell their stories, and speak to military groups whenever I can. Those now serving on active duty in the military can be best described as our "Forward Line of Troops." This is a battlefield term of the United States Army Infantry and is abbreviated F.L.O.T. It refers to those combat troops that are dispersed to the farthest points of combat situations, forming the line of defense and point of attack. To those troops serving this country on the F.L.O.T. line now, I sometimes quote from a book written by Lieutenant Colonel R. B. Thieme and titled *Follow the Colors*.

To these who follow the colors, I tell them that I wear the Congressional Medal of Honor for them and for all the "silent heroes" who have served. I tell them that it is their medal, too. There are not enough medals of distinction to reward the military heroes of this country. Most must bear their heroism in their hearts. Everyone in uniform is a "silent hero," and no matter how manipulated a serviceman or servicewoman may feel in any given geopolitical military confrontation, his or her duty, honor, and responsibility is to follow the colors of individual and national freedom. Even to death. No matter how they are perceived by the civilian population, their personal goal must be to follow the colors.

I believe that only in America could I, a young Hispanic-Indian American, have risen to my place. That opportunity was won for me on the battlefields where American blood was spilled as cry after cry went out through the conflicts in our country's history for soldiers to follow the colors. I tell the new generation of military men and women that the guidon has been passed to them. The message of freedom and the cry of "Follow the colors" are their marching orders. I also pray that when they are in harm's way that God will keep them in the safety of His hands. One of my greatest concerns is the youth of America. As I travel this country speaking about the cost of freedom to the various business organizations who invite me, I consistently ask that they make arrangements for me to speak in the schools surrounding them. One of my efforts is to raise in the students interest in the politics of the Vietnam War.

I tell the students that those of us who served in the military did so because a torch of freedom had been passed to us from those who had served before. I tell them that it is their turn now and that it is my honor to pass on the command to follow the colors. I cannot count the number of young people I have addressed, nor can I express my joy at being invited to visit with them. Every time I approach a school audience I see the faces of the children that my fellow soldiers fought and died for. I must admit, however, that what I am now seeing in many of those eyes shocks me. I learn of dropout rates in schools, mostly Hispanic and black, that approach seventy-five percent. When I address these students I see poverty. Not just poverty of finances but poverty of values, morals, and purpose. It brings tears to my eyes and breaks my heart. I tell these students that an education and a diploma are the keys to success. I tell them I paid a large price for leaving school early. It was a bad decision on my part, and I have paid dearly for it my entire life. I had a good mind and I sold myself short. Many of these students belong to gangs. I tell them to stay away from gangs. If you're going to gang up, gang up on education. If you want to fight, fight drugs. If you want to join a gang, join my gang, the United States Army Special Forces. Our motto is *De Oppresso Liber* ("To free from oppression"). The Special Forces fly our colors just as some gang members wear certain colors, but we fly our colors with the pride of knowing that what we stand for advances the freedom of this nation. Our headgear is the green beret, and we have earned the right to fly our colors. Our colors stand for freedom, not oppression and fear. President John F. Kennedy himself told us, "The Green Beret is the symbol of excellence, mark of distinction, badge of courage in the fight for freedom."

I have a code name, too, just as some gang members do. It's Tango Mike/Mike, and it stands for "That Mean Mexican." That Alpha code name was given to me by my gang—the Special Forces. The youth gangs these days fight with firearms, often injuring innocent people. Conflicts are no longer settled with a fistfight as when I was young. I tell the youngsters that there's nothing wrong with fighting. It just depends on what you're fighting for. I was called upon by my country to fight for freedom. That's always something worth fighting for. I never murdered a man out of revenge, hatred, or for racial feelings. I killed that others might be free. There's a big difference between murdering and killing. I tell the students that there are no good excuses for any of them to claim that they are what they are because of racial bigotry. I know what racial bigotry is. I was confronted with it daily as a young Hispanic-Indian American growing up in South Texas.

I had to make decisions quickly in my life, and I chose to rise above that prejudice and prove that I was a better person than those bigots. In order to do that I had to start making more good decisions than bad ones. Good decisions from a position of strength, not weakness. I tell the youngsters that bad habits and bad company will ruin them. I tell them that friends don't get friends into trouble. My prayer is that I reach them.

One last group of people I give some time to is the survivors of Vietnam soldiers who were killed or are missing in action. I constantly receive letters or am approached by parents, widows, and orphans. There is one universal theme in the questions that they ask: "Sergeant Benavidez, was it worth it for me to give up my husband or father?" "Sergeant Benavidez, I never knew my father because of Vietnam." "Sergeant Benavidez, my father was never there for me. Why?"

Oh, God, how my heart breaks each time I read or hear those words. How can a feeble, mortal man like me answer such questions! My answers to them are based on my own personal experiences and those of my family. I tell them that I believe that there is no greater calling for a man or woman than to serve in the military of a free nation. I believe that it is a calling that transcends all others because imbedded deep within the soul of every free man or woman is the knowledge that every freedom we have was earned for us by our ancestors, who paid some price for that freedom. Each and every generation must relearn those lessons, and they are best learned by doing. The strength of every free nation depends on this transfer of knowledge. Only through the transfer of knowledge from generation to generation will free men survive.

I ask myself again and again if it would have been worth it to my family if I had been killed and my body never returned. The answer is yes! Even if I was deceived by my commander-in-chief and my fight was for the preservation of rubber plantations rather than for freedom for the Vietnamese people, would my death have been worth it? Why?

I know the content of my heart. I am a good soldier. I go where I am ordered. That kind of loyalty, at least, is noble and vital for the preservation of freedom.

When I am asked if it is worth it to lose a loved one in military service I answer "Yes." Our duty as survivors is to pass on the pride in the noble sacrifice made by our child, parent, spouse, or buddy. The reason that he or she served, the reason that all American men and women serve, is best expressed in that portion of the West Point motto: "Duty, Honor, Country."

Postscript

My last military unit in Vietnam was the Fifth Special Forces Group. This unit was awarded the Civic Action Medal from the chief of staff of the armed forces of the Republic of Vietnam for its efforts in setting up almost 50,000 economic aid projects, 35,000 educational projects, over 35,000 welfare projects, 11,000 medical projects, and 1,500 transportation facilities; supporting nearly a half million refugees; digging 6,500 wells; and repairing almost 2,000 kilometers of roads. Also, 130 churches, 275 markets, 110 hospitals, 400 dispensaries, over 1,000 classrooms, and 670 bridges were built.

Contact Address:

MSG Roy P. Benavidez, USA SF (Ret.)
P.O. Box 909
El Campo, Texas 77437

Glossary

AK-47—Russian-made assault rifle normally used by the North Vietnamese and Vietcong. It fires a 7.62-mm bullet from a thirty-round clip and weighs a bit over eleven pounds, loaded.

ARVN—Army of the Republic of Vietnam, was rebuilt with the assistance of the U.S. advisers between 1957 and 1959.

BASE CAMP—A permanent base of operations. The Special Forces had such camps spread throughout South Vietnam.

C&C—Command and Control. A pilot who flies his chopper above, over, and through a battle area, usually at three thousand to five thousand feet, so he can see what is happening to ground troops. He reports back to headquarters and keeps in radio and visual contact with those on the ground. He radios for air strikes and calls in artillery, as well as directs extraction helicopters to a PZ.

C-4—An explosive material called plastique. Many GI's in the jungle used shavings from C-4 to start a fire. It burned like Sterno and was used to warm coffee or as a smoke signal.

CIDG—Civilian Independent Defense Group, made up of South Vietnamese who volunteered to fight to defend their village and country. The United States trained these combat soldiers and many worked with Special Forces teams to aid as interpreters, trackers, and combatants.

CLAYMORE—A fragmentation, antipersonnel mine that sends a swath in an arc-shaped pattern to its front. In large letters, it reads FRONT, foolproof so it will not be turned the wrong way.

CP—Command post.

DMZ—Demilitarized zone.

DZ—Drop zone, an area where a parachute jump is to be made. Could signify one parachutist or an entire regiment.

FIREBASE—A temporary combat base set up in hostile territory from which patrols are sent out to search for the enemy.

FREE-FIRE ZONE—An area that is not supposed to contain any allies and in which the soldier is free to fire at anything. During the early days when the United States was not supposed to be in Laos or Cambodia, in the event a Delta or SOG team was in the area, it was a free-fire zone for them.

GRUNT—Slang term for infantryman.

GUNSHIP—An attack helicopter, heavily armed with two M-60 machine guns, a six-barrel Gatling gun, some added armor plating, and a 36-, 48-, or 52-cylinder pod for rockets. Used for extractions in "hot" zones. During the course of the war in Vietnam, the United States lost 4,869 helicopters.

HO CHI MINH TRAIL—A well-known trail that started in North Vietnam and ran along the Anamese Mountains, through Laos and Cambodia, and ended in the Mekong Delta in South Vietnam. The NVA and VC used this trail to move men and equipment (food, ammunition, weapons). In 1959 it was truly a trail that took close to three months to travel from end to end. By 1975 travel took less than a week.

HOOCH—A Vietnamese jungle or country dwelling for humans, regardless of how primitive. Could be a thatched-roof house, a few boards with tin for a roof, or a hole in the side of a mountain with a canopy-type awning in front made of canvas. GI's in 'Nam often referred to their personal living quarters in the field, maybe their tent (with or without a wooden floor), as their hooch.

HUEY—Yet another name for a helicopter or chopper. The Huey was a series of helicopters used in Vietnam starting with the UH-1A, UH-1C, and UH-1D.

KLICK—Service term for kilometer; measures out to be a bit over six tenths of a mile.

LZ—Landing zone, a place large enough for a chopper to land and let troops out for combat or reconnaissance.

M-16—The standard U.S. infantryman's weapon. A lightweight rifle, manufactured by Colt Firearms. It has a twenty- or thirty-round belly-clip and fires 5.56-mm bullets. The M-16A1 was fitted with a 40-mm M203 grenade launcher under the barrel, enabling the weapon to propel small-spin stabilized grenades to a range of about 350 meters. Loaded with a thirty-round clip, it weighs just a tad over eight pounds and is the Western world's answer to the AK-47. A simple movement with the thumb can move it from safety, to semiautomatic, to full auto.

MERCENARY—A term meaning anyone who fights for money.

NVA—The North Vietnamese army, composed of regular army troops who were highly skilled and well supplied with Russian armaments.

POINT MAN—The first man heading a squad or platoon walking along a trail or through the jungle. The point man (or point) is the first one to encounter mines, booby traps, or the enemy.

PZ—Pickup zone, the same as an LZ (landing zone), and is usually a predetermined spot for ground troops to meet their extraction chopper.

R&R—A vacation, one where you get rest and relaxation, usually a three-day pass but can be longer.

SEAL—Elite combat group of the U.S. Navy (Sea-Air-Land). SEALS were at home in the air, on or under the water, on

or under land (many SEALS worked as "tunnel rats").
They were taught to avoid or take out the enemy, infiltrate
an objective, and carry out their mission. They would
gather intelligence, kidnap, sabotage, rescue, or assassi-
nate. Skilled with knives, weapons, and explosives.

SHAPED CHARGE—Any number of explosive charges, the
energy of which is focused in one direction. (For example,
the Claymore.)

SHRAPNEL—Term used for any filler in an explosive charge. It
could be nails, glass, or pieces of metal, but usually the
outer core of a shell, mortar round, hand grenade, or metal
from a helicopter, truck, jeep . . . any pieces of metal that
fly through the air because of an explosion.

SLICK—A helicopter used to lift troops or equipment, armed
with two M-60 door guns. A warrant officer acts as pilot,
and another WO as co-pilot. Travels with two door gunners
(usually enlisted men) and a bellyman, who assists with the
McGuire rig, and, in combat situations, maybe a medic.

SOI PAPERS—Standard Operating Instructions. Usually has
twenty-four-hour radio frequencies for patrols needing to
be extracted to call the C&C chopper or FAC airplane to
direct extraction choppers to the PZ, as well as maps of the
area, certain checkpoints for a possible rendezvous with
other teams, or other information that was classified as to
location of camps or troop movement.

USOM—United States Operation Mission.

VC—Vietnamese Communist or Vietcong. These were bands of
ragtag guerrilla fighters and sometimes skilled volunteers
who knew the jungles well. They were from the north (or
believed the doctrine of communism) and tried to force
their beliefs on the South Vietnamese.

Appendix A: Special Forces Medal of Honor Recipients

Eugene Ashley, Jr., Sergeant First Class, intelligence sergeant, Detachment A-101, Fifth Special Forces Group. Born 12 October 1931 in Wilmington, North Carolina. Entered service at New York, New York. No date of entry available.

Personally led five counterattacks on 7 February 1968 at Camp Lang Vei, Quang Tri Province, Vietnam, in effort to break through to comrades in overrun camp before he was killed.

Gary B. Beikirch, Sergeant, medical specialist, Detachment B-24, Fifth Special Forces Group. Born 29 August 1947 in Rochester, New York. Entered service at Buffalo, New York. No date of entry available.

Retrieved and treated disabled soldiers on 1 April 1968 at Camp Dak Seang, Quang Duc Province, Vietnam, under heavy fire despite serious wounds.

Roy P. Benavidez, Staff Sergeant, headquarters, B-56 (Project SIGMA), Fifth Special Forces Group. Born 5 August 1935 on a small farm near Cuero, Texas. Entered service June 3, 1955, at Houston, Texas.

Voluntarily accompanied evacuation force from his forward headquarters on 2 May 1968 and rescued several isolated patrol members in heavy combat near Loc Ninh, five kilometers inside Cambodia.

William M. Bryant, Sergeant First Class, adviser, 321st CIDG Company, 32d Mobile Strike Force Battalion, Detachment B-36, Fifth Special Forces Group. Born 16 February 1933 at Cochran, Georgia. Entered service at Detroit, Michigan. No date of entry available.

Enabled his surrounded company to escape by charging several Vietcong positions before he was killed by a rocket on 24 March 1969 in Long Khanh Province, Vietnam.

Brian L. Buker, Sergeant, adviser, 513th CIDG Company, 1st
Battalion, 5th Mobile Strike Force Command, Detachment
B-55, Fifth Special Forces Group. Born 3 November 1949 in
Benton, Maine. Entered service at Bangor, Maine. No date of
entry available.

Led the attack against a heavily defended mountain
fortress on 5 April 1970 at Nui Khet, Chau Doc Province,
Vietnam, during which he was mortally wounded assault-
ing a bunker.

Jon R. Cavaiani, Staff Sergeant, platoon leader, Task Force 1
Advisory Element. Born 2 August 1943 in Royston,
England. Entered service at Fresno, California. No date of
entry available.

Defended Hickory Hill radio relay site (Hill 953) in
Quang Tri Province, Vietnam, on 4–5 June 1971 against a
North Vietnamese army battalion until overwhelmed and
captured.

Drew D. Dix, Staff Sergeant, reconnaissance team leader (mixed
LLDB/U.S. Navy SEAL), MACV Combined Studies
Division (Central Intelligence Agency). Born 14 December
1944 at West Point, New York. Entered service at Denver,
Colorado. No date of entry available.

Helped lead repulse of Vietcong from Chau Phu, Chau
Duc Province, Vietnam, with jeep-mounted machine gun from
31 January to 1 February 1968, single-handedly assaulted
building and rescued personnel inside.

Roger H. C. Donlon, Captain, commanding officer, Detachment
A-726, Seventh Special Forces Group. Born 30 January 1934
in Saugerties, New York. Entered service in Fort Chaffee,
Arkansas. No date of entry available.

Heroically defended Camp Nam Dong, Thua Thien
Province, Vietnam, on 6 July 1964 despite serious wounds.

Loren D. Hagen, First Lieutenant, reconnaissance patrol leader,
Task Force 1 Advisory Element. Born 25 February 1946 in
Fargo, North Dakota. Entered service in Fargo, North Dakota.
No date of entry available.

Courageously defended patrol perimeter inside
Demilitarized Zone on 7 August 1971 and repelled numerous
charges until killed extracting comrades from imperiled bunker.

Charles E. Hosking, Jr., Sergeant First Class, adviser, 3rd Mobile Strike Force, Fifth Special Forces Group. Born 12 May 1924 in Ramsey, New Jersey. Entered service at Fort Dix, New Jersey. No date of entry available.

Wrestled a Vietcong prisoner with a live grenade to the ground and saved his men by absorbing the blast on 21 March 1967 in Phuoc Long Province, Vietnam.

Robert L. Howard, Sergeant First Class, reconnaissance patrol leader, MACV Studies and Observation Group. Born 11 July 1939 in Opelika, Alabama. Entered service at Montgomery, Alabama. No date of entry available.

Rallied surrounded platoon and covered its aerial extraction despite severe injuries on 30 December 1968 in Laos.

John J. Kedenburg, Specialist Fifth Class, reconnaissance patrol leader, MACV Studies and Observation Group. Born 31 July 1946 in Brooklyn, New York. Entered service at Brooklyn, New York. No date of entry available.

Defended landing zone and covered team aerial extraction on 13 June 1968 in Laos, giving his place to another team member, who suddenly came to pickup zone, and remained alone on LZ until overwhelmed and killed.

Franklin D. Miller, Staff Sergeant, reconnaissance patrol leader, MACV Studies and Observation Group. Born 27 January 1945 in Elizabeth City, North Carolina. Entered service at Albuquerque, New Mexico. No date of entry available.

Repelled several attacks on his patrol despite serious wounds on 5 January 1970 in Laos.

George K. Sisler, First Lieutenant, exploitation force leader, MACV Studies and Observation Group. Born 19 September 1937 in Dexter, Missouri. Entered service at Dexter, Missouri. No date of entry available.

Destroyed machine gun and personally counterattacked NVA assault, at which point he was killed, on 7 February 1967 in Laos.

Charles Q. Williams, Second Lieutenant, executive officer, Detach-ment A-342, Fifth Special Forces Group. Born 17 September 1933 in Charleston, South Carolina. Entered service at Fort Jackson, South Carolina. No date of entry available.

Directed defense of beleaguered compound at Camp Dong Xoai, Phuoc Long Province, Vietnam, on 9 and 10 June 1965 despite grievous wounds, destroying numerous key Vietcong positions.

Gordon D. Yntema, Sergeant, platoon adviser, Detachment A-431, Fifth Special Forces Group. Born 26 June 1945 in Bethesda, Maryland. Entered service at Detroit, Michigan. No date of entry available.

Carried several personnel to safety from 16 to 18 January 1968 near Thong Binh, Kien Tuong Province, Vietnam, and returned to trenchline, which he defended until ammunition was exhausted, after which he used his rifle as a club until he was killed.

Fred W. Zabitosky, Staff Sergeant, reconnaissance patrol leader, MACV Studies and Observation Group. Born 27 October 1942 in Trenton, New Jersey. Entered service at Trenton, New Jersey. No date of entry available.

Defended landing zone against determined NVA attack on 19 February 1968 in Laos and rescued pilot from downed helicopter before he passed out because of multiple wounds and burns.

Appendix B: Special Forces Personnel Missing in Action in Indochina 1957–1975*

Arthur Edward Bader, Jr., Sergeant, reconnaissance patrol member, Command and Control North, MACV-SOG. Born 12 July 1934 in Atlantic City, New Jersey.

Missing in action since 30 November 1968, 10 miles inside Laos east of Tchepone, when returning from patrol aboard a Vietnamese H-34 helicopter that was hit by 37-mm antiaircraft fire; aircraft fell out of control from altitude of 3,000 feet and exploded upon impact with ground. No ground search was initiated because crash site was located in a denied area.

Earl Roger Biggs, Sergeant First Class, light weapons leader, Detachment A-411, Fifth Special Forces Group. Born 23 March 1932 in Concho, West Virginia. Entered service on 31 May 1950 at Colcord, West Virginia.

Missing in action since 16 January 1968, 16 miles northwest of My Tho, Vietnam, when camp strike force was involved in a firefight; CIDG and LLDB survivors report that the Vietcong captured and summarily executed him, but actual confirmation of death was impossible.

Klaus Yrurgen Bingham, Staff Sergeant, reconnaissance team member, Task Force I Advisory Element. Born 14 December 1943 in Metz, France. Entered service on 17 June 1965 at New Orleans, Louisiana.

Missing in action since 10 May 1971, after his long-range reconnaissance team "Asp" was inserted into western Quang Nam Province 12 miles from Laos on 3 May; past initial radio contact, no further contact was ever made.

*Source: USARV USPW/CI detainee files and MIA Board Proceedings of Fifth Special Forces Group and MACV-SOG.

John Arthur Boronski, Staff Sergeant, reconnaissance patrol member, Command and Control Central, MACV-SOG. Born 24 July 1944 in Northampton, Massachusetts. Entered service on 22 June 1964 at Springfield, Massachusetts.

Missing in action since 24 March 1970, when UH-1H helicopter lifted him and other team members from landing zone in the tri-border area 14 miles inside Cambodia; aircraft racked by explosions during ascent, continued forward aflame for 200 yards, and disappeared into the jungle, where it crashed.

Russell Peter Bott, Staff Sergeant, patrol member, Detachment B-52 DELTA, Fifth Special Forces Group. Born 5 September 1936 in North Easton, Massachusetts. Entered service on 22 March 1954 at Worcester, Massachusetts.

Missing in action since 2 December 1966, 1.5 miles inside Laos west of the DMA with a reconnaissance patrol which had two skirmishes with Vietcong on 29 November and was last seen by Vietnamese patrol survivors attending to wounded comrade, Sfc. Willie E. Star, whom he refused to abandon although they were surrounded by a superior force.

Alan Lee Boyer, Sergeant, reconnaissance patrol member, Command and Control, MACV-SOG. Born 8 March 1946 in Chicago, Illinois. Entered service on 11 January 1966 at Butte, Montana.

Missing in action since 28 March 1968, when last seen 15 miles inside Laos northeast of Tchepone during extraction, having started to climb a rope ladder that broke as the Vietnamese H-34 helicopter moved away because of hostile weapons fire.

George R. Brown, Sergeant First Class, reconnaissance patrol leader, Command and Control, MACV-SOG. Born 19 September 1935 in Daytona Beach, Florida. Entered service on 22 October 1952.

Missing in action since 28 March 1968, when last seen alive and unwounded with two other Special Forces sergeants and one Vietnamese sergeant awaiting extraction from an area 15 miles inside Laos northeast of Tchepone by helicopter, which was driven off by ground fire; later search of area failed to reveal any trace of the team.

William Theodore Brown, Staff Sergeant, reconnaissance patrol member, Command and Control North, MACV-SOG. Born 20 February 1945 in Chicago, Illinois. Entered service at La Habra, California. Date of entry not available.

Missing in action since 3 November 1969, when his reconnaissance patrol was attacked by a numerically superior force 30 miles inside Laos near Ban Chakevy Tai; he was shot through the body just below the rib cage in the initial burst of automatic weapons fire and was last seen lying wounded on the ground as their position was about to be overrun, as related by an indigenous team member who evaded capture.

Michael Paul Burns, Specialist Fourth Class, reconnaissance patrol member, Command and Control North, MACV-SOG. Born 25 April 1947 in Oconto Falls, Wisconsin. Entered service on 14 February 1968 at El Paso, Texas.

Missing in action since 31 July 1969, when his reconnaissance patrol was attacked 1.5 miles inside Laos west of Hue just prior to extraction; last seen by Pan and Comen, the surviving commandos, lying on his back with severe head wounds, possibly dead, after incurring blast of a B-40 rocket.

Johnny C. Calhoun, Staff Sergeant, reconnaissance patrol leader, Command and Control, MACV-SOG. Born 14 July 1945 in Roanoke, Alabama. Entered service on 18 January 1963 at Atlanta, Georgia.

Missing in action since 27 March 1968, when his team was attacked 1.5 miles south of Ta Bat in the A Shau Valley and he provided covering fire for rest of patrol while ordering the other five members to withdraw; hit several times in the chest and stomach and last seen by interpreter Ho-Thong as he slumped to the ground, pulled the pin from a grenade, and clutched it to explode among advancing enemy, but his ultimate fate was unknown because of the rapid retreat of the survivors.

Donald Gene "Butch" Carr, Captain, assistant launch officer, Mobile Launch Team 3, Task Force 1 Advisory Element. Born 10 December 1938 in East Chicago, Indiana. Entered service on 12 October 1961 at East Chicago, Indiana.

Missing in action since 6 July 1971, while flying a visual reconnaissance mission in an Air Force OV-10 aircraft from the 23d Tactical Aerial Surveillance Squadron (tail number 634) piloted by Lt. Daniel Thomas, which disappeared 15 miles inside Laos west of Ben Het.

James Derwin Cohron, Staff Sergeant, reconnaissance patrol member, Command and Control North, MACV-SOG. Born 11 November 1938 in Leon, Iowa. Entered service on 9 January 1968, in Centerville, Iowa.

Missing in action since 12 January 1963, while a member of Spike Team "Indiana," as the second man from the rear of the team formation, when ambushed 1 mile inside Laos south of Khe Sanh; team broke contact by evading through a gully and set up defensive position on a small hill where called for helicopter extraction while waiting in vain for Cohron and two indigenous soldiers; tall elephant grass obstructed their vision, and efforts to reach him via squad radio failed.

William Michael Copley, Specialist Fourth Class, reconnaissance patrol member, Command and Control North, MACV-SOG. Born 22 May 1949 in Columbus, Ohio. Entered service on 31 July 1967 at Los Angeles, California.

Missing in action since 16 November 1968, when patrol was ambushed 16 miles inside Laos west of Ben Het prior to establishing overnight positions; he was seriously wounded by automatic weapons fire and cried out to S. Sgt. Roger T. Loe, "Help me, I'm hit!"; Loe carried him on his back until he tripped after traveling a short distance, tried to administer first aid until Copley's face showed signs of death, and was forced to leave because of pursuit by hostile forces.

Douglas Edward DaHill, Specialist Fourth Class, patrol member, Detachment B-52 DELTA, Fifth Special Forces Group. Born 6 March 1949 in Lima, Ohio. Entered service on 28 June 1966 at Columbus, Ohio.

Missing in action since 17 April 1969, when Reconnaissance Patrol 6 was ambushed by numerically superior Vietcong force in Thua Thien Province 9 miles from Laotian border; last heard from by radio transmission to circling aircraft requesting assistance, whereupon radio contact was lost.

David Arthur Davidson, Staff Sergeant, reconnaissance patrol member, Command and Control North, MACV-SOG. Born 8

March 1947 in Washington, D.C. Entered service at East Riverdale, Maryland. Date of entry not available. Reenlisted on 18 May 1968 in the Republic of Vietnam.

Missing in action since 5 October 1970, after his patrol had established its overnight position 12 miles inside Laos west of Ta Bat and was attacked by a hostile force; according to the two surviving indigenous patrol members, Davidson was hit once in the head and fell down a ridge, after which he lay motionless with a probable fatal head wound.

Ricardo Gonzalez Davis, Sergeant First Class, reconnaissance patrol leader, Command and Control North, MACV-SOG. Born 17 March 1941 in Fort Stockton, Texas. Entered service at Carlsbad, New Mexico. Date of entry not available. Reenlisted on 30 May 1967 at Fort Campbell, Kentucky.

Missing in action since 20 March 1969, when his six-man patrol was attacked 11 miles inside Laos west of Kham Duc; Sgt. James C. La Motte was two feet away when Davis was hit by rifle fire in upper chest and face and said, "Jim, Jim!" and fell; the assistant patrol leader advanced to Davis's position seven minutes later but detected no signs of life, whereupon the patrol was forced to evacuate the area because of advancing hostile soldiers.

Ronald James Dexter, Master Sergeant, reconnaissance patrol member, Command and Control, MACV-SOG. Born 23 July 1933 in Chicago, Illinois. Entered service on 2 September 1951 at Chicago, Illinois.

Missing in action since 3 June 1967, when last seen exiting a downed CH-46 helicopter as it was being grenaded by approaching hostile forces 15 miles inside Laos west of the A Shau Valley; the Nung commander, Mr. Ky, saw several men in a large bomb crater firing red star clusters from a flare gun as Ky was lifted out on the last helicopter.

Edward Ray Dodge, Sergeant First Class, administrative supervisor, Detachment C-1, Fifth Special Forces Group. Born 16 December 1933 in Norfolk, Virginia. Entered service on 21 December 1950 at Norfolk, Virginia.

Missing in action since 31 December 1964, while an observer aboard an Air Force 01-F aircraft (Number 572823) of the 336th Tactical Fighter Squadron piloted by Capt. Kurt C. MacDonald, on a reconnaissance flight over the A Shau Valley, as the aircraft failed to return to Da Nang.

Raymond Louis Echevarria, Master Sergeant, reconnaissance patrol leader, Command and Control, MACV-SOG. Born 16 September 1933 in Brooklyn, New York. Entered service on 3 December 1950 in New York City.

Missing in action since 3 October 1966, when patrol was inserted 1 mile inside Laos west of the DMZ and immediately engaged in firefight under adverse circumstances; sole survivor, interpreter Bui Kim Tien, last heard of him when Sfc. Eddie L. Williams had told Tien, "Jones is dying and Ray (Echevarria) is the same way."

Lawrence Jesse Englander, Sergeant, radio supervisor, Detachment A-109, Fifth Special Forces Group. Born 19 April 1943 in Las Vegas, Nevada. Entered service on 4 August 1964 at Van Nuys, California.

Missing in action since 2 May 1968, when participated in a CIDG heliborne assault that came under intense automatic weapons fire from fortified NVA positions 8 miles southwest of Thuong Duc; last heard from by Sgt. John M. Vincent on radio stating he was wounded in foot and arm and pinned down in open field behind dead Vietnamese radio operator, refused help because he claimed to be "zeroed in," that any movement would bring heavy fire, and that he would try to crawl back to friendly lines; LLDB Lt. Ho Tang Dzu stated he saw him hit by machine gun fire in back and head, but attempts to reach him failed and battlefield was abandoned.

Danny Day Entrican, First Lieutenant, reconnaissance patrol leader, Task Force 1 Advisory Element. Born 12 August 1946 in Brookhaven, Mississippi. Entered service on 1 October 1969 at Fort Devens, Massachusetts.

Missing in action since 18 May 1971, after his reconnaissance team "Alaska" was inserted into the Da Krong Valley in Vietnam on 15 May and overwhelmed in a firefight three days later 1 mile from the Laotian border; surviving commando Truong Minh Long and interpreter Truong To Ha stated that they rolled downhill after hostile search party detected them hiding in bush, at which point Entrican was apparently wounded and yelled at them to move out.

Richard Allan Fitts, Specialist Fifth Class, reconnaissance patrol member, Command and Control North, MACV-SOG. Born 23 February 1946 in Weymouth, Massachusetts. Entered service on 18 January 1966 at Boston, Massachusetts.

Missing in action since 30 November 1968, 10 miles inside Laos east of Tchepone when returning from reconnaissance mission on a Vietnamese H-34 helicopter that was hit by 37-mm antiaircraft fire; aircraft fell out of control from altitude of 3,000 feet and exploded upon impact with the ground. No ground search was initiated because the crash site was located in a denied area.

John Theodore Gallagher, Staff Sergeant, reconnaissance patrol member, Command and Control North, MACV-SOG. Born 17 June 1943 in Summit, New Jersey. Entered service on 25 December 1962 at New Haven, Connecticut.

Missing in action since 5 January 1968, when aboard the second helicopter transporting patrol 20 miles inside Laos south of Lao Bao, which was struck by 37-mm antiaircraft fire at an altitude of 2,000 feet; it went into an uncontrollable spin and exploded in flames upon impact with ground; heavy ground fire prevented search attempts.

Fred Allen Gassman, Sergeant, reconnaissance patrol member, Command and Control North, MACV-SOG. Born 5 September 1947 at Eglin Field, Florida. Entered service at Fort Walton Beach, Florida. Date of entry not available. Reenlisted on 10 February 1969.

Missing in action since 5 October 1970, after his patrol had established its overnight position 12 miles inside Laos west of Ta Bat and was attacked by a hostile force; Gassman radioed the overhead aircraft for emergency extraction and, as he attempted to retrieve the homing device, stated on the radio, "I've been hit, and in the worst way," followed by several groans before the radio went dead. According to the two surviving indigenous patrol members, Gassman was last seen lying motionless with a large hole in his back.

Stephen Jonathan Geist, Specialist Fourth Class, heavy weapons specialist, Detachment A-332, Fifth Special Forces Group. Born 12 April 1946 in Philadelphia, Pennsylvania. Entered service on 9 May 1966 at Baltimore, Maryland.

Missing in action since 26 September 1967, when aboard an aircraft of the 74th Aviation company piloted by Lt. Lynn R. Huddleston on a visual reconnaissance mission north of Minh Thanh 4 miles from the Cambodian border; aircraft disappeared and never reached destination.

Douglas J. Glover, Staff Sergeant, reconnaissance patrol member, Command and Control, MACV-SOG. Born 2 May 1943 in Cortland, New York. Entered service at Cortland, New York. Date of entry not available. Reenlisted on 17 October 1965 at Fort Myer, Virginia.

Missing in action since 19 February 1968, when reconnaissance team was being extracted 4 miles inside Laos west of Dak Sut; as the helicopter ascended from the landing zone, it nosed over and crashed, bursting into flames; the pilot, copilot, and one team member survived but left six persons missing because of hostile fire; later recovery efforts detected only five badly burned unknown remains.

Roger C. Hallberg, Staff Sergeant, platoon leader, III CTZ Mike Force (Detachment A 302), Fifth Special Forces Group. Born 18 September 1944 in Visalia, California. Entered service on 11 October 1963 at Los Angeles, California.

Missing in action since 24 March 1967, when his Mike Force company conducted a heliborne assault 7 miles east of Bu Dop; shortly after landing they were engaged by two NVA battalions armed with automatic weapons and recoilless rifles, and supported by mortars, forcing company elements to retreat under extremely heavy pressure. Attempts to consolidate positions around the landing zone supported by air strikes failed; communication was lost with the Mike Force and never regained.

Kenneth Hanna, Sergeant First Class, heavy weapons specialist, Detachment A-101, Fifth Special Forces Group. Born 28 April 1933 in Scranton, South Carolina. Entered service on 28 April 1951 at Scranton, South Carolina.

Missing in action since 7 February 1968, during NVA tank-infantry assault on Lang Vei Special Forces Camp, when last seen with wounds to scalp, left shoulder, and arm, administering first aid to Sfc. Charles W. Lindewald, at the mobile strike force outpost as it was about to be overrun.

Gary Alan Harned, Sergeant, reconnaissance patrol member, Command and Control Central, MACV-SOG. Born 7 July 1950 in Meadville, Pennsylvania. Entered service on 10 September 1968 at Pittsburgh, Pennsylvania.

Missing in action since 24 March 1970, when UH-1H helicopter lifted him and other team members from landing zone in the tri-border area 14 miles inside Cambodia; aircraft racked by explosions during ascent, continued forward aflame for 200 yards, and disappeared into the jungle, where it crashed.

James Arthur Harwood, Sergeant, reconnaissance team member, Detachment B-43, Fifth Special Forces Group. Born 10 March 1950 in Omaha, Nebraska. Entered service on 10 October 1968 at Dallas, Texas.

Missing in action since 15 January 1971, when attached to the Reconnaissance Platoon, 2d Company, 1st (later the 6th) Cambodian Battalion, which was ambushed in thick bamboo on the slope of Hill 282 (Nui Ta Bec) northwest of Chi Lang and 2 miles from the Cambodian border; last heard when he radioed 1st Lt. James J. McCarty that he was moving up toward the point, could not see anything, and was receiving direct fire from the front; communication was then lost and McCarty's shouts to him received no response.

Robert Dale Herreid, Specialist Fifth Class, demolitions specialist, Detachment A-402, Fifth Special Forces Group. Born 13 June 1946 in Williston, North Dakota. Entered service on 11 July 1966 at Chicago, Illinois.

Missing in action since 10 October 1968, as part of the 47th Mobile Strike Force Company advancing up Nui Coto near Chau Doc, which was blasted by heavy bunker fire and withdrew to pagoda, where set up perimeter; radio operator gave Herreid's weapon to commanding officer, stating that Herreid was dead; Nguyen Van Liet and other soldiers said Herreid was shot in left temple and lying by a leafless mangrove tree, but body never found.

Barry Wayne Hilbrich, Captain, operations officer, Company B, Fifth Special Forces Group. Born 25 June 1947 in Cuere DeWitt, Texas. Entered service on 28 December 1965 at Corpus Christi, Texas.

Missing in action since 9 June 1970, when flying on a visual reconnaissance mission 7 miles south of Ben Het in an Air Force O-1F aircraft (tail number 890) of the 21st Tactical Aerial Surveillance Squadron, piloted by 1st Lt. John L. Ryder, which disappeared west of Pleiku.

Cecil J. Hodgson, Sergeant First Class, patrol member, Detachment B-52 DELTA, Fifth Special Forces Group. Born

28 July 1937 in Campbell, Texas. Entered service on 15 June 1955 at Greenville, Texas.

Missing in action since 29 January 1966, in An Lao Valley of Binh Dinh Province 12 miles west of Tam Quan when his reconnaissance team was split during firefight; last seen with 9-mm pistol in tall grass within arm's reach of M. Sgt. Wiley W. Gary and S. Sgt. Ronald T. Terry, when they opened fire on a hostile element blocking their escape and became separated during skirmish.

James William Holt, Sergeant First Class, senior medical specialist, Detachment A-101, Fifth Special Forces Group. Born 19 September 1941 in Hope, Arkansas. Entered service on 18 June 1959 at Little Rock, Arkansas.

Missing in action since 7 February 1968, when the Lang Vei Special Forces Camp was overrun by NVA tank-infantry assault; destroyed three North Vietnamese army tanks with a recoilless rifle before forced to abandon the position; last seen by S. Sgt. Peter Tiroch running to the ammunition bunker to look for light antitank weapons.

William Balt Hunt, Staff Sergeant, replacement platoon leader, III CTZ Mike Force (Detachment A-302), Fifth Special Forces Group. Born 31 July 1935 in Priest River, Idaho. Entered service on 13 November 1953 at Spokane, Washington.

Missing in action since 4 November 1966, when lifted into battle by helicopter to evacuate wounded northeast of Soui Da 10 miles from Dau Tieng and voluntarily left aircraft to reinforce remaining troops on ground; after two days of heavy fighting and numerous casualties, the Mike Force was overrun by numerically superior forces on 6 November 1966; as he carried the wounded company commander, Sfc. George H. Heaps, out of danger, he was gravely wounded by a bullet that hit him in the shoulder, penetrated his upper back, and exited his side, but still succeeded in moving Heaps to a covered position where they passed out from loss of blood; both later awoke and crawled toward landing zone, passing out periodically; Nung soldier stayed behind with Hunt and later reported that Hunt had died, but the body was never found.

Charles Gregory Huston, Sergeant, reconnaissance patrol member, Command and Control, MACV-SOG. Born 29

September 1945 in Houston, Ohio. Entered service on 5 October 1965 at Cincinnati, Ohio.

Missing in action since 28 March 1968, when last seen alive and unwounded with two other Special Forces sergeants and one Vietnamese sergeant awaiting extraction 15 miles inside Laos northeast of Tchepone by helicopter, which was driven off by ground fire; later search of area failed to reveal any traces of team.

James Emory Jones, Sergeant First Class, reconnaissance patrol member, Command and Control, MACV-SOG. Born 3 September 1939 in Enigma, Georgia. Entered service on 23 July 1957 at Milledgeville, Georgia.

Missing in action since 3 October 1966, when patrol was inserted 1 mile inside Laos west of the DMZ and immediately engaged in firefight under adverse circumstances; sole survivor, interpreter Bui Kim Tien, last heard of him when Sfc. Eddie L. Williams had told Tien, "Jones is dying and Ray is the same way."

John Robert Jones, Sergeant, light weapons leader, Task Force 1 Advisory Element. Born 20 February 1949 in Louisville, Kentucky. Entered service on 1 July 1968 at El Paso, Texas.

Missing in action since 5 June 1971, at Hickory Hill radio relay site north of Khe Sanh in Quang Tri Province, which was overrun in heavy combat by a battalion-size North Vietnamese force in adverse weather which prevented air support; he was not found despite search by helicopter and low-flying aircraft.

Gerald Francis Kinsman, First Lieutenant, training officer, Detachment B-43, Fifth Special Forces Group. Born 12 June 1945 in Boston, Massachusetts. Commissioned on 11 July 1969 at Fort Benning, Georgia.

Missing in action since 15 January 1971, when attached to the Reconnaissance Platoon, 2d Company, 1st (later the 6th) Cambodian Battalion, which was ambushed in thick bamboo on the slope of Hill 282 (Nui Ta Bec) northwest of Chi Lang and 2 miles from Cambodian border; Kinsman was severely wounded and unconscious as Lt. James J. McCarty attempted to pull him out of a bamboo thicket, but a machine gun wounded McCarty and forced him to abandon the effort.

Harold William Kroske, Jr., First Lieutenant, reconnaissance patrol leader, Command and Control South, MACV-SOG. Born 30 July 1947 in Trenton, New Jersey. Entered service on 29 June 1966 at Mercer, New Jersey.

Missing in action since 11 February 1969, when patrol was engaged 12 miles inside Cambodia west of Bu Dop and he killed several hostile troops along a trail; he then motioned the point man, Diep Chan Sang, to come with him; there was a sudden burst of gunfire, Kroske dropped his weapon, grabbed his stomach, and fell; Sp. 4th Class Bryan O. Stockdale tried to approach him, received no response when he called out his name from twenty feet away, whereupon the patrol was forced to withdraw because of heavy automatic weapons fire.

Frederick Krupa, Captain, platoon leader, Exploitation Company A, Task Force 2 Advisory Element. Born 2 September 1947 in Scranton, Pennsylvania. Entered service on 25 June 1965 at Wilkes-Barre, Pennsylvania.

Missing in action since 27 April 1971, when his special commando unit was about to conduct a helicopter insertion 2 miles from Laotian border northwest of Plei Djereng, Vietnam; hostile forces opened up on his UH-1H helicopter when it was three feet off the ground, and he fell forward; SCU Company A commander Ayom grabbed his right shoulder but let go when Ayom's hand was struck by bullet; last seen lying next to a log sprawled out on his back, not moving or making a sound, by crew chief Sp. 4th Class Melvin C. Lew during helicopter ascent.

Gary Russell LaBohn, Specialist Fourth Class, reconnaissance patrol member, Command & Control North, MACV-SOG. Born 28 December 1942 in Madison, Wisconsin. Entered service on 29 December 1966 in Detroit, Michigan.

Missing in action since 30 November 1968, 10 miles inside Laos east of Tchepone when returning from patrol aboard a Vietnamese H-34 helicopter, which was hit by 37-mm antiaircraft fire; aircraft fell out of control from altitude of 3,000 feet and exploded upon impact with ground. No ground search was initiated because crash site was located in a denied area.

Glen Oliver Lane, Sergeant First Class, reconnaissance patrol leader, Command and Control, MACV-SOG. Born 24 July 1931 in Diboll, Texas. Entered service on 30 June 1951 in Odessa, Texas.

Missing in action since 23 May 1968, after his six-man spike team "Idaho" was infiltrated just across the Laotian border west of A Loui by helicopter on 20 May 1968, and all further contact with patrol was lost; spike team "Oregon" inserted into area for search on 22 May immediately contacted large hostile force and was extracted.

Billy Ray Laney, Sergeant First Class, reconnaissance patrol member, Command and Control, MACV-SOG. Born 21 August 1939 in Blanch, Alabama. Entered army 3 August 1960 with two years of navy service.

Missing in action since 3 June 1967, aboard CH-46 helicopter downed 15 miles inside Laos west of the A Shau Valley; last seen by Sfc. Wilklow and Nung soldier lying wounded on floor of helicopter, between one crew member with a broken back and the door gunner with head wound, as hostile forces approached, tossing grenades at aircraft.

Charles W. Lindewarld, Jr., Sergeant First Class, platoon leader, 12th Mobile Strike Force Company, Company C, Fifth Special Forces Group. Born 30 July 1938 in La Porte, Indiana. Entered service on 2 August 1955 at La Porte, Indiana.

Missing in action since 7 February 1968, at Lang Vei Special Forces Camp when overrun by NVA tank-infantry assault; last seen severely wounded in chest or abdomen by automatic weapons fire and being treated at mobile strike force outpost by Sfc. Kenneth Hanna just as it was about to be overrun.

James Martin Luttrell, Staff Sergeant, reconnaissance team member, Task Force 1 Advisory Element. Born 14 December 1935 in Milwaukee, Wisconsin. Entered service on 29 March 1954 at Wamatosa, Wisconsin.

Missing in action since 10 May 1971, after his long-range reconnaissance team "Asp" was inserted into western Quang Nam Province 12 miles from Laos on 3 May 1971; past initial radio contact, no further contact was ever made.

Michael Howard Mein, Specialist Fourth Class, reconnaissance patrol member, Command and Control North, MACV-SOG. Born 13 March 1945 in Oneida, New York. Entered service on 17 February 1967 at Syracuse, New York.

Missing in action since 30 November 1968, 10 miles inside Laos east of Tchepone when returning from patrol aboard a Vietnamese H-34 helicopter that was hit by 37-mm antiaircraft fire; aircraft fell out of control from altitude of 3,000 feet and exploded upon impact with ground. No ground search was initiated because crash site was located in a denied area.

Michael Millner, Staff Sergeant, light weapons leader, Detachment A-341, Fifth Special Forces Group. Born 17 December 1942 in Alhambra, California. Entered service on 11 January 1960 at Marysville, California.

Missing in action since 29 November 1967, when accompanying a CIDG unit on a search-and-destroy operation 6 miles east of Bu Dop, which was begun 26 November; against advice of senior adviser, Capt. Matthew J. Hasko, the LLDB commander stopped the troops for lunch, and unit was attacked by a Vietcong company; the CIDG became completely disorganized and ran from field as Special Forces personnel tried to cover the rear and carry the wounded; Millner was missing when unit was finally reconsolidated.

James Leslie Moreland, Specialist Fourth Class, medical specialist, 12th Mobile Strike Force Company, Company C, Fifth Special Forces Group. Born 29 September 1945 in Bossemer, Alabama. Entered service on 27 September 1965 at Anaheim, California.

Missing in action since 7 February 1968, at Lang Vei when overrun by NVA tank-infantry assault; severely wounded and became delirious in command bunker as it came under sapper attack, preventing his extraction when bunker was later abandoned; last seen by 1st Lt. Thomas E. Todd in the bunker ruins, apparently dead and covered by debris.

Dennis Paul Neal, Captain, reconnaissance patrol leader, Command and Control North, MACV-SOG. Born 1 February 1944 in Quincy, Illinois. Entered service on 28 June 1966 in Clearwater, Florida.

Missing in action since 31 July 1969, when his six-man patrol was attacked just prior to extraction 1.5 miles inside Laos west of Hue, and last seen by Pan and Comen, surviving commandos, after he was severely wounded in chest by a B-40 rocket blast, when they turned him over to take off one of his emergency UHF radios prior to retreating because of wounds and intense fire; forward air control aircraft heard the second emergency radio transmit "Help, help, help, for God's sake, help," but search teams later dispatched to area were unsuccessful.

Charles Vernon Newton, Staff Sergeant, patrol leader, Detachment B-52 DELTA, Fifth Special Forces Group. Born 10 May 1940 in Canadian, Texas. Entered service on 16 December 1959 at Canadian, Texas.

Missing in action since 17 April 1969, when Reconnaissance Patrol 6, which had been inserted into Thua Thien Province on 14 April, was ambushed by numerically superior Vietcong force 9 miles from Laotian border; last heard from by radio transmission to circling aircraft requesting assistance, whereupon radio contact was lost.

Warren Robert Orr, Jr., Captain, civil affairs officer, Company C, Fifth Special Forces Group. Born 20 March 1943 in West Frankfort, Illinois. Entered service on 22 March 1963 at Moline, Illinois.

Missing in action since 12 May 1968, when arrived at Kham Duc Special Forces Camp to assist in evacuation efforts, and last seen loading Vietnamese civilians aboard an Air Force C-130 aircraft, which crashed 1 mile from the camp; Vo Dai Phung claimed he saw Orr get on aircraft after everyone was aboard before the tailgate closed; later search of wreckage impossible because aircraft was totally destroyed except for tail boom.

Robert Duval Owen, Staff Sergeant, reconnaissance patrol member, Command and Control, MACV-SOG. Born 21 December 1938 in Lynchburg, Virginia. Entered service on 30 July 1954 at Pine Bluff, Arkansas.

Missing in action since 23 May 1968, after his six-man spike team "Idaho" was infiltrated just across the Laotian border west of A Loui by helicopter on 20 May, and all further contact with patrol was lost; spike team "Oregon" inserted into area for search on 22 May immediately contacted large hostile force and was extracted.

Norman Payne, Sergeant, reconnaissance patrol member, Command and Control North, MACV-SOG. Born on 14 July 1939 in Greenville, Alabama. Entered service on 8 July 1957 at Cleveland, Ohio.

Missing in action since 19 December 1968, when his reconnaissance team was attacked 6 miles inside Laos west of the A Shau Valley just before nightfall; last seen by the team leader, Sp. 4th Class Donald C. Sheppard, as Payne left the team to join another group, which had slid down an embankment; Sheppard later followed this route along a creek bed, but efforts to locate Payne failed. During extraction, Sheppard heard garbled emergency radio transmission, the last word of which sounded like "bison" (the code name for Payne), but a later ground search was blocked by hostile activity.

Thomas Hepburn Perry, Specialist Fourth Class, medical specialist, Detachment A-105, Fifth Special Forces Group. Born 19 June 1942 in Washington, D.C. Entered service on 10 March 1966 in New Haven, Connecticut.

Missing in action since 10 May 1968, when Ngok Tavak base south of Kham Duc was overrun by NVA ground assault; last seen by Sgt. Cordell J. Matheney, Jr., standing twenty feet away as Capt. John White (Australian army) formed up the withdrawal column at the outer perimeter wire on the eastern Ngok Tavak hillside; noted missing during later extraction. A ground search was prohibited by hostile activity in overrun area.

Daniel Raymond Phillips, Specialist Fifth Class, demolitions specialist, Detachment A-101, Fifth Special Forces Group. Born on 7 August 1944 in Philadelphia, Pennsylvania. Entered service on 18 March 1966 in Harrisburg, Pennsylvania.

Missing in action since 7 February 1968, at the Lang Vei Special Forces Camp when overrun by NVA tank-infantry assault; last seen wounded in the face and attempting to evade North Vietnamese armor by going through the northern perimeter wire.

Jerry Lynn Pool, First Lieutenant, reconnaissance patrol leader, Command and Control Central, MACV-SOG. Born on 2

April 1944 in Sinton, Texas. Entered service on 11 April 1964 at Austin, Texas.

Missing in action since 24 March 1970, when UH-1H helicopter lifted him and other team members from landing zone in the tri-border area 14 miles inside Cambodia; aircraft racked by explosions during ascent, continued forward aflame for 200 yards, and disappeared into the jungle, where it crashed.

Charles Francis Prevedel, Sergeant, patrol member, Detachment B-52 DELTA, Fifth Special Forces Group. Born 18 November 1943 in St. Louis, Missouri. Entered service on 14 September 1965 at Florissant, Missouri.

Missing in action since 17 April 1969, when Reconnaissance Patrol 6 was ambushed by numerically superior Vietcong force in Thua Thien Province 9 miles from Laotian border; last heard from by radio transmission to circling aircraft requesting assistance, whereupon radio contact was lost.

Ronald Earl Ray, Staff Sergeant, reconnaissance patrol leader, Command and Control North, MACV-SOG. Born 11 August 1947 in Beaumont, Texas. Entered service on 21 June 1965 at Port Arthur, Texas.

Missing in action since 13 November 1969, when his six-man reconnaissance team was attacked and overrun 16 miles inside Laos west of Thua Thien Province; sole survivor Nguyen Van Bon stated that Ray was hit in an exchange of gunfire, fell to the ground, groaned, and then was silent; Bon shook him but received no response, and noted that Ray's weapon was smashed and that Ray had been hit in the chest and arm.

John Hartley Robertson, Sergeant First Class, operations sergeant, FOB #1, Command and Control North, MACV-SOG. Born 25 October 1936 in Birmingham, Alabama. Entered service on 15 June 1954 at Birmingham, Alabama.

Missing in action since 20 May 1968, when aboard a Vietnamese H-34 helicopter on a medical evacuation mission 4 miles inside Laos south of A Shau; as helicopter was landing it was struck by hostile fire, smashed into the trees, and burst into flames. Vietnamese ground unit could not reach the wreckage, and no survivors were spotted.

Robert Francis Scherdin, Private First Class, reconnaissance patrol member, Command and Control North, MACV-SOG. Born 14 February 1947 in Somerville, New Jersey. Entered service on 15 August 1967 at Newark, New Jersey.

Missing in action since 29 December 1968, when part of the rear element of a reconnaissance team that was split during a skirmish 4 miles inside Cambodia west of Dak To; Montagnard soldier Nguang in same element saw him fall on his right side and tried to help him stand up, but Scherdin only groaned and would not get up; Nguang was then wounded himself and realized he had been left by the other three Vietnamese of the rear element, whereupon he left Scherdin and was extracted along with the remainder of the team.

Klaus Dieter Scholz, Staff Sergeant, reconnaissance patrol member, Command and Control North, MACV-SOG. Born 20 January 1944 in Bad Warmbrunn, Germany. Entered service on 17 May 1965 at Amarillo, Texas.

Missing in action since 30 November 1968, 10 miles inside Laos east of Tchepone when returning from patrol aboard a Vietnamese H-34 helicopter that was hit by 37-mm antiaircraft fire; aircraft fell out of control from altitude of 3,000 feet and exploded upon impact with ground. No ground search was initiated because crash site was located in a denied area.

Mike John Scott, Sergeant First Class, aerial observer, Command and Control Central, MACV-SOG. Born 2 September 1932 in Gostynin, Poland. Entered service on 13 September 1956 at Newark, New Jersey.

Missing in action since 13 May 1969, when aboard an aircraft of the 219th Aviation Company, piloted by Lt. Bruce C. Bessor, just inside the Laotian border west of Kham Duc, attempting to locate ground reconnaissance team whose members heard aircraft engine noise followed by fifteen rounds of 37-mm fire and engine sputtering but no sound of crash, then a large volume of rifle fire from same direction. Efforts to locate the aircraft failed.

Lee D. Scurlock, Jr., Staff Sergeant, reconnaissance patrol member, Command and Control, MACV-SOG. Born 10 November 1943 in Restful Lake, Ohio. Entered service on 22 September 1961 at Restful Lake, Ohio.

Missing in action since 21 December 1967, during extraction of team on Laotian-Cambodian boundary of the tri-border region 18 miles west of Vietnam, while climbing a rope ladder to a helicopter ("Gator 376") of the 119th Aviation Company; he climbed only three rungs on first attempt before losing grip, removed rucksack and radio, and slowly climbed ladder, appearing weak and possibly hurt as the door gunner and a Special Forces sergeant shouted encouragement; just before he reached their out-stretched hands, he fell off the ladder fifty feet to the ground, landed on his neck and head, and rolled down hill-side until a small tree stopped his movement. The heli-copter came under automatic weapons fire and was forced from the area.

Leo Earl Seymour, Staff Sergeant, reconnaissance patrol leader, Command and Control, MACV-SOG. Born 14 May 1942 in Sayre, Pennsylvania. Entered army 28 June 1963 with four years' marine service.

Missing in action since 3 July 1967, when his reconnais-sance team "Texas" was readying ambush positions near a trail junction 11 miles inside Laos northwest of Ben Het in the Dale Xow river valley; two large hostile columns con-verged and noticed a propaganda poster tacked to a tree that had not been there previously and began searching area, spot-ting the forward security element, which opened fire; team split up by skirmish, and upon rallying a distance away could not find Seymour.

Jerry Michael Shriver, Sergeant First Class, exploitation platoon leader, Command and Control South, MACV-SOG. Born 24 September 1941 in DeFuniak Springs, Florida. Entered ser-vice on 9 December 1958 at Sacramento, California.

Missing in action since 24 April 1969, when his platoon was engaged by intense fire 1.5 miles inside Laos west of the DMZ's southern boundary of Vietnam; last seen by Capt. Paul D. Cahill, moving against machine gun bunkers and entering the woodline, whereupon he continued radio contact until transmission ceased. Ten air strikes and 1,500 rockets were required to extract the few survivors of the platoon from the battlefield.

Donald Monroe Shue, Sergeant, reconnaissance patrol member, Command and Control North, MACV-SOG. Born 29 August 1949 in Concord, North Carolina. Entered service on 26 June 1967 at Charlotte, North Carolina.

Missing in action since 3 November 1969, when his reconnaissance patrol was attacked by a numerically superior force 30 miles inside Laos near Ban Chakeny Tai, and he was hit by grenade fragments; last seen lying wounded on the ground as their position was about to be overrun, as related by an indigenous team member who evaded capture.

Burt Chauncy Small, Jr., Specialist Fourth Class, psychological operations specialist, Detachment A-108, Fifth Special Forces Group. Born 2 September 1946 in Long Beach, California. Entered service 19 January 1966 at Savannah, Georgia.

Missing in action since 6 March 1967, when accompanying a twenty-man Vietnamese patrol of the 142d CIDG Company, which was ambushed near Minh Long; during the skirmish Sgt. Jacob G. Roth, Jr., and Small tried to stop the CIDG radio operator, who was running away, when Small was wounded in the left leg, captured by North Vietnamese troops, and never seen again.

Raymond Clark Stacks, First Lieutenant, reconnaissance patrol leader, Command and Control North, MACV-SOG. Born 6 March 1948 in Memphis, Tennessee. Commissioned on 6 September 1966 at Memphis, Tennessee.

Missing in action since 30 November 1968, 10 miles inside Laos east of Tchepone when returning from patrol aboard a Vietnamese H-34 helicopter that was hit by 37-mm antiaircraft fire; aircraft fell out of control from altitude of 3,000 feet and exploded upon impact with ground. No ground search was initiated because crash site was located in a denied area.

Willie Ernest Stark, Sergeant First Class, patrol leader, Detachment B-52 DELTA, Fifth Special Forces Group. Born 7 October 1932 in Martinsburg, Nebraska. Entered service on 21 July 1950 at Waterbury, Nebraska.

Missing in action since 2 December 1966, 1.5 miles inside Laos west of the DMZ with a reconnaissance patrol on 29 November 1966, which had two skirmishes with Vietcong, and last seen wounded in thigh and chest and being guarded by S. Sgt. Russell P. Bott, as related by Vietnamese patrol survivors.

Jack Thomas Stewart, Captain, commanding officer, III CTZ Mike Force (Detachment A-302), Fifth Special Forces Group. Born 30 March 1941 in Washington, D.C. Entered service on 27 February 1959 at Washington, D.C.

Missing in action since 24 March 1967, when his Mike Force Company conducted a heliborne assault 7 miles east of Bu Dop; shortly after landing they were engaged by two NVA battalions armed with automatic weapons and recoilless rifles, and supported by mortars, forcing company elements to retreat under extremely heavy pressure; attempts to consolidate positions around the landing zone supported by air strikes failed; communication was lost with the Mike Force and never regained.

Madison Alexander Strohlein, Sergeant, parachutist commando, Task Force 1 Advisory Element. Born 17 May 1948 in Abington, Pennsylvania. Entered service on 8 July 1968 at Philadelphia, Pennsylvania.

Missing in action since 22 June 1971, after being parachuted into the Ta Ko area of Vietnam at night on a reconnaissance mission with Sgt. Maj. William D. Waugh and Sfc. James O. Bath; last heard from by radio requesting evacuation because of injuries; his transmissions were monitored until 11:00 A.M., when he stated hostile forces were approaching; thereafter transmissions ceased. Rescue team inserted on 23 June found only his weapon, scattered gear, and indications that his parachute had been pulled from a tree.

William Wentworth Stubbs, Staff Sergeant, reconnaissance patrol member, Command and Control Central, MACV-SOG. Born 6 August 1949 in Oak Harbor, Washington. Entered service on 26 October 1967 at Newport, Washington.

Missing in action since 20 October 1969, when his reconnaissance team was attacked 20 miles inside Laos northeast of Nakhon Phantom and he was at the point of immediate contact; according to surviving indigenous patrol members, three bursts of automatic fire were directed at him from a distance of two feet, striking him in the head, followed by three grenades thrown onto his position. The rest of patrol was unable to move up the steep slope to reach him and were forced to withdraw five minutes later because of renewed hostile assault.

Randolph Bothwell Suber, Sergeant, reconnaissance patrol member, Command and Control North, MACV-SOG. Born 22 May 1947 at Albuquerque, New Mexico. Entered service on October 26, 1967, at Albuquerque, New Mexico.

Missing in action since 13 November 1969, when his six-man reconnaissance team was attacked and overrun 16 miles inside Laos west of Thua Thien Province; sole survivor Nhuyen Van Bon stated that he last saw Suber trying to gain contact on his URC-10 emergency radio, then pick up his weapon and aim at four approaching hostile soldiers, but that the rifle did not fire because it became jammed, and Suber was hit immediately afterward and fell to the ground; Bon called to him, but he did not move or answer, and Bon was forced to leave the area.

Samuel Kamu Toomey, Major, special mission officer, Headquarters, MACV-SOG. Born 30 December 1935 in Honolulu, Hawaii. Entered army on 13 April 1956 after service with the marines.

Missing in action since 30 November 1968, 10 miles inside Laos east of Tchepone when returning from patrol aboard a Vietnamese H-34 helicopter that was hit by 37-mm antiaircraft fire; aircraft fell out of control from altitude of 3,000 feet and exploded upon impact with ground. No ground search was initiated because crash site was located in a denied area.

Glenn Ernest Tubbs, Staff Sergeant, reconnaissance patrol member, Command and Control South, MACV-SOG. Born 24 January 1940 in Sulphur Springs, Texas. Entered service on 21 June 1959 at Olton, Texas.

Missing since 13 January 1970, when his reconnaissance team was crossing the Se San River close to the Cambodian border 12 miles northwest of Duc Co; Tubbs was the last member of the team to cross; near the center of the channel he was swept from the rope by the swift current, tried to swim against the current, and was last seen when he went under for the sixth time while being carried over some deep rapids about fifty feet downstream from the rope. Team members chased after him, two by swimming back across the stream, but he had disappeared.

Gunther Herbert Wald, Staff Sergeant, reconnaissance patrol member, Command and Control North, MACV-SOG. Born 7 January 1944 in Frankfurt, Germany. Entered army on 13 June 1967 with four years' marine service.

Missing in action since 3 November 1969, when his reconnaissance patrol was attacked by a numerically superior force 30 miles inside Laos near Ban Chakevy Tai, whereupon he was hit by a grenade while trying to make radio contact; last seen lying on the ground with multiple wounds and possibly dead as their position was about to be overrun; related by an indigenous member, Pong, who evaded capture.

Lewis Clark Walton, Staff Sergeant, reconnaissance team member, Task Force 1 Advisory Element. Born 13 May 1934 in Providence, Rhode Island. Entered service on 21 June 1952 at Providence, Rhode Island.

Missing in action since 10 May 1971, after his long-range reconnaissance team "Asp" was inserted into western Quang Nam Province 12 miles from Laos on 3 May; past initial radio contact, no further contact was ever made.

Charles Edward White, Sergeant First Class, reconnaissance patrol member, Command and Control North, MACV-SOG. Born on 18 May 1933 in Union Town, Alabama. Entered service on 23 May 1950 at Columbus, Georgia.

Missing in action since 29 January 1968, when he was being extracted by McGuire rig hoist by helicopter 16 miles inside Cambodia west of Kontum along with team members Nang and Khong; after being radioed by White that the trio was ready to be lifted out, the pilot increased his altitude to 200 feet, at which point White fell into the jungle. Later ground search on 31 January found path that falling body made through jungle canopy into thick bamboo, which was surmised as being enough foliage to have safely broken his fall, but no trace was ever found of him.

Eddie Lee Williams, Sergeant First Class, reconnaissance patrol member, Command and Control, MACV-SOG. Born 10 February 1935 in Miami, Florida. Entered service on 30 November 1953. No location of entry available.

Missing in action since 3 October 1966, when patrol was inserted 1 mile inside Laos west of the DMZ and immediately engaged in firefight under adverse circumstances; sole survivor, interpreter Bui Kim Tien, last saw him on 4 October while they were trying to evade capture; Williams sent him to investigate some caves, at which point Tien was spotted by hostile forces and forced to run from area.

Peter Joe Wilson, Staff Sergeant, reconnaissance patrol leader, Command and Control Central, MACV-SOG. Born 23 August 1938 in Ridley Park, Pennsylvania. Entered service on 17 February 1961 at Long Beach, New York.

Missing in action since 19 October 1970, when his reconnaissance patrol was attacked 2 miles inside Laos in the tri-border area southwest of Ben Het and forced to abandon the battlefield with hostile forces in close pursuit; last seen by Sgt. John M. Baker when Wilson directed him to the front of the patrol and told him to continue to the east if the column was split; at that time Wilson was covering the rear of the patrol and assisting a wounded indigenous solider, Djuit; later Baker heard Wilson transmit "May Day, May Day" on his emergency radio and the sounds of a firefight from the direction of the separated patrol element.

Remains Recovered

Frank Collins Parrish, Sergeant First Class, senior medical specialist, Detachment A-411, Fifth Special Forces Group. Born 19 September 1931 in Big Springs, Texas. Entered service on 14 October 1948 at Cleburne, Texas.

Missing in action since 16 January 1968, near My Phuoc Tay, when camp strike force was involved in a firefight; CIDG and LLDB survivors reported that the Vietcong captured and summarily executed him, but remains were not recovered until 30 April 1973.

George Quanmo, Major, deputy commander, FOB #3, Command and Control North, MACV-SOG. Born 10 June 1940 in Lynn, Massachusetts. Entered service on 23 October 1958 at Averill Park, New York.

Disappeared on 14 April 1968, when aboard a Vietnamese U-17 aircraft (tail number XT) flown by Chinese contract pilot, as courier en route from Khe Sanh to Da Nang. Remains recovered on 28 June 1974.

Index